ENDORSEMENTS

Creatively written and imbued with passion, *Lost and Found along the Way* relates not only the experience of Willie's journey to and along the Camino, but includes beautifully written historical fiction. These set the stage for the impact that the life of St. James has had on the church, both while he was living and after his passing.

Willie's self-deprecating honesty speaks to the challenges any pilgrim faces not only along The Way but even in getting there in the first place. For the new pilgrim, this book can serve as a guide. And yet for all of us, the story of Willie's journey can serve as deep fodder for our own reflections on our personal journeys of faith and how to grow closer to God.

Most appreciated was the reflection in the final chapter on how to share one's faith. It is well written, and the advice applies universally to people in any type of ministry.

—Deacon John Green
Founder, Emmaus Ministries
Senior Mission Expansion Officer, Evangelical Catholic

This book was a gentle wake-up call to the complacent attitude I was carrying in my own faith walk. The bits and pieces of the five hundred miles transported me and allowed me to visualize something that most people will never see. I felt the experiences with Willie, even the blisters and physical challenges. I laughed with him, prayed with him, and even cried with him. But most gratefully, I felt that I walked every step of the Camino with Willie.

Not only that, I felt the Spirit within Willie. Details of his spiritual insights begged that I put down the book and *listen* for God's messages for me. With the end of Willie's pilgrimage came insight for my

Camino, that is, my faith walk. *Lost and Found along The Way* has led me to find greater purpose, greater meaning, and infinitely more joy in my journey toward Him.

Thank you for documenting your journey, sharing your heart, and for changing mine.

—Teena Medick
Chief Administrator, Peyton's Promise

Lost and Found along The Way: Stories for Your Faith Walk from the Camino de Santiago is a wonderfully written virtual experience of walking the Camino. Willie takes you on a geographical, historical, and spiritually reflective journey that is heartfelt, honest, insightful, and inspiring. Willie does more than share his journey—he paves the road for your own. Enjoy the walk! I did!

—Frank Mercadante
Executive Director, Cultivation Ministries
Author, *Make It Real* and *Engaging a New Generation*

Lace up your hiking boots, grab your trekking poles, and walk with Willie on this ancient trail of the Camino. Whether you're traveling with boots on the ground or just in your imagination, Willie will guide you well. You will be encouraged, uplifted, and challenged to journey into the depths of your own life experience and there encounter an intimacy with God many of us have never known.

When I considered walking the Camino with several friends, I turned to Deacon Willie. We got plenty of practical wisdom, but more importantly he helped us reframe the experience as a unique opportunity to hear God's voice. Now Willie's words are available to the world. A natural storyteller, Willie weaves history imaginatively retold, sage advice on how to prepare for the journey, and vividly written details of the lush landscape. With a dose of self-deprecating humor, Willie shares his own missteps and learnings, but the heart of this book is an invitation for each of us to walk our own pilgrimage of spiritual discovery. There's a reason why people from all over the world have been walking this sacred path for more than a thousand years. Delve into these pages and you'll not only understand why, but you'll find yourself walking your own Camino.

—J. Michael Sparough, SJ
Retreat Director, Bellarine Jesuit Retreat House
Co-author, *What's Your Decision? An Ignatian Approach to Decision Making*

Willie's book is an invitation to walk in true friendship with our Lord and Savior. It is a brilliantly woven together work of art that draws me deeper into the mysteries of faith and the absolute reality that God is intimately present in every moment of my life, whether I recognize Him or not. Willie's Camino became my Camino. His openness to experience whatever the Lord would bring his way on The Way provides a profound testimony to the graces that flow into the heart of a person who submits to the will of God. Willie eloquently and practically draws me into his life, story, and journey. He inspires me to see that my experiences change my life and, if I allow Him to, God uses those experiences to grow my life from good, to better, to the best that it can be. This book is a call to deep discipleship overflowing with wisdom and filled with practical examples and reflections on how to deepen my relationship with Jesus Christ. I can't wait to read it again.

—Eric Groth
President/CEO, ODB Films

For anyone who has considered walking the Camino de Santiago or wanted to make a pilgrimage, Willie has crafted a narrative that gives the reader the spiritual experience of the Camino. For those seeking answers to life's biggest questions or those looking to understand their personal sense of purpose, this is the book for you. It is an invitation to realize every day is a pilgrimage along life's rugged and spectacular landscapes.

—T. J. Berden
Producer, *Paul, Apostle of Christ*

St. John Paul stated that all of our life is a pilgrimage to the heart of the Father. Each one of us is journeying on a trail of life that is taking us somewhere. But where? Is the path we are on taking us to the heart of the Father? For over one thousand years pilgrims have been on the Camino to the burial place of St. James asking this very question. Where am I going with my life? What's my purpose? Am I on the right path?

Through personal stories of his own Camino, as well as many others, Deacon Willie Williams walks us through these questions and leads us to a place of discovery. As we walk with Deacon we discover fellow pilgrims whose stories of joy, suffering, doubt and faith resonate with our own experience. In the end, we are led to discover Jesus who, while not always recognized, has journeyed with us each step of the way and is leading us to the Father.

—Fr. David Pivonka, TOR
President, Franciscan University, Steubenville, Ohio
10-Part Series—"Metanoia" by Wild Goose Ministries
Popular YouTube presenter, Wild Goose Ministries
Author, *Hiking the Camino: 500 Miles with Jesus* and *Metanoia Prayer Journal*

LOST
AND
FOUND
ALONG
THE WAY

Stories *for* Your
Faith Walk
from the
Camino de
Santiago

by
RON "WILLIE" WILLIAMS

ISBN—13: 9781632695659
Library of Congress Control Number: 2021902963

Printed in the USA
2021—First Edition
30 29 28 27 26 25 24 23 22 21   10 9 8 7 6 5 4 3 2 1

DEDICATION

To my precious grandchildren
Brady, Clara, Mila, Lily Mae, Giada, and Leo

"The only thing a man keeps is that which he gives away."
It's a Wonderful Life

With great love,
Papa

CONTENTS

FOREWORD

Vierge de'Orrison is a tiny refugio in the foothills of the Pyrenees. It was here in April 2013, over our evening meal and after our first day's climb from St. Jean Pied de Port in France, that my wife Joyce and I first met Willie Williams—or, as we came to know him, Deacon Willie. The following day we summited the Pyrenees; and on the third day, before we set out for Pamplona, Deacon Willie, having heard that Joyce and I had previously walked the Camino, asked if he could join us. We both spontaneously agreed and for the next thirty-four days, all the way to Santiago, we were a "trio." For Joyce and me, our Camino was deeply enriched by having Deacon Willie as a companion and fellow pilgrim. We would not have wished it any other way! We both knew that we were walking with a man of God, a man who gloriously reflected the light and grace of God in all that he did and said. And it is that same light and grace that shines through the pages of *Lost and Found along The Way: Stories for Your Faith Walk from the Camino de Santiago.*

This is not just a book about the Camino, though it is that. It is so much more! This is an inspiring devotional book in which Willie brilliantly weaves a glorious tapestry in which he reflects first on "The Camino," then on "My Camino," then on "Our Camino." Everyone who walks the Camino will in some way either encounter God, or be changed, or both! This book will do the same for you, and I have no hesitation in encouraging you to read *Lost and Found along the Way*. You will be informed, you will be inspired, you will be challenged, and perhaps changed!

—Bishop Eric Pike,
former Anglican bishop of Port Elizabeth, South Africa;
marcher against apartheid with personal friend Nelson Mandela;
author, *Who Do You Say That I Am?* and *Waymarks for the Way*

INTRODUCTION

"Let us decide to take our first steps without knowing how the journey will turn out. If that defines us as reckless and crazy, then let us accept that fate and celebrate the fact that we shall not be cowards."

"Motivation Manifesto," Brendon Burchard

I am leery of any "this will change your life" claim. Hearing it strikes me as a desperate plea to lure me into someone else's quick-fix experience. Add to this: I am not sure I *want* my life changed. Nonetheless, I threw my inner warning aside and accepted an invitation to "change my life" and attend a "Christ Renews His Parish" church retreat.

That was February 1989 and yes, God did change my life during that retreat. He changed me through testimonies, which were the heart and soul of this retreat. These testimonies are the stories of individuals—personal reflections on major events in their lives and how God saw them through those events. For me, a startling commonality in each story became increasingly clear: God is intimately present in *every* moment of our lives, whether we recognize Him or not. As I listened, I discovered that my life story was woven into each one of their life stories. Details of the good, the bad, and the ugly might have differed, but God's love and mercy were universally present. Their expression of His unconditional love during illness, near-death encounters, deaths of loved ones, and joys of love in relationship bonded me to each testifier. Their stories were my story! What an experience!

Yet, I had to ask, was it the retreat that changed my life?

Or was it the power of God in people's stories—their experiences— that changed my life forever?

It became clear: It was the stories. It's our experiences that change our lives and how we allow God to use those experiences to grow our lives from good to better—or to the best they can be. My experience at the retreat reflected this. I allowed God to use that experience to salt a thirst in me to serve in that retreat ministry. Over time, experiencing more retreats led me on a path to become the retreat director for those retreats. Now, nearly three decades later, I have heard more than seven hundred testimonies. My faith has been strengthened, my hope has grown brighter, and my love for God has deepened. I owe it all to the power of God's presence in those testimonies—real stories—which worked their way into my heart. I'm convinced hearing and sharing those experiences are what God used to call me to become an ordained deacon in the Catholic church. The stories God gifted to me during those many retreats dramatically grew my faith in God and radically changed me.

Christian believers commonly quote 2 Corinthians 5:7 to describe their life experience: "for we walk by faith, not by sight." One's testimony can also be represented by more contemporary labels. "My witness," "journey of faith," "walk with the Lord," "my story," or simply "my walk" are just some of those well-known labels. Personally, I am partial to calling my life with the Lord my "faith walk." Spanish speakers use the word "camino," from the verb *caminar*, which in English means "to walk." Whichever word we use represents a person's walk, journey, or way in life.

For the first twenty-five years I served in ministry, my "faith walk" or "camino" had been routinely rewarding. However, we all know that life is filled with change and challenges. After the privilege of hearing hundreds of faith walk stories, I found myself becoming complacent with my own faith. I was too busy doing ministry. I could listen and offer meaningful advice to those I mentored, but I was growing numb to God's messages for me. I was newly semiretired and consumed with boredom and lone-liness. In addition, I was trying to build esteem and respect in my new part-time job as a corporate chaplain, coping with the death of our adult son, and being swallowed in grief over the loss. My life felt like a kite on a string in unsteady breezes.

My prayer time typically sounded like this: *What am I to do, Lord? I try to pray to you. I try to talk to you, but my prayers bounce off the ceiling. So many share their beautiful faith walk stories and my hard heart isn't even moved any more. Nothing seems satisfying or complete. My faith has no fire, no passion, no hunger for You. Lord, where are you?*

Are . . . You . . . even . . . listening?

This was my prayer time one arid month after another for nearly two years.

Then, on March 23, 2012, during what I thought would be another dry morning of prayer and meditation, a surprising storm shower of grace broke through. It was intimate and unmistakably from Him. During a precious contemplative moment, God gave me a powerful call: I was to walk the ancient pilgrimage of el Camino de Santiago de Com-postela. With this realization, my "faith walk, my Camino" erupted into something that almost had a life of its own.

Talk about an experience that changed my life! Preparing for a year to walk a 790-kilometer (500-mile) trail, living the thirty-three-day experi-ence itself, and gaining the body, mind, and soul benefits that come with completing the pilgrimage all radically changed my life completely. Yet I had no idea how consuming this would become.

God's call and experience did not occur as just one pilgrimage, but included another one in the fall of 2015. That's right, call me crazy! I walked the entire 790-kilometer (500-mile) Camino across Spain *a second time*. Call me crazier—I walked the last 325 kilometers (200 miles) again in the spring of 2018.

Each one of these experiences on the Camino with the Lord brought me into a deeper, more intimate, and personal relationship with Him. These experiences with Him also changed my life in innumerable other ways. *So, so precious!* He chose these Camino experiences and fellow pilgrims on the trail to draw me closer to Him. I merely said, "Yes." The Camino was the setting where He chose to do His mighty transformation.

However, let me make this point clear. The Camino did not change my life. God did.

This book comprises the most potent experiences, insights, and spiritual lessons that were instilled in me along the Camino trail over those three pilgrimages. It describes how I changed, how I grew, and how I was transformed. The following chapters contain a hybrid of the best-of-the-best blessings God offered me on my journey. Hopefully, they will bless you as well.

St. James in the Scriptures

Before sharing my journey on el Camino de Santiago de Compostela, The Way, a question begs to be answered. Who was Santiago? That is, who *was* the apostle James? ("Santiago" is Spanish for St. James, the main focus of the Camino.) Scripture is the necessary and enlightening foundation on which to start.

Let's string together the Scripture references to the apostle James (not to be confused with the epistle writer, James) woven throughout the New Testament. These Scriptures teach us who James is and about his privileged company with Jesus, along with his brother John, and another apostle, Peter. How Jesus viewed James and his brother is implied by the nickname He gave them: "the sons of thunder." Zebedee was the father of James and John, and his wife, Salome, was their mother. Her presence in the Scriptures is also worth consideration. How James died reveals much also.

Let's unveil some of the mystery of this intimate friend of Jesus.

Threading the Story of St. James through the Scriptures

- James, along with his brother, John, leave their fishing nets and their father Zebedee to follow Jesus's call (Matt. 4:21–22; Mark 1:19–20).

- James and his brother John are nicknamed by Jesus as "Sons of Thunder" (Mark 3:16–18).

- James's fiery zeal is shown when Jesus was not welcomed into a Samaritan town. James is quoted, "Lord, do you want us to tell fire to come down from heaven and consume them?" (Luke 9:54–55).

- Salome requests of Jesus that her sons be allowed to sit on His left and right when He comes into His glory (Matt. 20:21; Mark 10:38–39).

- Salome was present at Jesus's crucifixion (Matt. 27:56; Mark 15:40).

- Salome was at Jesus's tomb after the resurrection (Mark 16:1–8).

- James, John, and Peter were the only apostles who were present with Jesus during these private moments:
  - Raising of Jairus's daughter to life (Mark 5:37)
  - Transfiguration (Matt. 17:1; Mark 9:1; Luke 9:28)
  - Agony in Gethsemane (Matt. 26:37; Mark 14:33)

- King Herod Agrippa I, grandson of Herod the Great and the ruler at the time of Jesus's death, sought to please the Jews so he had James beheaded (Acts 12:1–3).

- James was the first apostle to be martyred.

St. James in the Legends and Strongly Held Beliefs

With more than 1,200 years of Camino history, stories abound; and Camino walkers of the past have added to the stories about St. James and the pilgrim trail. Some tidbits are tantalizing folklore to consider, some are held cautiously, and some contain more historical truth.

The list below contains some of the more popular legends that have circulated for centuries. Some of the items have become endearing, strongly held beliefs for pilgrims and non-pilgrims alike who want to learn about the Camino journey.

- St. James's ministry was in a small fishing village in Spain's Finisterre along the country's western coast, immediately adjoining the Atlantic Ocean. James ministered to fierce pagans there, the Druids, pre-Christian Celts who worshipped the sun.[1]

- It is conjectured that James may have taken Jesus's last four words literally: "Go ye therefore, and teach all nations . . . and, lo, I am with you always, even unto the end of the world" (Matt. 28:20, KJV). In the first century, Finisterre, Spain was known as the "end of the world." *Finis* means "finish" or "end"; *terra* means "land," thus the name Finisterre, "end of the world."

- Some question, where else would a "man of thunder" go to "spread the good news"?

- James had two disciples who served with him in ministry: Theodore and Athanasius.[2]

- James, according to legend, received a calling to leave his ministry in Spain and return to Jerusalem.

- Upon his entry in Jerusalem, James's fiery and bold preaching agitated and angered the Jews. Herod had James beheaded in order to appease Jewish religious leaders and hopefully gain their favor.

- James's executioner was so moved upon hearing James's teaching about Jesus that at James's execution, this man claimed the faith that James had just shared with him. As a result, Herod had that man executed by the same blade that killed James.[3]

- Theodore and Athanasius stole James's body from his fresh grave in Jerusalem.[4]

- Theodore and Athanasius returned James's body via boat across the Mediterranean Sea to western Spain, to the province of Galicia where the apostle had preached. There, Theodore and Athanasius gave James an honorable burial.[5]

- Theodore and Athanasius lived out their lives by continuing James's ministry in Galicia.[6]
- After their deaths, the location of St. James's burial site remained unknown for centuries.
- In the year AD 813, a hermit named Pelayo lived in utter seclusion in Galacia. He claimed that one night he heard mysterious music—a beautiful melody. It was coming from where he witnessed starlight hitting a field amongst a forested land in Padron, a Galician province near Finisterre, Spain.[7]
- Following the mysterious clues of melody and starlight, Pelayo discovered the grave of the apostle James. The gravestone inscription read: "Here lies James, apostle of Jesus AD 44."[8]
- The term, Santiago de Compostela, originates from the Spanish *compo*, meaning "field," and *stella*, meaning "star." The "Field of Stars" references how and where the grave was found.[9]
- Pelayo solicited his bishop to officially explore the mysterious site. The bishop confirmed the discovery of the long-lost apostle's grave.[10]
- Graves of Theodore and Athanasius were found nearby.[11]
- Word of the location of St. James's burial site spread throughout Europe. Devout believers from all over Europe left their homes and began walking to the holy site. They were the first pilgrims who blazed the trail to the apostle's grave.
- During the Middle Ages, more than a million pilgrims walked el Camino de Santiago de Compostela, also known as, "The Way" "The Way of St. James," or simply "The Camino." Its popularity has continued for centuries.
- Many have walked the trail in hopes of experiencing God's graces along The Way, and many as penance for their sins. For this reason, el Camino de Santiago de Compostela has also been referred to as "The Penitent Trail."[12]

- The Cathedral de Santiago de Compostela was constructed in 1075 (officially completed in 1211), just a few short years after the last crusade.
- The crypt and the apostle's relics were laid to rest in the cathedral and the town was named Santiago in St. James's honor.
- El Camino de Santiago de Compostela, the 790-kilometer (500-mile) pilgrimage trail has been walked upon for twelve centuries by millions and millions of pilgrims.
- As many as 325,000 pilgrims from two hundred different countries walk it every year.

Trail Map

Every good journey needs a map. Hopefully the historical references above serve as signposts for us all to begin our journey together. However, as important as these details are, this apostle's dramatic faith walk and martyrdom begs for an attempt to visualize and paint it.

To that end, I used historical fiction to depict James's faith walk. Chapters 1, 2, and 3 are a creative work of my imagination and were driven by the scriptural facts and ancient legends. The stories—how James gave his life for the faith, how his grave was discovered, and how The Way to Santiago started—make for a dramatic faith walk story. History and well-documented legends drive these stories. However, in one short episode, I exercised a creative retreat from the facts. Out of respect to the reader, I offer this heads-up: I included a phenomenon that has been discovered with many saints after their death—their bodies were uncorrupted. The corpse showed no signs of physical deterioration, no change in skin color, no odor of death, and no deathlike appearance. The common testimony is that the deceased saint just appears to be sleeping. I took literary license to include this incorruptible aspect to St. James as a vehicle to move the storyline.

A respectful Camino story must honor St. James. After all, for centuries people have walked this pilgrimage in hopes of paying respect to this faithful follower of Jesus at his gravesite and the magnificent cathedral bearing his name. My fondest hope is that the fruit of my imagination brings the apostle to life for you as it did for me. Hopefully his life and journey will linger in our minds as we become fellow pilgrims on this journey.

Following the narrative chapters about James, the balance of the book is nonfiction and describes key experiences during my three Camino journeys. The book reads as one continuous pilgrimage when, in fact, it is a hybrid of the best of the best of my experiences over the three separate treks. I also include a short "Pre-Camino" chapter that launches my pilgrimage experience in Spain.

Each chapter includes three segments which form a unique triad: "The Camino," "My Camino," and "Our Camino." This approach offers the reader three unique lenses in which to see, to feel, and to gain wisdom from the Camino de Santiago with or without actually walking the trail.

The Camino

Each chapter begins with a segment called "The Camino." It contains descriptions of actual locations along el Camino de Santiago de Compostela. You will start the walk with me in southern France and climb 1,500m (5,000 ft.) while I cross the Pyrenees Mountains all along The Way to the Cathedral of Santiago. In each "The Camino" segment, I employ vivid descriptions of the geography of *where* I was so that you may enjoy the natural beauty just as I saw it.

Our own lives have an interesting personal history, and the history of "The Camino" is no less marvelous. I am optimistic that the history embedded along the trail will captivate you as it did me and the millions of pilgrims over the centuries.

My wish is that you visualize the beauty and fascination of "The Camino" and more fully understand the challenge of walking all 790 kilometers (500 miles). Perhaps one day you will accept a call to walk it yourself!

My Camino

The second segment of each of these chapters is "My Camino." These are my personal faith walk stories, insights, and spiritual lessons that occurred during my own pilgrimage. The thoughts and epiphanies often describe how I wrestled for answers. I did my utmost to share the exact wording that expressed my actual thoughts, and invite you as the reader to share my reflective thinking. I also endeavored to capture the specific language of my thoughts and prayers. These can be easily recognized; they're shown in *italic*.

While soaking in the breathtaking Spanish countryside and immersed in long hours of silent contemplation, Jesus often knit insightful parables into my life. These revelations are some of the heart treasures contained in the "My Camino" segment of each chapter.

Our Camino

The final segment within each chapter is called "Our Camino." In this section, I offer some teaching related to the chapter's message. The content is based on solid teaching from respected Christian teachers and the saints. For many "Our Camino" explanations, I encourage you to dig deeper into self-reflection and the truth of who you are. This encouragement springs from my own training and wisdom God has granted me throughout my spiritual formation. In many "Our Camino" segments, I also share spiritual challenges and lessons—situations we all face—in an honest, thought-provoking way. My fondest hope is that "Our Camino" provides new answers, direction, reason to hope, and a new hunger for the gift of faith.

Faith walk stories close the end of each "Our Camino" segment to illustrate the chapter's central message. Most of these testimonies were shared with me over the years in retreat work or through involvement in a ministry I conducted. All are included with the wholehearted support and approval of the ones who shared their faith walk story for inclusion in this book. They contain real life dramas that will inspire, captivate, and bring "Our Camino" to life.

This unique triad—"The Camino," "My Camino," and "Our Camino" will serve as a format for us to share the truth of Jesus alive in us. This is evangelization! These faith walk stories will inspire those who have "found" their faith and guide them on how to share it with those who have "lost" it.

This is the mission of *Lost and Found along The Way.*

"The preaching that this world needs most is the sermons in shoes that are walking with Jesus."

D. L Moody

*   *   *

Okay, fellow pilgrim, before we take our first hiking step, you'll want to learn something of the man to whom the trail is attributed and some history behind the pilgrimage. It is a fascinating, centuries-old story.

Be reminded! This section is a creative work of my imagination.

Buen Camino! (Have a good journey!)

Love your enemies

Chapter 1

THE MEASURE OF A MAN

Jerusalem 44 AD

James made his approach into Jerusalem with bold, long strides of confidence far greater than when he had left for Spain and the "end of the world." Dressed in a coarse brown cloak and tunic, he carried a long walking stick. Attached to the top was a gourd of water and some seashells that were abundant along the seaside where he preached. His reputation as one of Jesus's apostles held a level of curiosity and respect by only a small number of the Jews. It didn't matter. James's face was set like flint as a man with a calling from God to return to Jerusalem.

James's message thundered above the din of hundreds gathered for the Festival of Unleavened Bread. As he walked, the message provoked attention: "Jesus taught us, 'Love your enemies. Do good to those who hate you. Bless those who curse you.'" His voice now pierced the crowd's chatter. "Pray for those who mistreat you."

Within the throngs were some Jews, agitated at yet another one of these Christ followers. They screamed themselves hoarse with their reprimand, "This is not our Law, the Law of Moses and Abraham. Go back to where you came from!" At that, a raucous argument erupted. James and his two disciples, Theodore and Athanasius, were like an island encircled by a sea of growing ferocity. One protester momentarily blocked James's path with a vicious challenge, "Be gone, Christ follower!" This brash confrontation emboldened more and more of the mob to join the rage. None of the waves of bitter emotion caused James even a pause in his long-legged march through town. The apostle was unmoved and unyielding on his new mission to return to Jerusalem. *I must forgive them.* The moment of reassurance would be short-lived.

A splat of spittle struck James above one eye. "May Yahweh curse you, Christ follower," one jeered. James pushed forward undeterred, his stride unchanged. Many were now kicking dust on him as they swung their fists in the air. Falling behind James and Theodore, Athanasius was swallowed up in the fuming crowd. One threatened with a stone, poised overhead and ready to strike. The disciple cowered under his tunic sleeve. Peeking underneath, he caught sight of the fearless James paused and looking at him with love.

The stone bounced off his chest with a painful thud. It stole his breath, but emboldened his resolve. He staggered to his feet holding his chest as he stumbled to join the two just ahead.

James resumed Jesus's message. "If you love only those who love you, what honor is there in that? Sinners love sinners. If you do good to only those who do good to you, what honor is there in that? Even sinners do that! Do to others what you would have them do to you."

Spit from the crowd was now raining down on James's dust-covered clothing. The crowds grew deafening while the faces in the swarm fumed their rejection. "Death to you! Death to all you Jesus followers!" The fracas became frenzied with the crowd's yelled chant, "Death! Death! Death! Death! Death!"

Observing the crowds from a balcony was Titus, chief Roman guard. Not only did he keep a watchful eye over the city's peace; he had the intimidating reputation as one of Herod's most proficient executioners. Step out of line, and Titus's simple report to King Herod Agrippa would be a certain death warrant. Witnessing the Jews' reaction to the apostle warranted an accusation to Herod. Titus reported, "The entire city of Jerusalem is ready to riot over this James. It will take every guard available for mob control. We cannot afford the chance of having his followers somehow rescue him during all this mayhem. This would threaten Roman rule."

Herod shouted, "Throw him in jail!" He thrust a fierce look and pointed his finger in Titus's face. "I want you to guard him. Watch him like your life depends upon it!"

He confidently paced his headquarters and crisply added, "Post this decree throughout Judea: 'On the twenty-fifth day of the seventh month of this forty-fourth year of Julius Caesar (25 July) James, son of Zebedee, will be publicly executed.'" Turning to Titus he ordered, "Secure the execution platform for all of Jerusalem to witness." With a self-satisfied grin he added, "One day from now I will not only be ruler, but the Jews' beloved ruler for many years to come." Titus understood his king's methods all too well. First, execute James, and next, the leader of the Christian radicals, Peter. With James now arrested, the crowd dispersed. Theodore and Athanasius were seized by Roman guards and escorted out of town.

Down a narrow flight of stairs, the bound James descended into a maze of prison cells. The stench of poor sanitation and death made both men gag. With a strong shove, Titus thrust James to his jail door. "Get in!" Titus commanded.

James faced his executioner, bowed his head slightly, and looked upon him with a kind expression, a humble submission, a brotherly love. At that, Titus's swift backhand struck James. Blood trickled from the side of his mouth and his cheek reddened. The blow stung Titus's hand as well. A fierce glare into James's face surprised him. There was no hatred or fear in James.

Titus raised his left hand, prepared to deliver another strike.

James fixed his eyes gently on Titus's face. Without comment and ever so gently, he turned his other cheek to him in expectation of another blow. The executioner was unaccustomed to such a reaction.

"Just what I thought. You Jesus followers are all cowards." Titus belittled.

James broke his silence, "Jesus taught us to love our enemies and if they should strike us on our cheek, we should give them our other cheek as well." With that, both men peered deeply into each other's eyes. One held confusion, the other a humble expression of love. For a few awkward moments, both men fixated on the other.

Titus broke first, shook his head, and began pacing awkwardly. He ran his hand over his head, and stared at the floor in hopes that some understanding would present itself.

"Ugh. Just, just, get in your cell." Titus ordered. Upon chaining and affixing the lock, he stole a curious look at James. "So what else did this Jesus teach you?"

From his jail cell, James proclaimed Jesus's messages unrelentingly to his sole guard, Titus. He recounted Jesus's miracle that brought Jairus's daughter back to life. He detailed the Transfiguration on Mount Tabor. He described their experience together at Gethsemane the night before Jesus's death. Each story, each word spoken by Jesus, and each loving act He performed was powerfully shared by James. "Your love for this Jesus makes Him come to life for me," remarked Titus.

After nearly twenty hours of the fiery apostle's messages, Titus stared through James in silent thought. It was daybreak and only the two were present in Jerusalem's jail. Sitting on a crude, wooden, three-legged stool was Titus, the executioner, staring with rapt attention into his prisoner's face. James stood tall and erect while Titus, short in height, resembled a gladiator with rippling arm and shoulder muscles. He took some pride in the fact that his sword swing dealt an immediate death blow to those he beheaded. The sheer power in his arms assured it. Linius was the Roman soldier who apprenticed under him. By contrast, Linius had displayed some colossally weak and misguided sword drops at executions he attempted. Hearing the victim's bloodcurdling cries haunted those who witnessed his blunders. On the contrary, Titus's strength was apparent, and death by his mighty blow was instantaneous and merciful.

Through the jail cell bars, Titus was riveted by the preacher's words. James paused and his gaze stabbed the heart of his executioner. "Be merciful, just as your Father in heaven is . . . merciful."

James knelt down. He was at eye level with the still-sitting Titus. With joy and certain peace, James humbly spoke the last of Jesus's message, "No greater love does a man have than that he lay down his life for a friend."

Titus felt the words eddy in his heart. He dropped his face into his stubby fingers and stroked his bare hands over his forehead and scalp. There was a tremor in his lips as anxiety and confusion rattled him. Finally, the combating beliefs exploded from the Roman guard.

"This can't be! I've always believed that there is no king but Caesar! The power of Rome—I've seen it. I am part of it. Nations tremble at our armies when we march in to conquer, plunder, and rule. That is power. Real power!" Titus argued.

James leaned into the jail cell bars, inches from Titus's stubbly bearded face. James's "truth" in Jesus confronted Titus's "truth" in Rome. James's voice softened, gritty in certainty, as he whispered into Titus's floundering life perspective, "You would have *no* power if it had not been given to you from our Father in heaven."

James stared deeply into Titus's green, bloodshot, and teary eyes. A long, awkward silence seized them both. In a shamed tone, Titus began. "James, I must beg your forgiveness. As chief officer to King Herod, I was the one who reported accusations against you. I was the one who cautioned Herod of a possible uprising to free you. I was the one who prompted Herod to sentence you to death. I was the one who acted as your fiercest enemy. Now I will be your executioner. How I wish I could reverse what I did!" Tortured in heart and spirit, Titus humbly begged, "Is it possible you could forgive someone who is both your accuser and executioner?"

James stood staring blankly at a corner of the ceiling. A short silence followed until he stretched his long-sleeved cloak through the bars and embraced Titus. In a strong and loving voice, James affirmed his forgiveness, "Peace be with you." He then kissed Titus on the crown of his head.

Both men exhaled deeply, releasing the emotion of the moment. Titus continued, "I . . . I want to live for your Savior." Through trembling lips and a heavy heart, Titus pleaded, "Please, baptize me."

A water gourd sat perched against the wall of another empty jail cell. Titus snatched it and brought it to James. Humbly, Titus knelt before James, his head bowed. Pronouncing the holy words, James emptied the gourd and completed the baptism.

Titus stood and embraced James with the jail cell wall between them. Long, deep breaths came in a peaceful rhythm. Titus stepped back and looked at James in a brand-new way. He affirmed, "Now your God is my God."

"It's time!" interrupted Linius, surprising them with his presence. "All are gathered for the execution. Titus, your accusation was all that was needed. We will have an execution today! Come on. We need to go!"

Terror transformed Titus's expression. In practiced sequence, he walked to the rack where his executioner's blade hung, grabbed the jail cell key, and brusquely opened the door. James stood confidently and walked into the streets brimming with brilliant and blinding sunlight. Linius led the way with James, who was still manacled, and Titus toting the blade. A small patrol of Roman soldiers managed to push back the crowds who jostled for a closer view. After all, this was the son of Zebedee who had the successful fishing business, and he was one of Jesus's apostles! The memory of Jesus's execution was still fresh. Who could blame them for wanting to see the plight of one of His followers?

The prisoner and his executioners marched ahead to the platform. Herod stood pompously on a balcony, which allowed a commanding view of the death blow. The crowds shouted commands through foaming lips and clenched teeth, "Death to the Christian!" Others screamed in passionate excitement, "Kill him!" Still others screeched, "Our allegiance is to Herod!" The cacophony of impassioned commands from the Jews fed Herod's confidence and he pronounced the sentence of death by the sword. The people shouted all the more, "Death to Christians! Death to all of them!"

James, Titus, and Linius stood on the executioner's stage. The crowd was rabid in determination for the sword to fall. With the word, "Death! Death! Death! Death!" pounding away in the confusion of noises, Titus stood contemplating his new faith. Linius, on the other hand, was swept up with the excitement of the crowd. James broadened his shoulders and stiffened his back. The fury of the crowd meant nothing to him, in fact, a fearless confidence overcame him.

Today I will be with Jesus in paradise.

During another long sweep of the crowd, James caught sight of inspiration. There, at a nearby balcony rail stood Mary, Jesus's mother, and his own faith-filled mother, Salome. Standing boldly behind them with his arms wrapping them like a shawl, stood "the one whom Jesus loved," his brother, John.

James tried to memorize every feature of the three. Their gaze was fixed upon him. Death chants and another promise by Herod to eliminate Christian radicals were muted while he drank in the vision of their love. Abruptly, Linius grabbed James by his tunic and led him to the crimson-stained block. With hands still bound, James was locked in position for the death blow. Anticipation reduced crowd noise to a murmur.

To everyone's shock, Titus took the opportunity to shout his declaration, "I stand . . . with the apostle . . . for . . . Jesus!" The crowd gasped into silence at this announcement. With but a brief moment to spare, Titus knelt and positioned his face just inches from the apostle's. Seeking assurance, he uttered, "There is no greater love than this?"

James's eyes pooled with love. "None," he confirmed.

Soldiers yanked Titus away as Linius was handed the sword. No time was wasted. With the chorus of "Death! Death! Death! Death!" still in the background, James's head was severed from his body. Cheers rose to a frenzy. Linius stood proud as a conquering hero.

Titus volunteered a step forward, then soldiers angrily laid him in position and secured him. Linius's intoxication with his power and prestige as the new executioner was sobered by his eye contact with Titus. Both knew well the incompetency of the new apprentice. Titus's look was meant to temper his executioner's overconfidence. Linius arrogantly dismissed his master's clue. He yanked the sword overhead, paused momentarily, and swung it madly. It missed its mark. Titus screamed in agony as the blade fell across his upper shoulder blades. This horror stunned the crowd.

"Again!" demanded Herod. Titus now strained a chant of his own. "Je . . . sus! Je . . . sus! Je . . . sus!"

Once more Linius swung the blade into position overhead; a moment later, the blade hit its mark.

Son, behold your mothers

Chapter 2

OF THUNDER AND STARS

Jerusalem, 25 July, AD 44

The crowds gathered for the execution had had their fill of blood and death and made their way home. Conversations and jeers amongst the exiting crowd became a blur of angry voices spilling out. One spoke confidently, "This should be the real end of these Christian radicals." Some argued, "We did away with Jesus. We will do away with whomever else tries to challenge our Jewish law." Others boasted, "Tear down our temple, will he? It hasn't happened and never will." Still others insisted, "Every Christ follower needs to feel the blade," with a thumb stabbed back in the direction of the executioner's platform, "just like that James character!"

As everyone trudged ahead, rumor sifted through the crowds that King Herod Agrippa I was determined to track down the leader of these Christ followers. The apostle Peter was to be seized and eventually executed. Surely doing away with him would silence these Christian zealots who were challenging centuries of Jewish traditions.

Heavy-hearted among the edgy, jostling crowd, three choked back the horror and grief imprinted by the execution. Mary, mother of Jesus, and Salome, mother of the slain apostle trudged wearily along with the masses. The man serving as son to both was John, the heartbroken brother of the executed. His arms were tucked strongly around each.

They arrived at a modest, yet comfortable home provided by Mary's uncle, Joseph.[13] It included one dim, large room with adobe walls and a foot-hardened earthen floor. Upon entering, the three collapsed into chairs. What started as a short stunned silence became a flood of heartbroken, uncontainable grief. Had what they just seen really happened? Center stage in their memory was the noisy confusion of the angry mob's hysteria, the flashing glint of the steel blade, and the quick end of their loved one's life. It was horrific, but real.

Mary reflectively broke the silence. "I remember when my Jesus first saw you boys by the sea. You were both hard workers and so diligent in obedience to your father, Zebedee. It was your loving respect of him that caught Jesus's attention."

John's heart was moved by so many memories. He began, "Rabbi Gamaliel determined our futures were not as rabbis. He encouraged us, 'Go home to the family trade.' For this reason," John added, "James and I were startled by Jesus's calling: 'Come follow me.' I'll never forget the day. Hearing it, we knew our father's life prayer was answered. He broadened his shoulders and stiffened his back as we had seen him do our whole lives when beginning solemn prayer in the synagogue. Without a single word, he watched us leave." John added, "It took only those three words from Jesus to change our lives forever."

Salome soulfully added, "I, too, will be forever grateful to Jesus for calling both of my sons to share in building the kingdom of heaven here on earth. How honoring it is."

Mary nodded. "I heard Jesus speak in love and gratitude for all of his apostles." She fixed her gaze on John and added, "Many fond stories of you sons of Zebedee." At that, she patted the hand of John, who was sitting between them both. "'Bold and courageous in faith,' Jesus would say."

John's mind drifted back to when he, James, and Peter were the only three privileged to see some of Jesus's miracles. They witnessed the raising of Jairus's young daughter from death, the Transfiguration, and the most painful: Jesus's agony in Gethsemane. His mind churned with so many of His teachings. And yes, those confrontations with the Pharisees and scribes! There were so many memories. Soon, another long silence captured them.

John's chuckle broke the chain of grief as he added, "I remember the day he nicknamed us. A Samaritan town had just turned us away. A righteousness boiled up in us, but more so in James. His indignation surfaced, 'Lord, do you want us to call down fire from heaven on that town?' We were chided with loving discipline as he declared, 'I shall call you both "Boanerges, Sons of Thunder."' Oh, how laughter broke out among all twelve of us! That was so special about our Lord; he could both love and correct anyone with but a simple message."

"He talked of this many times," Mary smiled. "'When those two men speak,' he would say, 'their faith shakes the world like thunder.'"

With conviction John said, "The good news cannot be hidden. Like loaves and fish for five thousand, it grows and grows. Love and mercy still overflow from Him. Faith brings sight to the blind and hearing to the deaf. It casts out demons, and it brings a young dead girl back to life. That's how it is with our Father in heaven. It can make the leper . . ." John caught himself mid-sentence and halted the thunderous discourse growing within. A sheepish grin broke out across his face.

"You cannot hide your love and faith in Jesus," Salome interrupted. "Loving Jesus means that we will someday die for Him. Your brother was the first of His apostles to do so. That will be the bitter cup of suffering from which we all must drink." At this, Salome grasped John's hand and used it to stroke her cheek. She gave it a mother's gentle kiss.

Mary softly closed both eyes and bowed her head in agreement.

Their grief imposed another reflective space of silence. The reality of the execution's horror again consumed them. Tears overwhelmed Salome's eyes and streaked down over her cheeks. John sat bent over, head in hands as his shoulders heaved rhythmically with each mournful wave. Mary fought back gasps of agony and grief. She fully understood what it felt like to bury a son. Her heart broke for her sister. She had these same feelings some years ago with the death of her Jesus. Grief leaves an indelible mark. Yes, she understood all too well.

John fought to collect himself. *How do I comfort them? What do I say? What would Jesus say now?* Then the message came flooding back, "Unless a grain of wheat falls into the earth and dies, it remains alone; but if it dies, it bears much fruit." At this, he excused himself and stood by the one window in the home. He looked out to where the sunset was complete and darkness hid the town. He released another long stretch of deep, soulful sobs.

A feverish drumming of fists on the door startled them. Roman soldiers? Was Herod now searching for them too? Rumor claimed a bounty was on Peter's life, but not theirs. After all, it was now past sundown. Arrests are made in broad daylight so that others can witness them. Why now? This made no sense. Did they think Peter was here? Mary whispered frantically, "Oh Lord, help us!"

Another round of drumming ensued, even louder. John offered, "If they've come to arrest someone, let it be me."

The steely look on Mary's face said it all. "John, you stay with your mother. If anyone must go, I will."

John broadened his shoulders and stiffened his back. "Let me see what this is all about. Call for Joseph back in Arimathea if they take me. He can help."

With but a sliver of the door opened, James's two disciples, Athanasius and Theodore, burst in and bolted the door. Athanasius asserted in a strained but panicked whisper, "We need your help. We have stolen James's body from his grave. It must be buried in Spain's village of Finisterre where he ministered to the pagans there. That is the only righteous way to honor him."

Theodore added in strong whispers, "We have his corpse still wrapped in burial cloths and hidden in a cart outside. We will leave by midnight to the coast of the Mediterranean where a small boat has been prepared. Hopefully Spain's coast will be in sight before Herod can react. We are determined to provide a proper burial and commit the rest of our days to continuing James's work."

Athanasius continued, "With news of James's execution, Joseph left Arimathea. Because his tin trade has been profitable, the many gold pieces he has delivered to us will more than cover expenses for our travel and to resume James's work there."

Mary asked, "How can we help?"

Both men spoke in unison, "We need your blessing." With that, the three laid hands on the men and called down the Holy Spirit on their mission.

*   *   *

The Arimathean's plans were perfectly prepared. Theodore and Athanasius arrived at the coast with their beloved James tightly bound in burial cloths. As they pulled the cart to the shoreline, a challenge lay ahead. This was no Sea of Galilee. The Mediterranean was far more treacherous. Their fishing vessel was made for the sea, but for such a distance as Spain? Of this they were unsure.

With Joseph's hired servants to help, James's corpse was carefully laid in the boat. Supplies were loaded. With a word of thanks and a fervent prayer for their protection, they pushed off. The Holy Spirit alone would be their Guide and Helper.

More than a month passed before the men arrived at the shoreline of Finisterre. Sitting in their boat, both took another long, hard look at their hero lying at the hull. Both marveled that after all those days, James's body was uncorrupted. There was no foul odor, no signs of decomposition, not even a discoloration of their hero's skin. Even in death, the apostle held a miraculous touch.

"*Jehovah Mekoddishkem* [the Lord who sanctifies]," uttered Theodore.

"Praise *Jehovah-nissi* [the Lord our protector]," reverently whispered Athanasius in reply.

An honorable burial was their mission, and it was time. Walking on solid ground again felt strange. On wobbly legs the men hefted the boat further ashore. While trying to steady themselves, they took a long scan of the ocean that dwarfed the sea they had just navigated. Its deep grey-blue color, distant white caps, sheer immensity, and the sunset gliding into the horizon stole their breaths away. Theodore broke their trance, "Finisterre," he declared. "Jesus said He would be with us even here, 'the end of the world.' Let's call upon Him once more."

At that, the men knelt on one of the abundant boulders, one as large as a fishing boat, making up the shore. With the power of ocean's wind and waves before them, they prayed. *"Adonai El Roi* [the God who sees us], we adore You for Your mighty strength. Your majesty is before us and we are in awe of it. We thank You for the long days of sea travel and how You protected us even as waves broke the bow and threatened us. We are humbly grateful for Your protection. Adonai, we beg Your guidance as we search for a proper burial place for Your faithful servant. Guide us, El Shaddai."

The wind intensified. Both men were rocked back and forth on their sandaled heels by the gusts. Their cloaks filled like small sails. Using their rowing oars, they fashioned a litter to carry their beloved inland to his final resting place. Their weakened sea legs, the buffeting wind, and the hilly, boulder-cluttered terrain stretched before them. No trees were even present to break the relentless wind. Added to the hours of physical strain was the darkness of night that made every footstep uncertain until the stars came out as brilliant, celestial lanterns. A couple hours passed before something of promise as a possible gravesite was detected on the horizon.

"Looks like a grouping of saplings and shrub," Theodore thought aloud.

Athanasius responded with new enthusiasm, "Yes! Yes! I see it now too." They plodded along awkwardly in the direction of the young plant line.

While getting closer and closer to the prospective site, Theodore stammered. "Listen! Can you hear that?" They paused for a few moments. "It's a strange kind of music. I've never heard anything like it, or more beautiful either." Both continued the last stretch captured in the joy induced by the mysterious tune.

Athanasius now added, "Look up there—in the sky! See the stars clustered over the site?"

Theodore saw them too. "So many stars I can't even distinguish much space between them. I couldn't even begin to count them if I tried."

The men contemplated, *Is this our sign? Our sign from the Holy Spirit?*

Theodore and Athanasius approached the cusp of this grove formed by young aspens and fragrant oleander. They pushed their way into the ring almost reverently. To their surprise, at the center was a grassy clearing. Their muscles screamed with gratitude as they laid their prized friend down. They surveyed the setting; it felt perfect. Just how perfect it was became clear when both men looked up. The three were bathed in starlight and swept away with the richness of the heavenly melody surrounding them. What they experienced could only be explained as holy. Assuredly, this was to be the burial ground for the dear apostle.

Centuries would pass before the story of James, "Son of Thunder," would be reignited.

Holy ground!

Chapter 3

THE LURE OF HEAVEN'S MELODY

813 AD

Living in western Spain holds many benefits. Spain's Galician province spans far with farms that are prolific with wheat, green olives, and acres and acres of plum-purple grapes bulging with sweetness. The bounty of these farms support the life ministry of the hermits living near the British Sea on Spain's western coast. Among those dedicated to this prayerful life was a devout hermit, Pelayo.

How he loved his monastic life in spite of its difficulties. He started his day in long hours of prayer, followed by tediously transcribing copies of St. Benedict's Monastic Rule. By early afternoon he began toiling away at the small farm that sustained him. His small cave's opening stood amid a field of mauve-colored heather and emerald, grass-covered hills. He lived alone, but would readily admit he was not lonely.

Steady ocean winds brought the sweet fragrance of blossoming oleander. The westerly breeze was ever present, although today he sensed something rather strange and delightful in it. *My cave has such an unpleasant staleness; I hope this breeze might float its way through it,* thought Pelayo.

It wasn't long before dusk swallowed the hermit's world. He was weary from a long afternoon tending his farm plot. Yes, it had been a productive day at his little hamlet. He sat on a bench just outside of the cave's opening. His limbs were limp from exhaustion. "Lord, you blessed me exceedingly this day. Your presence swirled around me with great delight. I am so grateful, my Lord."

The hermit's humble prayer was startled by the sound of music, soft and melodic. But it was more than that. Much more. It was soothing and soulful. "That's strange," Pelayo questioned. "Who could be playing such an instrument so far out here? And how could it reach me? I must be imagining something."

Teetered between allowing his evening prayers to float on the music or investigating its origin, Pelayo chose the former. His eyelids fluttered shut as the composition drifted with his meditation and drew him deeper in prayer with the Creator.

It felt like hours before his eyelids cracked open, with the realization that the music had picked up a stronger rhythm. Suddenly Pelayo was dumbstruck. There, about three hundred meters from the cave where a grove of towering trees and shrub lay, starlight pierced the evening sky. It descended in brilliant streams of light which silently kissed the ground and instantly faded. The ringlike cluster of trees was aglow with these celestial curiosities. "For the grace of God!" he exhaled reverently. It was a sight he could only comprehend as holy. He determined, *I must see what this is all about.*

With starlight so unusually bright this night, it was not difficult to make his way through the field to the ring of towering eucalyptus and erect, smooth-barked aspens. Their branches strained upward to the sky as if in prayer. Their sheer size could only be explained by the fact that they sat undisturbed for centuries. Beneath these stout giants was a strangle of sweet-smelling oleander, wild grape vines, prickly asters, and wild, fragrant fennel. These formed a natural barricade. In all of his years living here, he had never ventured into this clearing.

With bold inquisitiveness, Pelayo threaded his way through the outer ring. Once inside, he stood amongst tall grasses now matted down. At first impression he thought, *Just ordinary fodder grass.* However, with the holy starlight and the soothing melody surrounding him, he surrendered himself to what he could now tell must be a spiritual presence.

His gaze to the heavens above arrested his thoughts. A beam of light came from one bright star, surrounded by a ring of smaller stars. These smaller ones released streaks like sparks from a campfire, brilliant in pure white light. As they descended, they struck the grass he stood upon. Under a shower of heaven's light and sound, Pelayo stood mesmerized by how each sparkle of starlight was consumed in this clearing, yet never struck him nor started to flame. "Amazing!" he marveled.

Looking down to where the sparks landed, he made a startling discovery. Beneath his feet were the shapes of three rectangular scars concealed in the tall grasses. *They're like grave sites,* he thought. *Whose could they be? They are so overgrown and forgotten.* His imagination considered old legends that sifted throughout this end of Galicia. It was believed that the apostle James was buried somewhere nearby. Pelayo dared to speculate, *Could this be the resting place for the "Son of Thunder"?* The possibility excited his imagination. *After all, the apostle's ministry was just kilometers away near the Finisterre coast.* The possibility was quickly dismissed. *Not likely; that was eight hundred years ago.*

Starlight continued streaking a path to the clearing as he fell to his knees to explore. Pawing the ground and pulling out grassy clumps by the roots, the hermit worked feverishly in search of a stone, a marker, a clue. Anything. Nothing notable was to be found at the one spot in the center. He scratched and clawed at the two rectangles at each side. Still nothing. Crestfallen, Pelayo sat with bunches of grass cast about him and chilled fingers from clawing bare-handed in the cold soil. "Nothing. What a disappointment!" he muttered.

Surrendering to the thought that this entire adventure was just a wild hope imagined in the dull mind of a hermit, he prepared to leave. Standing, he studied the imprints one more time. *If these are graves, perhaps I was searching the wrong end of the grave,* he pondered.

Pelayo fell to his knees with a new hope, excitedly clawing the grass at the other end of the earthen scars. In quick order, his fingertips scraped across something coarse. Madly, he grasped and yanked clump upon clump of the grassy cover. As he pulled away more and more, a crude stone presented itself. Excitement boiled over inside of him until a stone slab was fully visible. Undeniably, it was a grave's headstone. With an anxious sweep of his palm, the inscription could finally be read: "Here lies James, apostle of Jesus AD 44."

"Holy ground," breathed Pelayo. He quickly scampered to the earthen scar to the right and commenced the grass clearing. It revealed a name he knew nothing of, "Theodore." Excitement was erupting inside him. He took several squatted leaps to the earthen scar to the left of James. His hands tore at the grass madly for a third gravestone. Engraved upon it was yet another unknown name to him, "Athanasius."

With fingers chilled and soil caked beneath his fingernails, it dawned on the hermit that nothing big had ever happened in his life. Certainly nothing like this. *Lord, why me? Why did you choose me to discover this—the gravestone of the first apostle martyred?* Pelayo tamed his excitement and raised his arms and voice in humble prayer, "Whatever the reason, Lord, thank you. I know that as big as this is, it's all for your greater glory." He then knew what his next step had to be: to share this good news with his superior, Bishop Theodomir of Iria Flavia.

*   *   *

All through that night, Pelayo churned with gratitude for heaven's gift that he experienced. *What might this all mean? Will people believe me? What if many do believe that the grave of the apostle is here? How might life for this forgotten land in Galicia be changed? People? Yes! Many, many people might come! If so, what will become of my solitude?* These and many more questions stormed his mind.

The lack of sleep didn't faze the hermit, for sunrise couldn't come soon enough. He was teaming with energy. He packed a small sack, some cheese and bread, and a water gourd. Pelayo half-walked, half-ran the twenty-three kilometers to the cathedral where the bishop resided. With surprising quickness, the bishop received him immediately. The story of the melodic music floating toward his rural dwelling, the bright star contained by the ring of stars, and starlight striking the ground gushed from him like a waterfall. Pelayo's excitement was not only unstoppable; it was infectious. Bishop Theodomir's face flushed when the animated hermit shared the discovery of the three headstones.

By mid-morning the next day, the bishop had already assembled a small patrol to accompany him and Pelayo to the place where the hermit had made the discovery. Six of them plodded along in single file. With but one exception, all were silent and reflective. Pelayo's robust enthusiasm could not be contained. The short, slender hermit's gamboling gait outpaced the bishop's entourage. Out of guilt, he would run back and gush with excitement, "It's not much further. Not much at all. It's holy ground, for sure, I tell you." Sunset came and went before the group arrived. By the time they finally rounded the Ligradon Mountains, their destination lay but three hundred meters before them. Even at that distance, the same enthralling melody could be heard. Pitch darkness swallowed the earth in all but one place—the grove ahead.

"It is just as you have testified," confirmed the bishop. There it was: the trees, the stars above, and the streaks of starlight shooting toward earth. Pelayo stole a long look at Theodomir. His countenance was enraptured, his skin color was now pale with shock, and his hands trembled. With his eyes fixated on the starlit site ahead, His Excellency stumbled occasionally, not watching where his feet were taking him.

The hermit directed them to the slim break between the branches where they might twist themselves into the central, grassy clearing. The grass he had madly pulled away still lay scattered about. The headstones were conspicuously visible just as Pelayo had reported: James in the center, Theodore to the right, and Athanasius on the left.

The instant the full entourage entered the grassy clearing, they fell to their knees. A silent awe overtook the six. "So the legend is true," uttered the bishop. He reached forward and with reverence, swept a hand over James's headstone. He gasped, "Son of Zebedee. Son of Thunder. So," he breathed, "Here is where you lie. And your two disciples lie as guardians at each side."

The bishop's confirmation validated the enormity of this discovery. With the glow of the starlight overhead and the heavenly melody swirling around them, the bishop lifted his arms toward the light of heaven. "No greater love does a man have than that he lay down his life for his friends."

"None," voiced Pelayo, his tears spilled with gratitude.

*   *   *

The discovery of James's final resting place marked the beginning of millions of pilgrims journeying the trail to see it. Heaven's lure to the gravesite of the Son of Thunder still attracts new pilgrims. Three pilgrimages across Spain later, I can claim that the experience remarkably changed my life. It all started in an intimate moment during prayer.

Chapter 4

GRACE

Definition: "a favor, goodwill, loving kindness . . . an undeserved help that God gives us to respond to His call to become partakers of divine nature and eternal life."

My Camino

"I do not at all understand the mystery of grace—only that it meets us where we are but does not leave us where it found us."

Anne Lamont

I welcomed this morning the same way I welcome every morning: I pulled back the drapes and hoisted open the blinds. Sunlight flooded the bedroom, allowing me an unobstructed view of the day. I settled into my high-backed Queen Anne-style chair and shed the last sleepy cast of the night. I tried to remain faithful to prayer in spite of my long spell of dryness with the Lord. For months now, my heart had not been in it and I had heard and felt nothing. I wondered, *Was He even listening?* A wise spiritual director had encouraged me: "Don't give up. Why stop talking to Him when you need Him most? Keep pushing forward."

I sat in my prayer chair and offered my usual question. *Is there something You want to teach me today, Lord?* I read some Scripture and some words in the day's verse salted my appetite. These I would use for my meditation. I closed my eyes and quieted my body—first my feet on the carpet, then my resting legs, my arms on the chair—even the movements of my breathing. These were unwelcome distractions. I was so thirsty for Him. I breathed His words in the Scripture slowly, deliberately, over and over in my heart of hearts.

After some time, I sensed my meditation growing deeper and becoming more contemplative. Reciting the Scripture and holding on to the initial verses were no longer necessary. The Holy Spirit was now leading and carrying my thoughts. I embraced the time to be silent and to listen—really listen—without expectation. I surrendered to this moment of prayer and felt such freedom. I was a little boy squeezed hip to hip alongside with my heavenly Daddy, my Abba. It had been such a long time since I felt His love so convincingly. I had known it in my head, but now there was a movement of love deep within me.

Relishing this moment, I was suddenly enveloped in a new, far deeper and richer faith encounter than I had ever experienced before. It was, dare I say, pure holiness. Long ago I had been blessed by holy, grace-filled moments in my life, but none compared with how powerfully present the Holy Spirit was to me right then. Joy buoyed within me. I wanted to pause and savor this moment, but I couldn't. I sensed something more, something good from God was coming. Approaching me was His grace—an instantaneous sense of His loving presence.

I've had times in my life when I looked back and thought, God's grace is here—even though I didn't deserve it. These were times when His grace alone saved me, healed me, protected me, forgave me, and much more. But this moment was far different. This time I believed, in faith, that grace was descending upon me, and even its approach was a gift. Anticipation consumed me. God delivered His grace as a drifting, floating, pure, rudderless feather. My heart drummed harder and harder as its gentle path headed directly toward me. Utterly stunned,

I could not think or speak. I was paralyzed in profound humility and gratitude, and suspense built within me for understanding. The Spirit's feather-like movement of grace swayed closer and closer, inch by inch, until it took its last, short, zigzagged dance immediately above me. I froze in breathless awe.

The Spirit's grace landed precisely on its target—my heart. The moment was so intimate, so precious. I felt only divine love—a pure and overflowing love, far richer than I had felt any other time in my life.

My body gasped for a new, long-needed breath. I suddenly wondered, *Dare I keep going? What if God wants to ask something of me? Would I be willing to say yes? Do I have enough faith to even face what might be ahead? Or should I just get out now?*

I had a choice. A scary choice.

I chose grace.

At that, a sunburst of warmth and light erupted in my heart. Somewhere in my soul the word "wonderful" whispered reverently. The mission of grace continued. Its warmth and light bore deeper into my spirit. God's love intensified until another pause occurred. A new choice emerged, *Do I allow grace to go even deeper?*

I chose grace—again.

No IMAX 3D movie could have captured the vividness of the image that formed in my mind's eye. In the distance were purple-gray, majestic mountain peaks dipped in snow. Some of the mightier crests hid in the clouds. Startlingly, I was in the scene, standing on a clay trail. It was abundantly littered with stones and skirted with deep green grasses, brilliant red poppies, delicate white daisies, and field upon field containing thousands of mysterious plants each abundantly covered in lemon-yellow blossoms. This scene stretched for miles. I had no clue why I was present in the scene, but it didn't matter. I was happy—so overwhelmingly happy. I gasped with delight. *Oh, Lord, how beautiful! What joy!*

There was no time to revel in the sight, for soon the image faded. What had been such a long, parched prayer period was now drenched in a storm shower of grace that drifted down upon me feather-like and peacefully. The vision ended, but I still thirsted for more of Him.

So many questions bounced around in my head like a pinball. I searched for connections. I strained for even a vague understanding of the final scene on the clay-colored trail. *Where had I seen that place before? Where? Where? Where, Lord? I sense You want to tell me more. Is there more?*

Ever so slowly, I remembered scenes from a movie I had watched nearly two years prior: *The Way,* starring Martin Sheen and his son, Emilio Estevez. The images in my prayer started to connect to that movie. Abruptly, like a crack of thunder, a revelation stunned me. God . . . was calling . . . me . . . to do the pilgrimage . . . el Camino de Santiago de Compostela, The Way of St. James! I was convinced of it. I was humbled, dumbfounded, and honored. All at once.

I had never considered doing a walking pilgrimage. I *never* had a single desire to do so even after watching *The Way*. I never had a five hundred-mile walk across Spain on my bucket list. Never.

Certainties and uncertainties began to stir within me. Practical realities confronted me. "How" questions plagued me like a swarm of mosquitoes. *Lord, how would I pay for this? How could I be gone from work so long? How could I walk through mountain ranges, cities, and along empty farm roads for hundreds of miles and not get lost?* (I have a strong reputation for this.) *How can I do this when I am forty pounds overweight and have never backpacked or hiked a long distance before? How can I do such a thing in my sixties while being so physically out of shape? How Lord, really? How?*

I finished my litany of questions and an anxious silence followed. The wait was so worth it. Our God is an awesome God. He unexpectedly breathed a rocket-fueled message of His wisdom, power, and love into my heart with just two mighty words.

"Have faith."

That was it. God had the last word. The imagery of grace faded. I was fully conscious and again physically aware of my surroundings. My eyes opened gradually and now stung from the sunlight streaming into the room beneath the blinds. My legs and arms were like concrete from the length of time spent sitting motionless in my chair. This prayer time was finished, but grace was still present. It remained within me as a precious gift still bearing some mystery. I wondered what this pilgrim calling would involve, what sacrifices it would require, and how to even begin.

But what I didn't know was not as important to me as what I did know. I knew I just had a spiritual encounter during my prayer experience. It was real. It was holy. I knew without a doubt God was calling me to go on a long walk with Him to talk of our love for one another. I believed this wholeheartedly. The words, "Have faith," returned me to my new spiritual reality.

It is said that a pilgrim's Camino starts on the day of God's call. That being true, then *my Camino* began on March 23, 2012. That was the day the Spirit's mighty grace called me to be a pilgrim on el Camino de Santiago de Compostela.

However, before I was to put my hiking boots to the Spanish soil of my Camino, God had a powerful lesson for me to learn first. And it occurred at an unexpected place: Munich International Airport.

Chapter 5

HUMILITY

"A virtue by which a man knowing himself as he truly is, abases himself."

St. Bernard

My Camino

"Something very beautiful happens to people when their world has fallen apart: a humility, a nobility, a higher intelligence emerges at just the point when our knees hit the floor."

Marianne Williamson

Body, mind, and spirit became my life's driving forces in preparation for a five hundred-mile walk on the Camino. I radically changed my eating habits. No more ice cream delights, just lots and lots of salads. Daily exercise was a serious commitment. I gave myself no excuse for not doing something, any kind of exercise regardless of how my day was or what little time I had. *Get down and at least do some sit-ups, do some push-ups, do something. You'll pay the price in those mountains if you don't.* I was relentless. I read countless books on the Camino. I watched many YouTube videos

from other Camino pilgrims. And I prayed. I begged God for strength
and inspiration to keep going.

Nearly a year later, the results were noticeable. It's a great feeling
when family and friends comment, "Wow! You look great." I was thirty-
six pounds lighter. I survived strenuous park district boot camps. I could
run 5K races with satisfying results for a sixty-something-year-old.

I had a list of eighty-eight friend and family names and their most desperate prayer needs on a notepad in my cell phone. I pledged to offer up
these needs to our Lord at the many ancient churches along the Camino.

I was also a student of the ancient pilgrimage. I could carry on
impressive dialogues of the history of the trail and places of interest well
before I took the first hiking step. I was already a bit of a Camino junkie.

Most importantly, my prayer time had come to life. The dry, des-
ert-like prayer routines were past. My conversations with the Lord
were rewarded with greater insight and encouragement. In short,
my strength and health were radically transformed, my mind keenly
informed, and my spiritual life overflowed with blessing. If anyone
was ever ready for such a daunting pilgrimage, it was me. I brimmed
with confidence. I caught myself feeling so proud. *What a great Camino
I will have*, I thought. *Just look at me, or just ask, and I will impress you with
how much I know.* I was ready!

My excitement grew when a surprise arrived. I had gained interest in
visiting Medjugorie, Croatia, a village gaining worldwide attention due to
firsthand accounts of miraculous occurrences. Pilgrims reported seeing
the sun dance in the sky. Some saw multicolored orbs dance before them.
Others witnessed the sterling silver chain of their rosary beads transform
into gold links. Reputation about Medjugorie and the presence of Jesus's
mother, Mary, brought thousands upon thousands of faithful believers.
Secretly embedded in my prayer time I asked, *Is there a miracle for me here, Lord?*

To my surprise, a friend presented a financial gift that would offset
travel expenses for me to visit Medjugorie. With permission to take additional time off from work, the opportunity had a green light. My heart
swelled with anticipation of not one but two spiritual encounters in my

near future. My revised travel plan lay before me. Spain and the Camino would immediately follow a short stay in Medjugorie.

Everything I needed was in a backpack that contained only the essentials for forty days. Unfortunately, it was five pounds heavier than the ideal weight for someone my size. Three of the pounds were a small laptop for my daily blog entries. My rationalizations overrode stringent advice by experienced Camino walkers. *I can't do without my laptop*, I determined. *Besides, I'm stronger and for goodness sake, what's three pounds?* I lifted the device between two fingers. *Come on, that's nothing. I can handle it.*

I was to travel from O'Hare International Airport en route to Munich, Germany. There would be a four-hour layover until my connecting flight to Dubrovnik, Croatia. I made arrangements through the hotel manager for a taxi to pick me up and drive the hour and a half through the mountainous countryside to my destination.

Two days before departure, my sinuses became heavily congested, depleting my energy and clear thinking. I saw a doctor for some antibiotics and other drugs, but the medicines didn't affect the severity of the infection that overwhelmed me like a tsunami. On top of this were final family issues and many people requesting last-minute information. My to-do list grew to a staggering length. I sacrificed sleep to satisfy the majority of these needs until I had slept only twelve hours out of the previous forty-eight. I was utterly exhausted.

I rationalized, *The flight's seven hours. I'll catch up then.* I took two decongestants with the warning "may cause drowsiness," and a sleep aid. I thought I would certainly drift into a deep sleep while airborne. But I was wrong. Very wrong. The aircraft jerked madly like a roller coaster from side to side; everything and everyone rattled in the turbulence. Add to that the all-too-frequent beverage cart interruptions and sleep was impossible. My infection grew stronger and aggressively attacked the rest of my sinus cavities. My head felt like a throbbing block of solid concrete. Changes in cabin pressure intensified the sinus headache agony.

Just two hours into the flight, I was a circus show of sneezing, nose blowing, and congested coughing. In jeopardy of the same sickness, disgusted passengers cast glances my way. Upon landing in Munich, I was zombie-like. Sleep deprived and overmedicated, I staggered under the effects of a sleep aid now ready to launch. I never looked nor felt more pathetic in all my life. I tried to reassure myself, *Just hours from now I'll be in Croatia. Plenty of peace and rest is waiting there.*

I arrived in Munich and found a seat just six feet from my new boarding gate. I planted myself in a black, stiff-backed vinyl seat. *I'll just rest here. I have four hours to kill.* The decongestants labeled "may cause drowsiness" went into full effect. The sleep aid overtook me in full force. Some of the minute-by-minute nose blowing and coughing retreated. I could finally rest uninterrupted.

I slept like the dead long forgotten. What a desperately needed sleep it was. But as my heavy eyelids finally opened, I made an odd discovery: no one was around anymore. No one. No ticket agent, no flight staff, no fellow passengers, no gangway toward a plane, no signage for Dubrovnik. Nothing was there, and there was no one to clear up my confusion.

A customer service sign led me to a long, slow-moving line and my only hope for answers. Anxiety brewed inside me as I waited for the agent.

"You miss because you sleep," he chuckled in his strong, ridiculing German accent. "You must call ticketing agent—rearrange new flight," he grinned arrogantly. I was brushed away with the call, "Next!" Shame washed over me. I was so bitterly angry at myself and felt worse as I imagined what others would think of my big blunder.

More bad news was ahead. I was trapped in a forty-minute conversation with the US ticket agent, using precious international calling minutes. My new flight would not depart for another twenty-six hours. The bad day was getting worse. I resigned myself to a night's sleep in the Munich International Airport, still sporting my ugly sinus mess and suffering profound humiliation over the last-minute travel costs.

With my phone still activated, I now was alerted to some emails that were sent hours ago from Medjugorie. "Oh my word, the *hotel*. I didn't contact the hotel!" With the slender amount of international calling minutes remaining on my new plan, I phoned Ivanka, the hotel manager.

She had sent the taxi I requested to pick me up in Dubrovnik and firmly asserted that the driver took the hour-and-a-half ride to the airport. He had waited and waited before deciding I was not to be found. Ivanka unleashed a storm of irritation upon me for causing such an inconvenience. I tried to explain my situation with every bit of grace I could muster. I pleaded my litany of pathetic excuses, "I was sick; I had not slept in days; I took medicine that was strong; I didn't want to miss the plane."

Her voice rose louder over my explanations. She made it abundantly clear how my negligence to call with my changed travel plans had inconvenienced many people trying to serve me. The infection left me with a crackly voice, also distorted by my stuffy nose. In spite of how terrible I sounded, I sweet-talked and apologized. She was hesitant to send another taxi. Who would blame her? Nonetheless, with my newly scheduled arrival time in Dubrovnik the next day, she agreed, but also added, "I be charging you for another taxi dis time too. Yes?"

What choice did I have? I thanked Ivanka for her kindness and assured her I would pay for the double expenses for taxi travel.

"If you no there, I charge you again," she asserted.

"I understand, ma'am. Thank you. I will be there," I assured her.

Shame and self-loathing bubbled up in me like a volcano. "How could I have done something so stupid? What an idiot!" I judged.

I was about to pay the price for my errors. I faced a night sleeping on airport chairs. I painfully maneuvered my body in and under the fixed chrome armrests, settling for the best spot near the new gate for tomorrow's late afternoon flight.

When I woke, I was in for a new experience: early morning personal hygiene in the airport washroom. With all the sinus mess and sweating on the vinyl chairs all night, I desperately needed freshening. I pulled off my shirt and took a bird bath of sorts. Using the pump soap, I washed my face, head, and chest in the sink. Talk about embarrassing—a grown man trying to dry himself on a wall-hung hand dryer. I was a sight.

Boarding my new flight could *not* come soon enough. What a contrast those vinyl seats were to the cushy airline seat I now enjoyed en route to

Dubrovnik. Walking out of that airport, I was grateful a different cab driver came for my travel to the hotel, sparing me direct apologies. Was this the end of my bad luck?

One must pass several security checkpoints when traveling through these small countries en route to Croatia. Security at those checkpoints was painfully slow. It was midnight before I arrived at the hotel with backpack in tow.

If Ivanka was upset with the inconveniences the day before, this late arrival roused a livid warning on her face. She had to wait six hours past her work shift for my check in, after starting at five a.m. With patience and grace stretched to the limit, she began, "Why you no call me? Why you make me send taxi and not call to stop him? Tell me why? Why you take medicine that make you sleepy when you going to ride airplane? Why? Why?" she challenged in her distinct Croatian accent.

I could only offer my pathetic and exhausted response, "I couldn't. I was so sick, so, so sick."

She riveted me with one exasperated glare, "OK, here your key. Breakfast until 9:30. Go sleep. Then we talk," she offered in a surrendered tone.

While walking through the hotel, I passed a group of Irish men enjoying a late night cocktail. I was introduced and one's shout filled the room, "You're the guy who slept!" All I could do was nod. It was true, but the comment grated my already broken spirit.

The next morning, I saw Ivanka long enough for a "Good morning" greeting. Sleep and a new day's outlook obviously transformed her disposition. There were too many new guests needing her for us to have a conversation. I set out for a full day of prayer and reflection at the holy shrines. Rest and energy returned as the medicines relieved my infection. I could finally think more clearly. Silent meditations allowed me to hear God breaking through my wounded spirit. As I reviewed "my terrible, horrible, very bad days," God revealed a new insight to me.

During a meditation, God showed me a movie of myself over the past months. I saw the attention and pleasure that occupied me in preparation for the Camino. I heard my own words as I told others of my journey ahead. How I enjoyed the admiring "Wow!" responses to the news of where I would be going and what the trail would involve. I recalled how important I felt during the little lectures I gave others of St. James, the Camino, and of Medjugorie. The truth of me was growing more and more real. I was ashamed of the replay of my overconfident voice as I talked to God about the upcoming pilgrimage.

I recognized that my missed flight in Munich was largely due to my stubbornness. My ego refused to allow me to even inform the gate attendant of the flight I was scheduled to board. He might have offered a wake-up call in time for the flight. All the out-of-my-control circumstances could win me sympathy, but the ugly hidden truth was my selfish, arrogant, "I'm so important" *pride*. This undeniable truth brought me to my knees.

I confessed it, and God forgave me. But could I forgive me? The regrets lingered; I needed help.

While having breakfast the next morning, I caught sight of Ivanka. Getting to know her better revealed a radically different Ivanka than my midnight arrival had. I came to relish her lovely Croatian-laced English accent that displaced "d" sounds for our "th" sounds. She sat across from me, and ever so gently slid her compassion my way, "How come you look so sad? You still sick? Or you sad?"

I confessed, "I am still upset with myself for causing so much trouble. I feel so sorry for what I did—missing the plane, the taxi, all the extra expenses. Just everything."

Ivanka's wisdom struck my heart like a lightning bolt. "What be da past is da past. No dink bout dat no more. Be dinking about now. OK?" She stared at me with a soft smile, her face seemed to glow. Then she followed with a simple, yet touching gesture: she patted my arm. I could almost smell the fragrance of the Spirit in that moment.

A smile overtook me—the first in six days. I found permission to forgive myself. For days I had tried to run from my guilt, complain of it, seek others' sympathy, and cling to the shame of it. In some distorted corner of my mind I believed I needed to suffer longer with my guilt before I could earn my own forgiveness. How foolish!

Ivanka's wisdom echoed, "What be da past is da past." The lesson I learned was a gift wrapped in one word: humility. I came to embrace who I am and *Whose* I am. With that, I saw that "my terrible, horrible, very bad days" were gifts to humbly empty me before the Camino. This would allow more space within me for Him.

An enigma about humility unknotted for me. God's full love cannot be grasped while holding clutched fists of denied faults, weaknesses, and imperfections. Love comes full measure to the open palms of beggars who offer their broken lives to God while on their knees.

"Humble yourselves before the Lord, and he will exalt you." (James 4:10)

You don't know what you don't know. Humility was a lesson I didn't know, at least not fully enough, but God knew I needed it. The test of how well I had learned would come five thousand feet atop the Pyrenees Mountains.

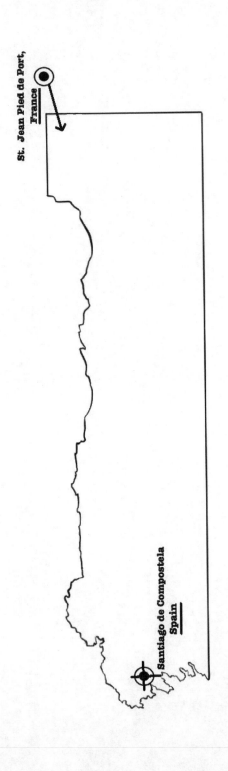

Chapter 6

OFFER IT UP

"A sacrifice to be real must cost, must hurt, must empty ourselves. The fruit of silence is prayer, the fruit of faith is love, the fruit of love is service, the fruit of service is peace."

Blessed Mother Theresa of Calcutta

The Camino

The historically famous el Camino de Santiago is known by several names. Some people use "The Camino Frances," others call it "Napoleon's Way,"[14] while others use its English translation, "The Way of St. James," or just its abbreviated identifications "The Camino" or "The Way." Whatever it's called, the most popular starting location for traveling the pilgrimage is the city, St. Jean Pied de Port, France.[15] This name means, "St. John at the foot of the mountain pass." The word, "port" means "passage." This little medieval village clings to the northern foot of the Pyrenees Mountains separating France and Spain. No airport is there; many pilgrims fly into Paris, France, or Madrid or Barcelona in Spain. Pilgrims coming to St. Jean from any of these major cities often choose to travel on high speed trains which exceed 200km per hour (roughly 125mph). The ride is most comfortable and lacks the jolts and bumps of standard trains.

Pilgrims who begin The Camino here will ultimately walk 790 kilometers (roughly five hundred miles) to the destination of the Cathedral of Santiago near the western coast of Spain. The Camino trail is made easy to follow by strategically placed yellow arrows. These road markers are of two varieties. Some are commercially casted yellow, horizontal streaks in the outline of a conch shell imposed on a distinct blue background. Most, however, are simplistically hand-painted, yellow arrows brushed across buildings, street curbs, and stone fences. Pilgrims need only to follow the yellow arrows, and they'll eventually arrive in the city of Santiago, Spain. This is the location where the body of St. James, apostle of Jesus, is buried.

Another noteworthy option is to begin the pilgrimage in the town of Aire-sur-l'Adour located east of St. Jean in southern France. This is the city that begins the "Le Puy Way."[16] The views here include the French Basque area, thirteenth-century castles, and the lengthy spectacular panoramas of the Pyrenees before reaching The Camino. This trail adds 155 kilometers (96 miles) and for those who endure the entire pilgrimage to Santiago it comes to just under a thousand kilometers (620 miles).

The more popular St. Jean Pied de Port is rich in history. Its strategic location has brought many famed military leaders. It was conquered by King Richard the Lionhearted,[17] and Charlemagne and Rome's mighty army marched through it, as did Napoleon's.

Three striking features are located in the center of this quaint, ancient village. One is the River Nive that runs through the center of St. Jean. Attractive white stucco buildings are adorned with striking red-orange shutters and wood balconies hang outside many homes allowing for a view of the river and the mountain horizon. The second feature is perhaps the most photographed site in St. Jean Pied de Port. It is St. James Gate at the bridge over the River Nive and the adjacent Church of Notre Dame dating from the thirteenth century. The third feature includes two statues situated in the brickwork overlooking the town's main cobblestone road. One is of St. John the Baptist and another of the Virgin with Child. This sight provides a divine inspiration while inviting a reflective pause for the pilgrim. *What awaits? Are injuries ahead? Who might I meet? Will I make it to Santiago?* Prayers abound for the month-long journey ahead.

The first order of business for all pilgrims before beginning their journey is to stop at the Pilgrim's Office. Multilingual clerks are there to officially register pilgrims, help them get their Camino Credentials, and to post the first rubber stamp graphic confirming their pilgrimage is beginning in St. Jean Pied de Port. A conch shell, the official symbol of a Santiago pilgrim, can also be purchased. Most buy one and tie it to their backpack. Maps with recommended distances to walk each day, as well as maps showing the elevations of sections on the Camino are provided. Pilgrims typically leave the Pilgrim's Office in search of their night's lodging.

Albergues, also known as hostels, offer a variety of sleeping arrangements based upon their quality and degree of privacy. Pilgrims pay a nominal fee each day ranging from five to fifteen euros (between six and eighteen USD) for a top or bottom bunk, access to a stationary tub for hand-washing their clothes, and use of bathroom facilities and showers. They may or may not have clothes washing machines or dryers. Sleeping quarters are shared by men and women, and could contain anywhere between six and twenty-six bunks in one room.

Most find simple sandwiches and snacks along the trailside cafes. The final meal for the day is at restaurants serving the "Menu de Perigrino del Dia"—that is, the "Pilgrim's Menu of the Day," ranging in price from eight to twelve euros (nine to fourteen USD). Almost without exception, the restaurant serves three courses. Water and wine is served without limit and is free of charge.

Pilgrims have concerns of how they might get medical help while walking. As an assurance, in larger towns, a *farmacia* (pharmacy) is easy to spot with its green neon sign forming what looks like a plus symbol. Here pilgrims can find reliable clinical advice and over-the-counter drugs at reasonable prices. For more serious ailments, medical treatment is available in larger towns. Taxis are readily available from most all locations to transport those in need.

Universally, accommodations along the Camino are easily available, safe, and clean.

My Camino

My first day in St. Jean Pied de Port was rewarded by a stay at a unique albergue. One of the proprietors, Eric, was endearing because of his philosophical nature. He waited until the registration line filled the small lobby and then stopped the proceedings. In his deep, French accented, Lloyd Barrymore stage voice, he began a dramatically delivered monologue. "Friends, you are about to embark on a rare life challenge. Many falsely believe that they are walking the Camino. Not true. The Camino walks you. Surrender yourself to her, listen to her speaking, and you will discover your real self." This Camino sermon continued with everyone's rapt attention. All of us were new pilgrims brimming with inspiration and silent fears.

Sacrifices came right away that first day on the Camino. What a cardiac stress test par excellence! The climb toward the mountain peak was torturously difficult for my sixty-two-year-old body. My clothes turned darker shades from heavy perspiration. Because the grade was so steep, I could not walk upright. My body leaned toward my boots. My trekking poles clawed at the gravely path and my biceps screamed in pain as they grew and tightened. With each straining step upward, my lungs stretched for another refill. The exertion allowed only panting breaths, clearly not enough for any length of time. As a sort of mind game to spur me onward, I would spot a tree or trail marker just a few hundred meters ahead as a goal. That would be my next desperately needed rest stop.

After long hours, I finally spotted a sign ahead indicating a short distance to the mountain peak. With my lungs starved for more of the thin mountain air, I leaned hard and pushed myself forward. My heart thumped madly and my strained calf muscles cramped, trying to reach my newly chosen rest stop near the mountain peak. Just when I thought the worst of my struggle was behind, a new, rude challenge presented itself.

Fresh gale force winds buffeted me face-on, indicating that a storm would follow. My clothes flared, and my pants rattled like a sail. I strained to push myself forward, struggling under my heavy backpack. The brutal winds made my trekking poles uncontrollable. I lifted one and it flew madly in the air with only my wrist straps to tether it to me. One pole after the other whipped in the wind, causing one wild arm wrestling match after another.

The devilish winds compromised my stride momentum and I rocked from my toes to the balls of my feet with each step. *This is insane*, I thought.

Then I tested a wild idea. I turned full-face into the wind and pulled back my poles from any support. I chanced a full body lean-in toward a free-fall forward. Shockingly, the wind levitated my weight, backpack and all, as I leaned forward suspended by the wind's force. With another 5 kilometers (3 miles) to go, my quads, my calves, and my back muscles quivered and twitched under the strain.

I am done, I thought. *I can't do this.* I had prayed for months in preparation for this Camino and on the first day I saw only failure ahead. However, there was no retreating. I was trapped on this mountain peak and didn't know what my next step should be.

Only two things were certain in that moment. There was my suffering, and there was my faith in a God, who, I believe, cares about my suffering. Prayer changes when facing only these two realities. My suffering took on new meaning. I stood paralyzed on the trail as an inspiration appeared in my mind's eye. I imagined Jesus's persecution. I recalled Him pleading, "Take this cup of suffering, Father." My physical suffering could relate, though minutely, with how Jesus's body must have ached under the physical brutality of Calvary.

I prayed, *Jesus, how You love us. How You suffered! And how You offered that love up for us.* Wait. My mind recoiled. *Your suffering was offered up . . . for me.* The last two words stuttered out of me with new insight. *Suffering, offered up to the Father, creates love.* Another quick realization dumbfounded me: *My suffering can move God to relieve another person's suffering. Accepting my suffering expresses love for another.*

To move beyond my pains, I must do as Jesus did. I must offer up my suffering here for another. A quick review of my prayer list and it came to me like a red flashing light. My mind flashed back to a conversation with a father of two toddler-aged girls, each in desperate need of a kidney transplant. Perhaps because of my compassion for their struggle, the dad shared with me a short video clip of the two girls at their kitchen table. One of the girls had a sickly complexion and a bloated appearance due to the kidney failure. I recalled the worry-worn look on his wife's face in the video, and the tender fear in the father's expression. This memory stole my heart and redirected a new dedication in me.

Lord, I accept my pain, present and future, in order to identify with Your suffering. Take my suffering and pain. I offer it up for those two little girls. I surrender all of it, in love of you, Lord.

Spiritually buoyed by my new epiphany in faith, I braved the trail's last four kilometers (more than two miles) along a precipitous descent leading to the village of Roncesvalles on the southern fringe of the Pyrenees. I registered at an albergue that housed several hundred pilgrims, showered, found a quick meal, and raced to my bed. With my muscles melting in my bunk, my new mantra recycled in a prayer loop, "Love grows when suffering is offered up for others."

Our Camino

Suffering is a part of life. We all have, had, or will experience the trauma of some suffering. It is the curse of Adam and Eve. So what form of suffering has been in your life? Is there something we can learn on Our Camino by the way we approach suffering?

Suffering patiently has not been a strong quality of mine, especially before the Camino. I am one who does not suffer silently, or well, for that matter. For most of my life when I faced some struggle, I would name the pain and plead with God to make it all go away and *quickly*, may I add. Can you identify with this thinking?

Don't get me wrong. It's not an unholy thing to petition God for relief from our suffering or the suffering of another. He hears our prayers. After all, Christ is the Gentle Healer in the Gospel accounts who cured many. However, one thought worth strong reflection is *what* and *how* to pray during periods of suffering.

A lesson on this can be learned from a woman during childbirth. She experiences contractions minutes apart that can last for hours. I've witnessed my wife in the agony of these pains. The "what" she would pray, and sometimes scream, was a short Scripture verse. Her favorite was, "I can do all things through him who strengthens me" (Phil. 4:13). This allowed her to identify with Christ's suffering. The "how" behind her prayers was to keep a single-minded focus on the hope to come. In this way she offered up the suffering in the hope of the new life coming. Simply put, when we have faith in His Word and grip tightly to His hope, we gain greater love.

My faith, hope, and love took on a new and deeper realization when I climbed Alto de Perdòn, the Mountain of Forgiveness. Climb this mountain with me and realize, as I did, the mountain of times God forgives. We may even realize the mountain of forgiving we need to offer others.

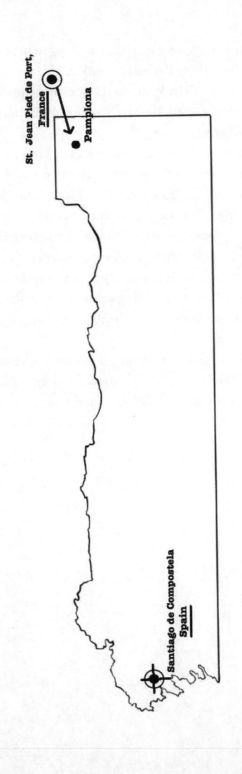

Chapter 7

A MOUNTAIN OF FORGIVENESS

Definition: "forgiveness—giving up my right to hurt you for hurting me" (Anonymous)

"God dealt with our whole situation on the cross: there is nothing left for you to settle. Just say to Him, 'Lord, I cannot forgive and I will no longer try to do it; but I trust that You in me will do it. I can't forgive and love; but I trust that You will forgive and love in my place and that You will do these things in me.'"

Corrie Ten Boom, Holocaust survivor

The Camino

A mere sixty-seven kilometers (forty miles) riding in a passenger vehicle can pass in a blink. Not so for walkers on the Camino, and certainly not so for pilgrims in Roncesvalles with the shadow of the Pyrenees behind them and a ski-slope descent to the city of Zubiri. They may stand at the base of the mountain's elevation of 950 meters (3,100 feet), proud of surviving the Pyrenees. They will soon encounter a new series of physical workouts in the next twenty kilometers (roughly 12.5 miles) on their next day. Overconfidence might draw them to think, *I've done those mountains; nothing can be as hard. It's just a different kind of hard that is ahead.*

The Camino from Zubiri to Pamplona is, for the most part, pleasant and peaceful. In sharp contrast, Pamplona teems with energetic city life. Following this, the trail envelops the pilgrim with stunning landscapes. The serenity of this stage of the Camino is rudely shaken by a new hard: the breath-stealing ascent of Alto de Perdón. Challenging? Yes, but not without rewards.

Pyrenees—the Last Descent

From the southern base of the Pyrenees, the Camino has several precipitous descents. They give the impression of a roller coaster track with a walk-down of one hundred meters (320 feet) then up another one hundred meters. This cycle occurs three different times before reaching Alto Mezquíriz, perched at the same altitude the pilgrim left at Roncesvalles. Pilgrims white-knuckle-grip their trekking poles while the trail descends 235 meters (eight hundred feet). The roller coaster continues with a new hundred-meter climb to Alto de Erro, only to be followed by a three-hundred-meter (roughly thousand-foot) descent over the scant distance of five kilometers (three miles). Its steep grade and abundance of loose, golf-ball-sized rocks over twenty-two kilometers (13.5 miles) are what make this single day on the Camino trail so physically taxing.

As challenging as the trail is, the views along this route more than reward the pilgrim with stunning natural and peaceful vistas. Farm fields display the year's crops with their green leaves waving in mountain breezes. Precise rows of spindly grapevines and branches stretch from vineyard to vineyard. Miles of short, succulent grazing grasses add to the fertile, verdant color of grazing land for livestock. The palette of the Creator's artistry is alive and vivid for the Camino sojourner.

Pamplona

Pamplona[18] claims credit as the most populated city on the Camino. It is rich in history and culture. First-century Roman occupation is evidenced by recently excavated streets and buildings. Later, Muslims conquered the city in the early 700s until overtaken by the Basques a few decades later. Charlemagne has the distinction of having destroyed the city walls around Pamplona around the year 800.

Pamplona also steals worldwide attention for the Fiesta de San Fermín—the Running of the Bulls.[19] Every July 6–14, tourists storm Pamplona for the event. Tall, double fencing erected along 825 meters (2,700 feet) of the city route corral the six, massive, long-horned bulls and six steers. More than twenty thousand predominantly young adult males participate. It is the custom to wear white shirt and pants, a red scarf for a belt, and a bright red kerchief around the neck. Contained within the fencing, these adventure seekers taunt the bulls to charge them as they run just ahead of the attacking beasts. Their goal is to lead them to the stadium's bullring while the masses watch from balconies overlooking the stampede. Widespread reports reveal that most who participate in the running are highly intoxicated. Numerous injuries and even deaths have occurred by being gored or trampled under the hooves of these charging, monstrous bulls during the festival. Roughly a million citizens and tourists strain to witness the life-threatening thrills these young adults voluntarily undertake.

It must be noted that the notoriety of the Running of the Bulls was enlivened by world acclaimed author Ernest Hemingway in his novel *The Sun Also Rises*. Traces of Hemingway's stays in Pamplona in the late 1920s are landmarked with statues and photos of him in hotels, restaurants, and open-air cafes.

Alto de Perdòn—The Mountain of Forgiveness

After leaving Pamplona, pilgrims travel a gentle and relatively level trail. A stark change awaits—the intimidating challenge of Alto de Perdón, the Mountain of Forgiveness. This cone-shaped mountain towers before its pilgrims. The mountain has briskly sweeping slopes for a climb of four hundred meters (just over 1,300 feet) to its peak. This entire height of Alto de Perdón is climbed within a span of a mere four kilometers (2.5 miles). The strenuous ascent travels long, steep inclines, and numerous switchbacks.

The heavy-breathing pilgrim lumbers up to the pike for a jaw-dropping reward. The panorama at the top is stunning! Stretching unobstructed is the large city of Pamplona to the east and many small towns to the west. Countless small farm plots are divided by irregularly shaped rows of small trees and flowering shrubs. The rich red soil provides a contrast to the many shades of green coloring the farm plots, vineyards, and almond trees. In stark contrast, the peak is skirted by massive windmills forming a string through the countryside.

Overlooking this landscape is the peak's unique central attraction. Inch-thick, wrought-iron figures of a dozen men, women, and children in garb representing pilgrims over the Camino's many centuries separate the mountain's peak from the peaceful countryside below. It is an irresistible stop for pilgrims to take a brief rest, drink in the natural beauty, and of course, take photos.

My Camino

It is said that lightning doesn't strike twice in the same place. Not true for me. God's spiritual lightning bolt struck me two different times on Alto de Perdón. Just when the level trail from Pamplona lulled me into a false sense of confidence, it was soon shaken by my daunting new test.

The blazing white and yellow sunrise broke the horizon behind me, like a million flood lamps. It lasted briefly before sliding behind the heavy cloud cover, yet long enough to illuminate the formidable Alto de Perdón, the Mountain of Forgiveness. Its massive height reminded me of an impressive sight in Chicago—Willis Tower, once the tallest structure in the world. Suburbs even thirty-some miles from the city marvel at it from their distance. Today it was not the tower in Chicago but Alto de Perdón which towered before me a scant two and a half miles away like a bully on the playground. I took a strong inhale, then exhaled. *I must be crazy to try this!*

Like muffled firecrackers, the day's rain shower sprung off my jacket and wide-brimmed hat. I gripped my trekking poles with numb fingers and white knuckles. Ducking my head from the rain, I was unaware of the seemingly endless trail ahead, but my shorter and shorter breaths told me I was approaching the steepest stretch to the peak. The rain made for cautious footsteps, so I concentrated on the multitude of rocks which rendered the trail maddeningly dangerous. *Just concentrate on your boots*, I reassured myself.

Fighting boredom, I began to mindlessly recite the mountain's name. It spilled out of me over and over again subconsciously: *A Mountain of Forgiveness. A Mountain of Forgiveness. A Mountain of Forgiveness.*

Strained breathing is not unusual while climbing a sharp incline. But this was different. I realized my struggling breaths were matching the words I was reciting. I inhaled the word "mountain" and exhaled the word "forgiveness." Inhale "mountain," exhale "forgiveness." Inhale "mountain," exhale "forgiveness." My very breath focused my attention solely on these words: mountain, forgiveness.

With each step upward, each breath was harder and stronger than the last. *Coincidence?* I wondered. *Is there something You want to teach me, Lord? Mountain, Forgiveness. Mountain, Forgiveness. Mountain, Forgiveness.*

Forgiveness of what? Oh so many sins. So many offenses against God. Too many to count or fully remember. I kept walking. *So many stones, so many sins! Stones made this mountain and my sins made a mountain.* A mental gasp stumbled out of me. *I have committed . . . a mountain . . . of sins. Ugh, such a mountain of sins.*

Rain still snapped at my rain gear as my boots trudged over the litter of stones.

Another thought seeped in. *Maybe this climb is like walking over my mountain of sins.* If so, it was not only an ugly picture—it was taking my breath away, figuratively and literally.

Could God forgive all of them? Could He love me that much?

The staccato pattern in my breath intensified just a hundred meters from the peak. I stopped for a short rest. I tilted my head to the right, looked skyward, and stared blankly. A lightning bolt struck my heart: *It's not about a mountain of sin; it's about a mountain of forgiveness. His forgiveness!*

Forgiveness. The word sprinted into my conscience. Scripture connections stirred. Testimonies I'd heard of His mercy returned. *My* faith story awoke memories of His forgiveness. My mind drifted to Psalm 103:8, 11: "The LORD is merciful and gracious, slow to anger and abounding in steadfast love. . . . For as high as the heavens are above the earth, so great is his steadfast love toward those who fear him."

The height of the heavens. Such a height certainly could be this mountain of forgiveness, I thought.

Turns out, the Lord's message was not about me and my sin. The lesson was all about God's towering mountain of mercy. "Amazing grace, how sweet the sound, that saved a wretch like me." The immensity of this amazing grace struck me like lightning. It brought a startling flash of insight into just how merciful God is.

Then the words of C. S. Lewis echoed inside me, *"Forgiveness is a beautiful idea—until you have something to forgive."*

Our Camino

We've all been there: an event with family, or perhaps a social gathering with a mix of friends. Plodding around is the elephant in the room: that person who has said or done something deeply hurtful. The whole world would agree they've terribly wronged us. To make matters worse, that person appears to be clueless about the hurt they've caused. Perhaps, even more bitter for us to accept, they seem like they don't even care. Or even remember. None of this is true for us, though, the wounded. We care, and we remember!

My mind teeter-tottered between what I felt and what I knew of Jesus's gospels about love and mercy. What if we were to consider that the problem really wasn't the elephant in the room? What if we were to consider that the true beast of burden is us? That it's our unforgiveness that is the elephant that keeps plodding around?

Even more challenging, what if our ability to forgive were greater? What if we could learn how to let transgressions slide off of us like Teflon? What if we could let go of anger, resentment, desires for revenge, ill will, or even a level of hatred for those who hurt us? What if our Camino could be that free? Where would we start? What would be our first step?

The Truth

Our road to freedom starts by first examining the truth behind what hurt us. We need to take a closer look and ask the hard question: Is it possible that the reason I am hurt might just be because of my perception of what happened? All too often what we perceive as hurtful is based upon faulty or incomplete information. We assume, think the worst, or don't give the benefit of the doubt. We make it all about us! So much emotional energy is wasted by our quick judgments. This is why we must first understand the truth.

But what if, after rethinking what happened, there truly is an offender who willfully hurt us? Given the facts, the whole world would agree that person did the unforgiveable. On top of this, that person might still be causing more hurt to you and others around you. There may be a storehouse of friction building between you and your offender.

Either way, is this a difficult mindset to overcome? Is this a real test? For sure! How can the Holy Spirit set us free?

We have to let Him show us the truth in us. We sin. We offend others. We say hurtful things and behave in hurtful ways. So how can we beg forgiveness from God for our offenses, and not extend it to our offenders? The following passage illustrates this:

> Therefore the kingdom of heaven may be compared to a king who wished to settle accounts with his servants. When he began to settle, one was brought to him who owed him ten thousand talents. And since he could not pay, his master ordered him to be

sold, with his wife and children and all that he had, and payment to be made. So the servant fell on his knees, imploring him, "Have patience with me, and I will pay you everything." And out of pity for him, the master of that servant released him and forgave him the debt. But when that same servant went out, he found one of his fellow servants who owed him a hundred denarii, and seizing him, he began to choke him, saying, "Pay what you owe." So his fellow servant fell down and pleaded with him, "Have patience with me, and I will pay you." He refused and went and put him in prison until he should pay the debt. When his fellow servants saw what had taken place, they were greatly distressed, and they went and reported to their master all that had taken place. Then his master summoned him and said to him, "You wicked servant! I forgave you all that debt because you pleaded with me. And should not you have had mercy on your fellow servant, as I had mercy on you?" And in anger his master delivered him to the jailers, until he should pay all his debt. So also my heavenly Father will do to every one of you, if you do not forgive your brother from your heart. (Matt. 18:23–35)

Forgive

The word "forgiving" is an action verb—both mentally and physically. The truth is His mercy is for giving to others, even the unforgivable. It is therefore loving like Jesus loves. Difficult? Impossible? How can we possibly grow to be more forgiving?

Cultivate an attitude of compassion

Nothing builds compassion like seeing the truth about ourselves. St. Ignatius wrote his 30-day Spiritual Exercises about the year 1524. Even today, faithful completion of the exercises are regarded as a gold standard for gaining profound spiritual insights. Interestingly, they are respected and practiced by Christians of many denominations. Contained within The Exercises is the Examen[20] prayer. Spending fifteen minutes toward the end of each day in this simple pattern of prayer focuses us on our need to forgive and the Spirit's involvement in it.

Pray the Examen from St. Ignatius's Spiritual Exercises:

1. Pray for God's help to see your day through His eyes.
2. Give thanks for the gifts of the day. Review the day and name the blessings.
3. Pray over significant feelings that surfaced as you replayed the day. Ask God to help.
4. Rejoice in times that brought you closer to God; seek forgiveness when resisting Him.
5. Look to tomorrow. Ask God to give you the grace you need.

Be on guard against a lazy spirit

Forgiveness sounds like so much work! It takes so much effort to keep forgiving one offense after another. Granting forgiveness is hard to give because of the pain endured. Besides, the person who keeps offending shows no sign of changing. It's easier to hold a grudge and not forgive. So why bother?

This is lazy thinking for believers who seek to live as Jesus taught.

The letters of Paul and Peter and James overflow with directives to accept, even be happy, during trials and sufferings. It is for our own good! God uses these tests of our faith to grow beauty and virtue in us. St. Paul wrote, "for those who love God all things work together for good" (Romans 8:28). Forgiving others points us to better days of peace and happiness. Who would not want that?

This is precisely why we should bother. It's been said, "Hurt people hurt people." The hurts we carefully bury deep inside inevitably spill out in hurtful words and actions upon family and friends close to us. We intuitively repay the hurt trapped within us with more hurt. The old adage comes true, "What we hate in others is that which we hate in ourselves."

As time goes on, "hurt people hurt people who hurt people who hurt more people." Over time, *we* can become the elephant in the room, and others now struggle with offering *us* forgiveness.

We need to bother! Learning how to forgive breaks the cycle of hurtfulness.

Okay. I Want to Bother. How Do I Do It?

Paul tells us why we should grip tightly to the truth: "Do not be conformed to this world, but be transformed by the renewal of your mind, that by testing you may discern what is the will of God, what is good and acceptable and perfect" (Romans 12:2).

The world lures us to hold on to the hurt, to withhold forgiveness, to grow in anger and resentment. The world says, "Don't forgive. Hold on to your hurt until you can pay them back—hurt for hurt. Forgiveness lets them off easy. You have a right to be angry."

These are prisons. Once again, our choice is not to be conformed to this world. But how? So how are we to act?

Get out of jail . . . FREE!

Wage a personal war on judgmental attitudes, memories, and behaviors. Refusing to engage in these allows room for virtue to grow. This creates an addition by subtraction.

Extend kindness and acceptance to that person, even if the offender doesn't deserve it. Begin with a simple, yet sacrificial act of kindness and service. It might be just a few kind words of interest. Initial efforts will likely feel awkward and almost irrational. After all, we're doing something new. We might be tempted to believe the effort is too much of a sacrifice. Some may think, *Why do I have to do all the work?*

Here is why: because this is precisely where growth in virtue occurs—right where we want to give up. God's way is not the easy way. But it's always the best way. Stay on His narrow path. He will bless our efforts.

Pray for the offender. God's perfect will is working in them as well.

In the end, we need only to remember this: forgiveness is the key to our jail cell keeping us from living in God's "good and acceptable and perfect" will.

*   *   *

Seeking forgiveness is one thing. However, granting forgiveness is hard sometimes. How do we forgive someone for a big offense? Mark's faith walk story will inspire our Camino.

Mark began his story by emphasizing that his life was blessed: beautiful wife, great kids, good job. He had it all, plus his passion in life—CrossFit exercise. One look at the tall, good-looking businessman confirmed it.

His big story began while driving home from an ordinary day at work. The speed limit on this patch of four-lane road was forty-five miles per hour, though he admitted most drivers exceeded it a bit. He was traveling in the left lane when a driver swerved into his lane and struck him head-on. He would find out later that this elderly driver was upset, and that this was his attempt at ending his life. The opposite effect nearly occurred for his victim, as Mark's life changed radically.

Paramedics, ambulance, and fire rescue arrived at the gruesome scene. Mark's car had folded like a collapsed accordion around him. Jaws of life carved the car away from his mangled body and he was urgently airlifted to the nearest hospital.

The medical assessment of Mark's condition was frightening. From head to foot, he had numerous broken bones, shredded muscle and tissue, and had a massive concussion. Doctors were astonished that he had survived. It was believed that the years of CrossFit exercise had kept his body clean of toxins and impeccably healthy.

Month upon month would pass as bones healed and multiple surgeries put Mark back together again. Nearly a year after, Mark was subpoenaed to appear in court regarding the accident.

Mark's wife and lawyer escorted him to the front of the courtroom. The prosecutor's table was to one side, and the judge was staged at center, slightly higher up. A glance across the aisle revealed a surprise. It was the first time Mark saw the man who deliberately caused the accident. (Talk about the elephant in the room!)

"It was so sad," Mark shared. "The man sat at the table with his head in his hands sobbing deeply. His adult children stood behind their father, crying uncontrollably. They looked scared, really scared. Maybe it was the shame of what their father had done. Maybe it was just fear of what might happen to their father after the verdict was served. I wasn't sure. It was just so emotional."

In short order, Mark was called to the witness stand. He was drilled with questions regarding his memory of the accident, how it occurred, and a report of his injuries. He answered them all as best he could.

Mark added, "Toward the end of questioning, the judge asked me, 'What do you think this man's punishment should be?'"

He told the judge, "I think this man should pay his debt to society. This should never happen to another person. But for me, I hold no ill will toward the man. And I forgive him."

At this point in his faith story, I could not resist asking, "How could you let that guy go scot-free? Shouldn't you be compensated for all your pain and suffering? That's only fair."

Here the sweet fragrance of forgiveness and trust in God was apparent. He responded, "I forgive him. And every day I thank God it was me in that accident. It could have been a young mom with children in the back seat. No, thank God it was me. All my physical training had made me strong enough to take the hit."

He added, "Getting revenge is like drinking toxins. It poisons you. I let God take care of what's fair."

*   *   *

Mark walked into the courtroom with the elephant and a powerful temptation before him. He passed the trial, and our Camino can take inspiration from him.

In our near future there will be a face-to-face encounter with "that person" in our lives. The elephant will stomp around unaware or uncaring of how hurt we feel. The world will scream in our heads, "Don't forgive!" All manner of anger and resentment will percolate inside and invite us to conform to the world's thinking.

Through a renewal of our minds we can see a new way of looking at forgiveness; we can reject the world's view. For this, our Camino can be lighter, less burdened . . . free!

The Mountain of Forgiveness is where I found a new depth of trust in His forgiveness. But that was not the end of what He had to teach me. God's spiritual lightning bolt struck me a second time on this same mountain while on a treacherous descent.

Join me as I take a giant leap of faith.

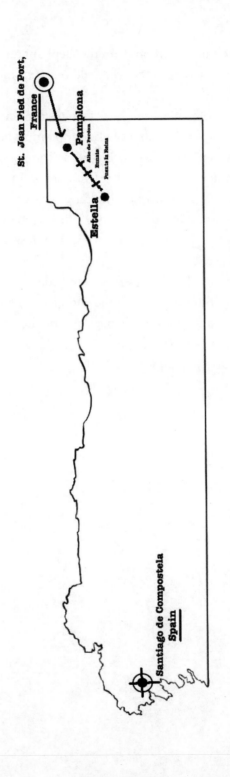

Chapter 8

A LEAP OF FAITH

Definition: "putting your belief and trust in something or somebody outside of yourself, and then acting on that belief"

Joseph Stowell, president, Crossroads University

"When God pushes you to the edge of difficulty, trust Him fully, because two things can happen. He'll either catch you when you fall, or he will teach you to fly."

Unknown

The Camino

Catholic churches are ubiquitous for all five hundred miles on the Camino. But why? The definition of a pilgrimage is "people on a journey to a religious place." Camino pilgrims are single-minded in their destination—Cathedral of Santiago. During the height of its popularity in medieval times, half a million pilgrims walked the trail per year. Churches provided places of worship, some food and rest, and some served as hospitals for pilgrims' excruciating pains and injuries due to the long walk on the rocky trail. Most churches were erected on mountain peaks, to be easily recognized by pilgrims. Many were constructed in the eleventh through fifteenth centuries by the Knights Templar, noble men of honor and fierce protectors of pilgrims. So many of these ancient churches still stand today like guardians over pilgrims. The legends surrounding them are fascinating.

This stretch of Camino from Alto de Perdón's peak to the city of Estella, thirty-two kilometers (twenty miles) away, is not without fascination. Five noteworthy places are included here: the descent from Alto de Perdón, the Church of Santa Maria de Eunate, the Queen's Bridge over the River Arga, the Church of the Crucifix in Puente La Reina, and the Church of the Holy Sepulcher in Estella. Centuries-old architecture and fascinating legends are concentrated in this day-and-a-half walk.

Alto de Perdón

The trek up Alto de Perdón, the Mountain of Forgiveness, is strenuously difficult, but the back side is steal-your-breath-away scary in places. Pilgrims' descent starts at 790 meters (2,590 feet) in elevation. The first rest stop comes three kilometers (about 1.5 miles) down the slope toward the town of Uterga. In that short distance, the elevation drops 290 meters (950 feet). Numerous caution signs warn pilgrims of this risky descent. It's the grade of this descent that is intimidating—nearly thirty degrees! Slick clay and a heavy coverage of loose golfball-to-softball-sized stones tempt every footstep to skid out of control. This would cast the pilgrim into a nosedive stumble down the mountainside. The balance of the day's walk is a moderate descent over six-plus kilometers (about 4.5 miles) to the popular city, Puente La Reina. This is followed by a twenty-one-kilometer walk to Estella, the ending point of this chapter's Camino journey.

Eunate

With the Mountain of Forgiveness behind and Puente La Reina nearing, resist the temptation to just push on. A short detour loop of five kilometers (about three miles) offers a great reward: Ermita de Santa María de Eunate: Church of Holy Mary in Eunate.[21] Known as the "Jewel of the Camino," this twelfth-century church's octagonal shape is believed to be modeled after the Church of the Holy Sepulcher in Jerusalem. Conflicting opinions are held as to its founders. Some claim it to be the work of the Knights Templar, who emerged after the final Crusade. Others believe a different crusading group of men, The Order of St. John, constructed it.

Current fascination with this gem along the Camino comes from the recent discovery of burial tombs along the church's exterior columns. These deceased had been buried with conch shells, a famous symbol of pilgrims on the Camino. The evidence suggests that Eunate might have been a hospital or hospice center for pilgrims who encountered life-threatening challenges.

Puente la Reina[22]

Pilgrims enter Puente la Reina by crossing its famed ancient stone bridge. It was named the Queen's Bridge after the wife of the once famous Mayor Sancho of Puente la Reina. Because of her dedication to the many pilgrims, the bridge was constructed to provide easy travel over the Arga River. The Roman architectural influence is fascinating, with six peaked, open arches in the bridge's base. This is uncharacteristic of any bridge along the Camino.

How astonishing to stand upon a structure constructed in the eleventh century, some three hundred years before Columbus discovered the New World! Even St. Francis traveled across it during his own pilgrimage. Its unique history and design make it one of the most photographed features on the Camino.

A short distance along the main street stands another Templar legacy: the Church of the Crucifixion[23] from the year 1325. Inside, a striking wooden crucifix, with the tree bark still attached, forms a Y shape. Christ's passion is portrayed with His arms excruciatingly stretched toward heaven forming a V shape, representing His cry for mercy for us.

His nailed feet point toward earth, completing the Y shape and showing that Christ's sacrifice was for us—sinners.

The legend behind this historic Y-shaped crucifix involves a group of medieval German pilgrims. They traveled through Puente La Reina, carrying this Y-shaped cross the size of an average adult on their shoulders, all the way from their hometown. Their ailments and injuries were treated in this town, after which they completed their pilgrimage to Santiago. In gratitude, these pilgrims carried the uniquely shaped cross all the way back to Puente la Reina and donated it to the town's church.

Estella

Embedded in Camino history is the legend that early pilgrims found direction to Santiago by following the stars in the Milky Way. This small town's name, Estella, is Spanish for "star."

Especially good food, drink, and nightlife make a stay in Estella a pilgrim's delight. How rich in history it is as well! Twice a year the town converts into a medieval festival. Locals dress in character, perform musical pieces, and demonstrate old-world craftsmanship by building tools, household items, and centuries-old crafts from that era. Rising over the costumed crowds are medieval tunes played in the authentic melody of the times.

Not to be missed, the Church of San Pedro de la Rua dates back to the twelfth century. Surprisingly, two walls are still standing. Pilgrims are drawn to this church because of holy relics—objects of religious significance such as bone fragments of men and women procured after their deaths, yet before being declared saints. Of the relics secured at this church, one holds a fascinating legend.

A pilgrim from Patras, Greece[24] was making his Camino pilgrimage. Word spread that he was carrying priceless relics he wished to donate to the Cathedral of Santiago. While passing through Estella, he died and was buried in the cloister surrounding the church grounds. After some time, a mystery developed surrounding this pilgrim's grave: it glowed! Church officials investigated and upon opening the grave, their suspicions were confirmed. The famed relics were discovered—a small fragment of the Holy Cross and a piece of shoulder bone from St. Andrew. Also inside the burial vault were a bishop's crosier and gloves. The deceased pilgrim was the Bishop of Patras, Greece.

My Camino

Two experiences on Alto de Perdón, the Mountain of Forgiveness, will be forever etched in me. The reason: God's spiritual lightning bolt struck me on the ascent and surprisingly again on the descent.

While crossing the Pyrenees on my first Camino day, I became friends with a man of deep and humble faith from South Africa. Bishop Eric was of the Anglican faith, seventy-six years old, and repeating the Camino with his wife Joyce and their close friend. Eric was one of those rare few who were blessed to have friendships with men of distinction and great faith. Desmond Tutu, a man renowned as a South African religious leader, was one. The other was Nelson Mandela, a man with whom he had marched against apartheid. These men of faith and peace had obviously left their fingerprints upon Eric's manner and the way he showed respect to others. His agile, six-foot-five-inch lean frame permitted an impressive Camino walking pace. He was a man of determination. He knew the Camino, and yet was a humble leader. Bishop Eric led with the confidence of Magellan, the famed sixteenth-century explorer who had traveled around the world. And he became my dear friend.

Then there was the weather. Since crossing the Pyrenees, the coldest, wettest season in seventy years ensconced itself upon us daily. Everything was soaked—clothing, backpack, boots, and most importantly, the trail. Not only was the clay growing slipperier, but the rocks that covered it were as slick as oil. Every slippery footstep up Alto de Perdón required vigilance for fear of falling.

The rain paused at the summit and I thought, *Ah, the worst is behind me.* I was standing on one of God's watchtowers overlooking His creation. Set along the rim were the intriguing wrought iron figures of Camino pilgrims over history. I relished the time to soak in the Spanish countryside's sheer beauty, contemplate my faith recharge, and rest briefly. I needed it. I knew the descent before me was well noted for its dangerously steep grade over the loose, rocky trail.

Eric and I took the lead for new friends now traveling with us. If the muddy descent wasn't enough to fear, the rain had returned hard and punishingly. This added painful stress to each step. No training back home could have prepared me for this. We struggled down a thirty-degree slope that became a stream coursing between our feet like small rapids. With it, the clay trail rapidly eroded, exposing more and more loose stone and rock. Every step was uncertain. The soles of my boots grew an inch with mud. This made them even more slippery and threatened me with a nasty fall. Soon we came upon the inevitable: a section of the trail had been washed away. It now exposed an eight-foot sheer vertical drop.

I stared bug-eyed and gulped hard like the cartoon character Wile E. Coyote on a cliff's edge. Eric caught up and whiplashed to an abrupt halt. I was paralyzed. We did a quick survey of where it was supposed to have intersected more of the trail below. Now it hugged a vertical mountainside drop off and plunged several hundred feet below. *If I make it beyond this washout, will I be able to stop abruptly, or even stop at all? Or will I face a headlong, rolling tumble of doom?*

My moment of problem-solving was abruptly interrupted. "We must go down," announced Eric matter-of-factly. I stood stiff-legged; my boots seemed super-glued to the cliff. Eric skirted me and the trail's washout, blazing a new trail. His tall, lean frame was ideal for the challenge. He positioned himself sideways to the steep grade, in line with a dense cover of stiff-stemmed, thorny aster bushes.

My eyes strained from their sockets with fear as I released my hold of Eric's hand before his first step downward. His long stride met the mystery of the thicket below. *Praise God!* Solid ground was at root level. He stomped the branches into a foothold and took his next long-legged stride down. Ever so cautiously, the new trail downward was successfully forged.

He stood safely where the two trails intersected. Immediately behind him was a drop of hundreds of feet.

I was stunned out of paralysis by Eric's call, "Willie, we must go down!"

I wondered, *Will these thorny shrubs hold my mud-caked boots? Will these slippery-wet shrubs even allow me to stop?* Terror rattled inside me as I looked for any other way around this. There was none. I panted in fear at the sight of Eric's new footprints in the shrubs. All of the frightening obstacles I faced and conquered before the Camino were nothing compared to the terrifying possibility of what falling here might mean. I stared motionless as if on a high-dive platform, mentally preparing for the plunge.

Lord, I can't do this. My short Italian legs won't make it. They can't make it. I can't make it! Never had I been so terrified. I imagined all kinds of brutal falls: a leg sliding out while carrying this backpack, an unstoppable roll downhill, a tumble in the thorny shrub, and many broken bones. I pleaded for God's help. *Lord, I beg you. Help me! I can't do this!*

Lightning struck my heart again. It came in the sound of a mighty whisper. I will not say it was God's voice, but I'm convinced, to my very core, that it was from Him. The moment of grace that called me to walk the Camino so many months ago returned with His same two words, "Have faith." That was it. Just two mighty words.

A new confidence churned. I took a deep breath and with all the heart and soul I could muster, I lifted one boot and aimed for Eric's first foothold, springing into thin air. A pole in each hand swung madly in hopes of catching solid ground and traction. Gratefully, my boots landed and stuck a few feet below. My body, weighed down with an overstuffed backpack and that bedeviling laptop, swayed wildly while I wrestled to control my momentum. After a short fight, a safe landing was my gift. *Thank you, Lord. You saved me. Oh, thank you!*

Quite literally, it was a "leap of faith."

A quick look around exposed more reason for gratitude. I was now aware of a knee-high, barbed wire fence exposed by our trailblazing.

No time to fear what could have happened, I reassured myself; *it is time to "have faith."* With one boot strained outward and only mountain air and the rapidly sloping terrain beneath me, I launched for the next foothold. I hit the ground with a strong, full-body wobble and swaying knees like a gymnast's poorly executed dismount. My shoulders, arms, and clutched poles spun for a few tense moments until I gained an upright posture. *Amen! Another safe landing.* Two more similar leaps later, I stood safely on the trail alongside Eric. As more pilgrims faced the same challenge, Eric and I assisted everyone until we were all safe again.

Alto de Perdón became holy ground for my pilgrimage. Two heaven-sent messages came into my life like lightning bolts there. They illuminated two precious areas of my faith walk—the gift of His forgiveness and His call to "have faith" in spite of my fears. God chose a mountain, this mighty mountain, as the stage for His messages to unfold.

Our Camino

How much do I trust God? I mean, *really* trust God? To be boldly self-revealing, I'd admit that many differing shades and intensities represent the ranges on my "trust meter" with God. Stretch your imagination with me for a moment.

Consider a vantage point where you are gazing upon a seascape. Nothing but vast waters stretch from shore to horizon. What shades of blue are there? Are the blue hues different at the shore than toward the horizon? Likely so. The shoreline color is likely the lightest blue, and the deepest blues are where waters are their deepest.

Here is the question: Is the entire seascape blue? Some might assert that there are many blue variations. Others might settle for a safe answer—blue is blue.

Imagine, if you will, that the color of *trust* in God is represented by the color blue. The deeper the blue, the deeper the trust in Him. A light blue could still represent trust, but perhaps a safe, shoreline-type of trust in Him.

I invite you to ask yourself, "If I were to draw myself somewhere on this 'sea of trust,' where would I drop anchor? What shade of blue would surround me there?"

Here is the big question for our Camino: How "true blue" is your trust in God?

*   *   *

Janina's faith story testifies to her "true blue" trust in God and a lesson for us on how to lift anchor and drift further out to the deep with Him.

I met Janina though her husband, Mitch, my coworker. He is a mid-fifties Polish immigrant with a deeply humble demeanor. He is hardworking, conscientious, and a "take pride in your work" kind of guy. He thrives on the love of his wife and their two children in late adolescence. Over the last few years, he has had a history of serious cardiac surgeries and related health issues. The latest challenge came in the form of a rare bone marrow cancer, settled into his lower spinal column. The diagnosis put his family and friends in a state of shock. Doctors gave him six to twelve weeks to live.

Mitch's cancer battle is captivating in itself. However, the far more dramatic testimony is Janina's. What she shared is not one big leap of faith but a series of leaps she took during Mitch's excruciating health trials.

"Mitch needed to have two of his lower vertebrae removed," she began. "Because he had so many heart problems and a recent open heart surgery, the doctors had to be careful with the strength of pain medicines. When Mitch came out of back surgery, he was in a crazy amount of pain." She paused to catch a breath and pinch back the tears. "He was in his hospital bed crying loudly in painful agony. Only so much could be done. Doctors were testing a delicate balance—enough pain medicine versus a dosage strength that would not compromise his delicate heart condition."

"But let me tell you," she restarted with a confident countenance. "I'm with my kids and we are terrified to see Mitch in this much pain. I say, 'We must pray for help.' So we knelt before his hospital bed, and we pray, *really* pray hard. We are Catholic so we prayed the Divine Mercy prayer, which in essence is this: 'Jesus, I trust in You.' That's all our minds and faith could manage with so much fear before us. We prayed it over and over again. My eyes pinched shut and I knew, Jesus is the only one who could help. I put everything, all my trust in Him. When we ended our prayers, we opened our eyes. We couldn't believe what we saw. Mitch was not crying anymore. He was resting calmly and he said the pain just left . . . had gone. And that pain never came back. Coincidence? I don't think so!" she assured me.

Janina went on to share another experience with even greater excitement. "The doctors said that Mitch would need a bone marrow transplant which I was to arrange. I have a terrible time on the phone trying to talk to many doctor offices because my Polish keeps getting in the way of my English. For days I tried to find a doctor who would take us. We needed to schedule this procedure, and soon! One after another refused us because our insurance and personal funds are both weak. What do I do now? I said the Mercy Prayer again and again and again." Her storytelling pace took a stronger tempo.

"I try another office and tell this nurse, my English is not too good. I told her my problem with all the other doctor offices I tried with no luck. I told her how sick my husband is. I told her about Mitch's many health problems and his need for this transplant. And I told her how I needed someone to help us.

"The nurse was silent for a long time before she replied, 'I'm going to help you. I have your information, the doctor's order, and your particular insurance needs.'"

Janina added, "I thanked her over and over. I didn't know how long it would take before it would be too late, but this was now my closest chance for help."

She held a constrained smile before continuing. "The nurse called the next day! She had the transplant arranged, insurance issues resolved, and a new doctor who took on the case."

She asked me, "What do you think is the doctor's name who agreed to do the transplant?"

I knew this was going to be good, "I have no idea, Janina. I'm guessing it's an interesting name, right?"

Like giving the final clue to a mystery, her answer came with deliberate confidence and gratitude. "The doctor's name is . . . Doctor Peace."

Didn't see that coming.

Janina went on to share several other "coincidences" that occurred immediately after reciting the Divine Mercy Prayer. Unexpected meals showed up when the pantry was thin or there was no time to fix something; a texted picture of a valentine heart at the exact moment she told God how her heart was breaking; a visit or call from family or a friend right after she prayed to God to show her some sign of His care for them.

Then she held up a finger to strengthen her most important point, "God's love is bigger than the ocean. I only have to believe."

Janina leaned closer and softened her voice. "God has a network. And all these people who help us are in His network. I know this for sure—God's network is love. And guess what? We are in God's network. I know. He's gonna take care of us."

I was utterly lost for words. In the face of complete despair came a sweetly fragranced grace born of her trust in God. Janina faced a series of intense trials during her husband's life and death struggle. Each test had only two choices: stay anchored safely near shore while hoping for luck, or pull up anchor and drift out to the deeper blue in God's "sea of trust."

As for Mitch, he has outlived the doctor's predicted timeline for survival and is doing well.

* * *

Our Camino will encounter a strong challenge one day. It is not a matter of if but when the challenge will come. Questions will lie before us. *Do I take a giant leap of faith? Am I strong enough to leave my comfort zone?* And then again, *Why take the leap when I can choose to play it safe?*

The answers lie in this simple Scripture verse: "No eye has seen, nor ear heard, nor the heart of man imagined, what God has prepared for those who love him" (1 Cor. 2:9).

His love is far greater than we can even imagine. We can't begin to see it, hear of it, or embrace it fully without more trust in Him.

When the big challenge arrives, how might we open our eyes, ears, and heart to accept more of His love?

Consider these suggestions.

Take a strong look at your "trust meter" with God. Ask yourself, "Where am I anchored on this 'sea of trust' of you, Lord?" Honest contemplation is where the journey begins toward more trust in Him and more peace in our heart.

Start with your prayer time. Ask God, "In what area of my life are You calling me to surrender control? What prevents me from pulling up anchor in order to journey deeper in trust of You?" In tense life moments, pray "Jesus, I trust in You."

Wait patiently. Be alert to everything around you. The Holy Spirit's movement cannot be detected when we're running through life like children on the playground. Yes, waiting is countercultural to our modern lifestyles. Remember though, God's ways are not our ways (see Isa. 55:8). And His ways and timing are infinitely wiser. The answers come precisely at the perfect moment. Watching and waiting grows a faith-filled trust in Him.

You might be thinking, "I'm not good at waiting when I have a difficult life challenge. Waiting doesn't feel like I'm doing anything about my troubles. What am I to do?"

Paul's advice is simply this, "Rejoice always, pray without ceasing, give thanks in all circumstances; for this is the will of God in Christ Jesus for you" (1 Thess. 5:16–18). Strive to do these three.

Before long, the "sea of trust" around you will be a deeper blue.

*   *   *

In reflection, my "leap" propelled me further into the "sea of trust." I'm convinced that heaven's lightning bolts that struck me two different times on the Mountain of Forgiveness were to prepare my heart for a powerful, yet comforting message.

Take a "leap of faith" and join me in a walk with My Encircler.

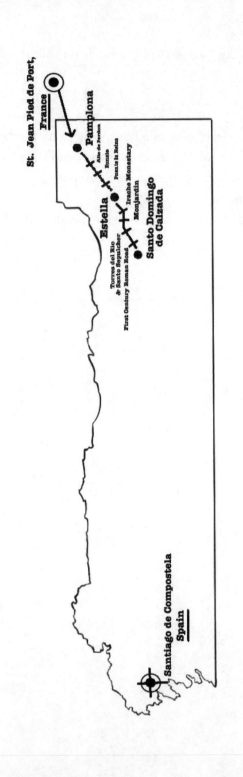

Chapter 9

MY ENCIRCLER

"God in all things."

St. Ignatius of Loyola

"Circle us Lord,
Keep love within, keep hatred out.
Keep joy within, keep fear out.
Keep peace within, keep worry out.
Keep light within, keep darkness out.
May You stand in the circle with us, today and always."

Ancient Celtic circling prayer[25]

The Camino

Stunning, breathtaking beauty awaits the pilgrim travelling from Estella to Santo Domingo de Calzada. It is an enriching four days over the next one hundred kilometers (roughly sixty miles). Pilgrims encounter but one strong incline of approximately two hundred meters (650 feet) each day. These are generously rewarded with Camino natural scenic beauties, intriguing history, and local cultural fascinations.

Five unique attractions worth noting for this stretch of the Camino are the Irache Monastery, Castillo de San Estaban at Monjardín, Torres del Rio's Santo Sepulcher, remnants of the Roman Road, and Santo Domingo de Calzada.

Irache Monastery and Outdoor Wine Fountain

Dating back to 958, the ancient Benedictine Irache Monastery[26] is well known for its vineyards and fine wines. Irache, now a museum, has a novelty about it: an outdoor, free wine fountain. Talk about generosity! Pilgrims eagerly wait in line for their turn to reach the stainless steel plaque adorned with a medieval coat of arms and two spigots—one for wine, the other for water. Even though many arrive in early morning with the aftertaste of breakfast still lingering, a cup or even a water bottle of free wine is irresistible. Pilgrims delight in taking a photo at the fountain at the Irache Monastery. Its novelty alone makes it a Camino "must do"!

Monjardín

Leaving Irache, pilgrims begin a long, sweeping ascent of 150 meters (just under five hundred feet) up the slender peak of Monjardín. For all nine kilometers (5.5 miles), the mountain captivates with its view of the remnants of the ancient castle at its pinnacle. This thirteenth-century structure strains conspicuously skyward above the humble farmlands.

One particular gospel verse captivates the pilgrim while walking toward this fascination born of nature and man: "A city set on a hill cannot be hidden" (Matthew 5:14). A nagging question accompanies each step toward the Castillo de San Estaban at Monjardín, the Castle of St. Stephen: How could such a fortress have been constructed atop this steep, conical peak? It's a mystery, but what a marvel to behold! The small, charming town of Villamayor de Monjardín sits at its base and serves as an appealing rest stop. Pilgrims soak in the marvelous panorama of countryside, vineyards, and grazing fields.

An intriguing legend from the year 1200 revolves around Monjardín.[27] The story holds that the famed Charlemagne fought Muslims there. Sometime between two battles, he asked God which of his warriors would die in the imminent fight ahead. As legend has it, about one hundred and fifty men were identified by a red cross appearing on their heads as the ones expected to die. Charlemagne ordered these men to remain in camp, away from the upcoming battle. The legend further claims that Charlemagne returned from battle to find that all the men marked with the red cross died in a fire at camp. This fascinating legend is just one of many along the Camino.

Torres del Río and Santo Sepulcher

Torres del Río is an octagonal church modeled after the Church of the Holy Sepulcher in Jerusalem. Like the church in Eunate, Santo Sepulcher Church may have also been connected to the famed Knights Templar. It is believed that this church's architecture contains both Muslim and Christian elements. Near the church's altar is a small indent that contains sacred art believed to represent Mihrab, the beads used in Muslim prayer.[28] A crucifix, crafted with strikingly realistic detail of Christ's brutal wounds, hangs above the church's altar. Many pilgrims stay for a brief, prayerful reflection while pondering the twelfth-century architectural details of Santo Sepulcher.

First-Century Roman Road

Continuing west, the clay and stone Camino trail seams into a few miles of ancient Roman Road. The historic, first-century road is made up of round, irregularly shaped rocks, fit tightly together as a continuous impenetrable barrier to erosion. Pilgrims find the contour of the rocks painful to walk on for any distance. For this reason, well-worn foot paths parallel its edges. The mere fact that something constructed about the time of Christ has endured, and so well, is fascinating. Imagining the labor involved in its construction causes the pilgrim to marvel even more.

Santo Domino de Calzada

From Monjardín, the Camino travels along miles of La Rioja vineyards producing fine quality wines known worldwide. The comfort of walking along
rolling vineyards is interrupted by a two-hundred-meter (650-foot) climb to
the Mountain of Roland. This is quickly followed by another 250-meter
(820-foot) climb to the town of Ciruenña. Beyond this point, pilgrims enjoy
a comfortable walk into the famed town of Santo Domingo de Calzada.[29] A
captivating story originated in this town, giving it Camino notoriety.

A pilgrim couple and their eighteen-year-old son, Hugonell, began
their Camino in their hometown in Germany. When reaching Santo
Domingo de Calzada, they stopped at an inn to freshen themselves. The
innkeeper's pretty daughter waited on them, and she took a strong liking
to the boy. Because he was pious and single-focused on his pilgrimage, he
shunned her advances. The young girl, angered by this, chose revenge by
hiding a silver goblet in his luggage. The family departed and while only
a short distance down the road, the young girl reported the goblet stolen
by Hugonell. The officials stopped the family to investigate.

The penalty for stealing on the Camino was execution. The innocent boy was quickly tried and sentenced to death by hanging. On top
of that, to serve as a deterrent to burglary, the dead were left hanging for
long periods in clear view of pilgrims crossing through. After their son's
punishment was administered, the heartbroken parents left the town and
continued their pilgrimage to Santiago. After their stay there, they headed
back home, determined to see Hugonell's remains on their return. Upon
arriving at the town's gallows, they were shocked to see their son miraculously alive. He told his parents that St. Domingo was kneeling below,
holding his feet up, and preventing strangulation.

The parents rushed to the town sheriff's home with the news, arriving at the family dinner time. The parents insisted that their son was not
dead; he had just spoken to them. Upon hearing this, the sheriff brushed
it off, saying, "Your son is as dead as these two chickens," pointing to the
cooked birds on the platter. At that, the two chickens grew wings and
feathers and flew off.

Today, the town of Santo Domingo de Calzada has monuments with roosters atop. The rooster is portrayed on buildings and artwork along the Camino. Within the church is a display of historic sacred art abounding with Camino stories. Most striking is a glass chicken coop perched in the back of the church with live roosters walking and eating within it. Sometimes the rooster's squawk will startle his visitors. A placard below the coop claims these birds are of the same breeding line as the chickens from those in the legend.

My Camino

Every morning before setting off on the Camino, Bishop Eric and a few others would huddle and pray Eric's adaptation of Carmina Gadelica,[30] a widely known Celtic prayer. This prayer is beauty in simplicity, and awoke something inside me through its curious name for God—"My Encircler."

> My Christ
> My Shield
> My Encircler
> Each day, each night
> Each light, each day
> Each step, each kilometer
> Over every hill and every valley
> Along every highway and every byway
> Be near us
> Uphold us
> Watch over us and
> All whom we carry in our hearts
> My Christ
> My Shield
> My Shepherd
> My Friend and Brother
> Amen

The Camino scenery before me, behind me, to my left, and to my right played a vital role to help me experience Him in this new way.

Along this stretch of trail, there was a climb up a quickly sloping mountain of 250 meters (650 feet) followed by miles of a long, comfortable walk. The incessant rain over the last two weeks finally broke, leaving behind a steely gray cloud cover. On rare occasions, these low lying cumulus clouds would unzip, gifting me with all-too-brief radiant sun blasts. Ironically, what happened in the sky had no effect on how picturesque the terrain was that stretched around me.

The Camino's rock-and-clay-colored trail snaked ahead in a series of rolling ups and downs. Its earthy color displayed a sharp contrast to some of nature's finest scenery. The trail's edges were hugged by a dense, steady stream of fire engine red poppies with intrusions of lavender plants. Petite white daisies squeezed their way through here and there in this flowery mix. Just beyond the wildflowers were fields upon fields of barley, cultivated in clean rows. From here and beyond were far-reaching farms of a plant I have never seen in the United States—canola plants, used in producing canola oil. These stunning beauties stood just under one meter, (just over two feet) high, and were heavily adorned with brilliant, lemon-yellow flowers. The farmland checkerboarded between vineyards and rich grazing grasses which stretched to the terraced foothills of the mountains far in the distance. A realization struck. *This is the scene that came during my prayer time calling me to walk the Camino. This was that place!* Stunning!

As enchanting as this vibrant living color was, another discovery stole the centerpiece of my day's reflection. I was completely surrounded by majestic mountains and high foothills. Their height and ruggedness were striking and I was enthralled by these snow-capped creations. Wow! God's handiwork in three hundred and sixty degrees!

My mind jetted back to a line from the bishop's morning prayer. I repeated the name reverently, "My Encircler." My spirit sensed there was something more of God contained in those two words. And there was. *These majestic mountains are encircling us—encircling me!*

I contemplated this. *The ring of mountains are as God's powerful arms. The mountains are immense and strong; God's love is immense and strong. God is wrapped around me; God is a protector. God's creation is beauty in flowers, crops, and vineyards; Creator God is beauty.* Years before, I had recognized God is my Lord, God is my Father, God is my Almighty One, God is my Savior, just to name a few. My Camino blessed me with a new name in which to embrace Him. God is my Encircler!

There was more. How easy it was to see, to feel God when standing within the natural beauty of His creation. His presence was tangible. *Yes, My Encircler is walking with me and His mountainous strength surrounds me.*

A challenging thought then intruded. *What about the times when these mountains of protection had not really protected me? What about the times when harsh storms had broken over the peak and overtook me?* I recalled hurtful gale-force storms that had knocked me down. Storms like my dad dying at the young age of sixty-four, my brother dying tragically of a drug overdose, my saintly mother's week-long, painful moans at death's door. And the most intense storm of all—the surprise heart attack and death of our oldest son. God had allowed storms like these to slip over the mountain peaks. *Where was He then? Where was His strength when I needed Him most?* I pondered this uncomfortably.

I had so many questions, I knew "why?" questions couldn't be among them. I learned long ago that "why?" questions are only a disguise for an argument I wanted to wage. I'd search and wait for a possible "God answer," only for it to be challenged by my "Yes, but why couldn't You have done . . . ?" Or, "Couldn't you have allowed something different to happen like . . . ?" Or, "But, that's not fair because . . ."

No! No "why" questions regardless of the storms. I already believed the valuable truth that came with loving Him: *The path to peace is a journey of surrenders.* Letting go of control during the storm allows Him to bring me through it.

I contemplated the gifts born of my surrenders. Storms dissipate. Situations change. Relationships change. Those I love change. Good things happen. And bad, even terribly unfair things happen as well. The truth is, God doesn't change!

As for my Camino, I believe His powerful arms are forever encircling me regardless of any and all the storms in my life. I believe He walks with me always. Yes, God is . . . my Encircler.

Our Camino

Is there more to the word "Encircler" and how its meaning might enlighten our Camino? To begin with, this name for God is rooted in ancient Celtic spirituality and particularly to St. Patrick's ministry in Ireland. Let's explore this background.

The symbol of the circle has been the focus of many belief systems throughout the ages. This was coincidentally true for the pagan Celtic Druid priests. Artifacts of their culture and stories of their fierce practices of human sacrifice included the circle[31] in their worship of the sun and moon. The pre-Christian Celtic clans and their Druid priests lived in the area of Finisterre, Spain where the apostle St. James preached to them during the first century. Interestingly, this same group thrived as far north in what we know today as Britain, Scotland, and Ireland.

Three centuries after St. James, another powerful preacher, Patrick, boldly confronted these same pagans about their worship involving the circle. One legend has it that St. Patrick was preaching about the cross of Christ crucified when he confronted the Druid king about the symbol of the circle they used in worship. He testified to the greater power of Christ's teaching and sacrifice in the symbol of the cross. In a way to connect to pagan beliefs, Patrick drew a circle over a cross's center, to demonstrate that God's power and care is all around us and that we are all invited into His circle of love. This, some believe, is the origin of the Celtic cross represented in sacred art past and present.[32]

Regardless of origin, the soul of Celtic spirituality embraces that God is always encircling us from all directions, in all things, in all matters of our hearts.

How might these encircling thoughts of God empower our Camino?

Begin by asking yourself, "What do I see surrounding me? Is it fear? Fear of what is happening? Fear of what could happen? Fear of losing what I have? Am I afraid of letting go and letting God's plan unfold?" Perhaps the problem is bigger than your own fears.

Ask yourself, "How big is God?" Challenge your paradigm of just how big your God is. The circle of mountains I experienced on my Camino provided an image of God's strength. Capture for yourself a God-image that is staggering in strength. Is it the ocean? The sands as far as the eye can see? A cloudless sky? A starlit night sky? Remember this: our grandest imagination pales in comparison to God's almighty power encircling us.

There is more. God also walks beside us in our circle of life that begins with birth and completes with our death. He stands with us and for us— especially during the storms of our life. Storms of anger, fear, worry, and darkness threaten us. We have used other names for these storms. Divorce. Addiction. Health challenges. Cancer. Lack of help for a struggling loved one. Death of a loved one. Anxiety. Depression. Inability to forgive. Bankruptcy. Whatever storm may break into the circle of our life, we need not be afraid. Our Encircler walks right alongside us. He surrounds us. Only a mighty God could do this and still be so intimately near. Jesus assures us of this. "I will be with you even to the end of time" (Matt 28:20b).

Take a reflective pause for this portion of the prayer inscribed on St. Patrick's breastplate.[33]

I Arise Today

I arise today
Through God's strength to pilot me
God's might to uphold me,
God's wisdom to guide me,
God's eye to look before me,
God's ear to hear me,
God's way to lie before me,
God's shield to protect me,
God's host to save me.
Christ with me, Christ before me, Christ behind me,
Christ in me, Christ beneath me, Christ above me,

Christ on my right, Christ on my left,
Christ when I lie down, Christ when I sit down, Christ when I arise,
Christ in the heart of every man who thinks of me,
Christ in the mouth of everyone who speaks of me,
Christ in every eye that sees me,
Christ in every ear that hears me.
I arise today.

*   *   *

These are all nice thoughts, but there's greater power in learning how to live it. So it was true in my dear Camino-walking partner and friend, Bishop Eric. His great faith and character can be witnessed in how our Encircler—his Encircler—surrounded him and walked with him through his recent storm with leukemia.

Eric faced many challenges throughout his life: a strained relationship with his parents; setting off for seminary training against their wishes; and the pain he felt over the practice of apartheid in his homeland, South Africa. He humbly shared the influence Bishop Desmond Tutu had on his ministry. His personal friendship with Nelson Mandela was his source of great joy, though overshadowed by the sting of the racial discrimination and injustice he and Nelson marched against. Then there was the heart-wrenching loss of his first wife due to cancer. At age seventy-four he walked his first Camino. Two years later, the celebration of his second five-hundred-mile Camino would be silenced by his life's most excruciating health storm. Here Bishop Eric's faith walk found a new challenge.

Leukemia struck. It overwhelmed his strength and movements. The stress of it induced two bouts of shingles in his left eye and on the left side of his head. It was agonizingly painful. This landed him for a spell in the hospital for a procedure to relieve intense shingles-induced headaches.

The storms grew scarier. Because of the shingles attack he was taken off chemotherapy. As a result, the chronic lymphocytic leukemia caused his white cell count to spike yet again, with intense complications. All that he had to clutch onto was his belief in the One who he called "my Encircler" to provide strength and to shield him. Christ's presence did surround him. For more than a year, scores of people lifted his name in prayer. They begged God to spare his life. And they expressed love for him in countless ways.

It became necessary for him to go back on chemotherapy. There were times he felt really weary, lethargic, and "down." Once again, God's people prayed and His power surrounded him. Eric would claim, "God's mighty presence has His arms wrapped around me tightly." Most times he did not know whether pain or strong suffering or even death was ahead. It didn't matter. He just believed and confidently told others, "My Encircler walks with me."

Many more months of suffering and sacrifices continued until God's mercy prevailed. It was not an overnight, miraculous cure, by any means. But his health improved in small doses; his strength was returning ever so slowly, and with it, more and more hope returned too.

Months of improvement brought him to the latest hematologist's report—a reversal! His white blood count hovered at normal readings. The tide had indeed turned. Eric's rejoicing was heard across South Africa, "It was the might of my Encircler! I praise Him! I arise today."

The bishop's own poem is a testimony of faith in life's storms. It was written at the onset of his leukemia.

I Wait for the Tide to Turn
inspired by David Adam's Prayer in *Landscapes of Light.*

Lord,
I wait for the tide to turn
Until the distant becomes close
Until the far off becomes near
Until the longed for becomes reality.
Until the ebb flows.
Lord,

I wait for the tide to turn
Until the medication has run its course
Until weakness is made strong
Until the shadows are filled with light.
Until the ebb flows.
Lord,
I wait for the tide to turn
Until the mist lifts
Until the sun breaks through
Until your glory shines in the haze
Until the ebb flows.
Lord,
I wait for the tide to turn
Until healing is restored
Until faltering strides are resolute
Until hope is fulfilled and I'm perfectly whole.
Until the ebb flows.

What is still true for my Camino, for our Camino, and for Bishop Eric's Camino is this: only God is constant. Storms come and go. They move in and out of our lives like the tides. My Encircler, our Encircler, is "God in all things; all things in God,"[34] as St. Ignatius writes. During our next storm, we need only rest in the circle of His strong embrace.

*   *   *

Walk the Camino a bit further with me. Listen. You, too, might share in some divine "Voice Lessons." The Good Shepherd is calling.

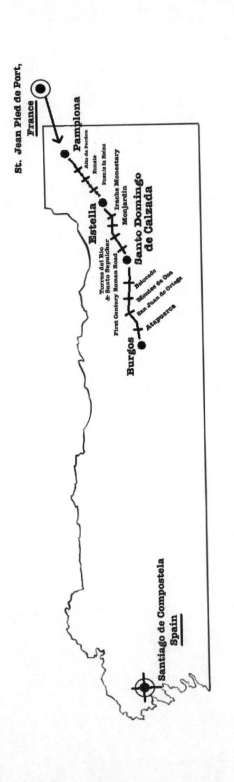

St. Jean Pied de Port, France

Pamplona

Alto de Perdon

Eunate

Puente la Reina

Estella

Irache Monastery

Monjardin

Torres del Rio
& Santo Sepulcher

First Century Roman Road

Santo Domingo de Calzada

Belorado

Montes de Oca

San Juan de Ortega

Atapuerca

Burgos

Santiago de Compostela
Spain

Chapter 10

VOICE LESSONS

Definition—worship: "an expression of our hearts toward God shown through song and praise. As we worship Him, we are drawn into His presence and experience His touch in our lives." (Unknown)

"The vibrations of the air are the breath of God speaking to man's soul. Music is the language of God. We musicians are as close to God as man can be. We hear His voice, we read His lips, we give birth to the children of God, who sing His praise. That's what musicians are."

Ludwig van Beethoven

The Camino

Two historically rich and captivating cathedrals bookend this span of the Camino, which traverses more than seventy-three kilometers (forty-five miles) from Santo Domingo de la Calzada to Burgos. Sandwiched between are fields where shepherds still tend their flocks, the historic town of Belorado, the intimidating ascent of Montes de Oca, the miracle attributed to San Juan de Ortega, the archeological site at Atapu-erca, and the robust city life of Burgos with its treasured cathedral.

Shepherd Fields

Intermittently from Ciruenña, six kilometers (just over 3.5 miles) east of Santo Domingo de la Calzada, and as far as west as Burgos, the pilgrim is treated to the rare sight of shepherds tending their flock of fifty to one hundred sheep. It is captivating for us urban folk to watch the intense attention the sheep pay to their shepherd's every movement—the tap of his wooden staff on their side, his slow deliberate strides, and especially his simple commands.

Belorado

This small, thirteenth century town has served pilgrims with hospitals, shelters, and, at one time, as many as eight churches. In the center of town is the famed Church of Santa María. Behind this ancient church are cliffs where hermits made their homes in caves. One pilgrim, San Capraiso, gave his life in defense of the faith there. For this, he was honored as the patron saint for Via Francigena, which leads from Belorado to Rome. Towering over the cliffs, caves, and the church are the remains of a castle with links to the early Romans.

Contained within the Church of Santa María[35] is a sculpture of Santiago Matamoros. It depicts the apostle James as Matamoros—the killer of Muslims. Legend claims that between the year 800 and the late 1400s, St. James appeared and served as a warrior in Spain's battle against the Muslim occupation. A famous image often seen along the Camino captures St. James as Matamoros, riding a white horse and wielding a deadly sword against Muslim soldiers during a battle. Images of beheaded Muslims provide a vivid representation of the saint's warrior prowess. However, Christian authorities are quick to refute this legend because it depicts an act so contrary to Christian teachings and Jesus's gospel of love, most notably the commandment "Thou shall not kill," and Jesus's command to "Love thy enemies." Nevertheless, this centuries-old image of Santiago

Matamoros frequents artwork found not only in this Belorado church but all along the Camino, as well as in the Cathedral de Santiago.

Montes de Oca

Beginning in Belorado, the climb is roughly four hundred meters (1,300 feet) over a total distance of fifteen kilometers (roughly 9.5 miles). The peak of Montes de Oca sits at 1,050 meters (3,700 plus feet). The ski-slope-like ascent stares down intimidatingly upon the lowly pilgrim. This climb alone is three hundred meters (980 feet) over the short distance of three kilometers (a little less than two miles).

Between gasping breaths, the pilgrim can enjoy the encircling countryside of natural oak, pine, and vast expanses of purple heather with hints of wildflowers hugging the trail. After a welcomed rest at the peak, the trail nosedives for 150 meters (just under nine hundred feet) before presenting another equally steep ascent. Beyond this climb, a gently rolling eight-kilometer (five-mile) walk leads to the town of San Juan de Ortega.

San Juan de Ortega[36]

A man named Domingo is remembered along this stretch of the Camino for his service to pilgrims. Out of compassion for their suffering he built bridges, roads, and hospitals along the Camino that served their needs. Domingo, who exhibited such sacrificial love, was later declared a saint.

Juan was a disciple of Santo Domingo. He helped in these construction projects as well as an Augustinian monastery in 1150. According to claims posted within the town, after Domingo's death, Juan went on a pilgrimage to Jerusalem. He was caught in a shipwreck and prayed to San Nicolás de Bari to intercede. (This is the same saint admired at Christmas; for a time, sailors of Bari, Italy, claimed God used Nicolás to intercede in saving them from a violent storm at sea.) San Juan's life was spared, and he returned to offer help to pilgrims making their way through the Oca mountains. He is believed to have constructed roads from these mountains to the town of Burgos.

Another of Juan's striking accomplishments is the construction of a Romanesque chapel he completed and dedicated to San Nicolás de Bari. This chapel is constructed precisely to capture an astonishing architectural feat. Within the chapel is a carving of Christ's mother depicted at the Annunciation. Precisely at 5 p.m. on only two days per year—the days of the fall and spring equinoxes, March 21 and September 22—sunlight pierces one window within the chapel. Miraculously, the light illuminates solely the carved image of Mary within the scene. Pilgrims today plan their Camino in order to personally witness this twice annual phenomena owing credit to Juan, later declared San Juan de Ortega.

Atapuerca

Just six kilometers (a little more than three miles) beyond the town of San Juan de Ortega is the valley of the River Vena. In this location, archeologists discovered the oldest human remains in all of Europe. Skull and bone fragments date back 900,000 years! The geographical elements of the river valley and the natural flora and fauna of the area explain why this area known as Atapuerca was such an ideal location to support human existence.

One of the many fascinating suppositions proposed by scientists is that these ancient humans not only ate from surrounding wildlife and vegetation, but also were cannibals! The full archeological story can be learned in Burgos. The Museum of Human Evolution allows visitors to read displays and view artifacts of these prehistoric people.

Burgos

After miles and miles of remote natural scenery, and with only a faded memory of city life in Pamplona weeks ago, a fresh excitement rises while approaching this next big city, Burgos. A high stone wall envelopes Burgos. The option to enter the town by way of the river and a boulevard of corkscrewed-limbed sycamore trees is enchanting. Just before entering the heart of the city, be sure to take notice of the Arch of San Juan.[37] It is here that Columbus was cheered by the city upon his return after discovering the New World.

Numerous avenues spider-web to the central plaza where pilgrims swarm like bees, reuniting with other pilgrim friends made along the way. Here sits the stunning Gothic architecture of the Cathedral of Santa María of Burgos. Numerous outdoor cafes and restaurants surround the plaza, begging pilgrims to drop their backpacks and enjoy refreshments and fine food. Mmm, Spanish paella!

The Cathedral of Burgos is an immense structure with pointed arches and spiked spires straining toward the heavens. Inside is awe-inspiring stained glass and numerous historical items of religious significance such as altar chalices, crucifixes, and vessels that once held the blessed Eucharist. Some date back to the twelfth century. One of the most intriguing pieces of sacred art is a sculpture of Jesus on the cross.[38] It is said to be made of real human skin and hair. Some legends claim that at times it needed to be shaved! Most salient is that it captures the brutality of Christ's suffering and death on the cross. This universally strikes a deep chord of sorrow and gratitude in the hearts of Christian believers.

My Camino

Hi! I'm Willie Williams. And I am a sheep.

An experience on this stretch of the trail led me to make this unusual claim. Once you read my Camino experience, I believe you will feel behooved to make the same claim.

One memorable day, just past Santo Domingo, I strained over a series of steep hillside climbs to a rolling plateau with several acres of green pasture. Upon an abrupt down slope, I was just as abruptly stopped by nearly a hundred roly-poly, ivory-colored, wooly sheep lumbering toward me. Standing tall between us was the shepherd—a lean, athletic-framed, middle-aged man with a weather-hardened complexion. He acknowledged me with a humble head nod and continued his slow, methodical advance through the field.

There was something special about him. I knew I needed to stand and just watch. *Lord, is there a lesson I need to learn here?* The shepherd had a strong military presence about him as a sentinel would. He stood for a while holding his walking stick, his eyes fiercely alert to his sheep surrounding him. Dumbstruck, I thought, *Here is one strong dude. Here is the epitome of meekness—a man exuding strength and confidence, and yet so humble. Here is a leader!*

I spent some time just observing the whole process of shepherding. There were about a hundred sheep grazing. Their heads were fixed on the grass below while chomping ravenously, oblivious to the entire world around them. A rarely seen drama in the relationship between the shepherd and his sheep was played out before me.

I was quick to notice that some sheep were attentive to the shepherd's every movement. Without announcement, he would plod forward and some heads would bolt up intently and gallop to stay abreast of him. Strikingly, they stared up at the shepherd's face as if to seek for any new clue of the shepherd's direction. As he walked, they followed in disciplined step with him.

Then there were sheep who missed the first cue and soon realized they were alone. They looked around, and their bewildered expressions suggested, "Hey, where did everybody go?" Seeing that the shepherd and other sheep had moved on, they scampered to rejoin their shepherd. What was particularly interesting is that the late arrivals maneuvered their way deep into the moving flock, nudging nearer and nearer to the shepherd.

Finally, there were those sheep who missed all the cues. They were far back in the field, lost in self-indulgent gorging on one luscious grassy patch after another. Their heads and eyes were fixated on one thing: overstuffing themselves on their pleasures.

I saw myself in those sheep.

Sometimes in my life, I gratefully recalled, I was so prayerfully attentive to my Shepherd's movement. Other times I was distracted and lost connection with Him. Other more faithful followers moved ahead, and

I was left to catch up to those who remained close to the Shepherd. And then, I sadly admit, there were times in my life when I abandoned any attention of the Shepherd in order to stuff myself with my own pleasures. So yes, I'm Willie Williams. And I am a sheep.

My Camino insight did not end there. The behavior of the shepherd himself on that field was fascinating as well. I watched in rapt attention as he moved in a deliberate, confident manner. His every step matched the speed of his sheep, or was it the other way around? Nevertheless, they walked together. When he stopped, they stopped, and immediately went back to grazing. Every so often, he would steal a short glance at any of his sheep left far behind.

With his head fixed forward, he voiced something that alerted all the sheep. It was not a word, but more like an utterance, "Che Che!" It was a short, staccato sound like the word "cheek," but without the "k" sound. However weird that might seem to us, the shepherd's voice had a startling, transformative effect on his sheep. They all reacted as if someone yelled, "Fire!" in a crowded building. All sheep heads bolted up, eyes searching for the shepherd, and instantaneous obedience followed. A few more steps, another "Che Che Che!" and the entire flock hugged close to the shepherd. Every so often a few sheep would start to stray just a few feet from his side. He used his staff, almost affectionately, to offer a gentle, redirecting tap. Any straggler quickly returned to walk in obedient progression with him once again. It was profound. The sheep knew his voice, and he loved his sheep.

This interaction between that shepherd and his sheep is branded in my memory. In it I saw Jesus's deeper message in the Good Shepherd story, "My sheep hear my voice, and I know them, and they follow me" (John 10:27). It may never be a "Che Che!" sound He makes, but His voice is distinct, confident, and protective of me. My Camino gave me a "voice lesson" that emboldened within me a yearning to be so in tune with my Shepherd and His every move that I am never separated from His side. After all, I am Willie Williams. I am a sheep—one He dearly loves.

Our Camino

Let's take an entirely different look at the idea of voice lessons. It will require some imagination.

What if we were to ask Jesus to give us voice lessons to sing His Father's praises? Would He be quick to agree? We can be certain that He would! Jesus said, "Whatever you ask in my name, this I will do, that the Father may be glorified in the Son. If you ask me anything in my name, I will do it" (John 14:13–14).

I contemplated this more curiously. Why? Because my singing to Him has been lackluster at times. Sometimes weak, sometimes more like a lip sync and far short of singing loudly and fervently. I had to admit, I needed a voice lesson. Perhaps you need one as well?

What happens at a voice lesson? What should a new voice student expect? Answers came in four elements that surprisingly align with our faith formation.

First, the teacher strikes a single note or chord that is true in sound, pitch, and quality. It may be struck over and over again to help the student really hear it, to create an auditory imprint in his or her mind. That note or chord becomes the standard the student must strive to emulate.

Similarly, the Scriptures are the standard for truth. There's no "close to the truth" or "my version of truth." The gospels, Jesus's words, the integrity of the Old and New Testaments ring a perfect pitch of truth.

Second, the teacher invites the student to match his voice to that first note or chord. The student may need to strain their talents and efforts to match that note of truth. Music sung off-key is painfully heard.

This is also true in our faith journey. When our life is "out of pitch" with the Scriptures, we may not hear it, but it is painfully "out of pitch" to those around us. We are called to "tune" our lives in order to match them to His truth in the Scriptures. This is painful and hard.

Third, the teacher will accompany the student in singing the notes. This guidance empowers the student to sing each note at its true pitch and quality.

Where can we get that help? How does God accompany us? The Holy Spirit is our Paraclete, our Helper, the One who will accompany us to live the true pitch and quality in the Scriptures. We do not have to do it on our own. We are empowered by His guidance and loving correction.

Fourth, the student sings the notes a cappella, that is, with no musical accompaniment.

Does our "Voice Teacher" ever really leave us to sing alone? Never. We have His Spirit with us and His truth within us. These are uncontainable gifts. How could we ever keep them to ourselves?

We can't! What joy the believer holds while lifting praise to heaven and imagining the pleasure the singing brings our Father. It's music to His ears!

So, let's dig deeper. What if we asked Jesus to be our voice teacher? Would not these same four lessons be true in our praises? A word in the Scripture will capture us. Like trying to sing that one note, we may think, "How can I get my life to match that scriptural truth?" We will attempt to make our lives sound like that truth. The Holy Spirit will join us, correct us along the way, and continually call us to become the best version of ourselves.

Now consider this: What if we could sing the Father's praises with Jesus as our voice teacher? Not too farfetched. Former Pope Benedict XVI spoke of a need for greater adoration using the Latin *ad oracio*, some translations of which are "to sing mouth to mouth." Imagine being on a stage with Jesus, singing adoration songs. What might be on Jesus's playlist? Maybe "A Mighty Fortress Is Our God," or even "Awesome God," and most assuredly, "How Great Thou Art." What additional song titles might we add to this list?

Imagine further that we're about to sing the first song with Jesus as our voice teacher. The first note of the song, born of Scripture, would be struck. We would start to sing it solo, then Jesus's perfect voice would glide harmoniously into ours. The Holy Spirit would lift the melody into the air. We would be singing, "mouth to mouth," the Father's praises. Imagine how this would please Jesus as our voices rise to the heavens! Soon more of the faithful would join us in chorus. It would grow into an ear-splitting, rapturous, ecstatic, heavenly worship. The "voice lesson" would climax with the song, "Joyful, Joyful We Adore Thee." Awesome—purely awesome!

Let that be the vision of our church worship and praise—singing *ad oracio* with Jesus.

But why would we want to sing the Father's praises better, stronger, louder?

I suspect many believers might answer, "Because we love our Father."

But why do we love Him? Better yet, why do *you* love the Father?

I've asked strong believers, and their answers have further inspired me to take a "voice lesson" in order to sing my Father's praises better.

"I love God because . . ."

Jennie: I feel His love and this makes we want to love Him back.

Tom: He created in me a thirst for Him that can only be satisfied by loving Him.

John: The 1 John message rings loudest, "God first loved me."

Barb: He forgave me.

Lambert: He suffered and died for me, to save me, and bring me to heaven.

Paul: My life only makes sense by His love for me, and me loving Him back.

Dave: His love is so overwhelming, and my service of others lets me love Him in return.

Jim: His love is unconditional. Loving others unconditionally brings me closer to Him.

Jen: I am nothing without His love. Nothing. With it, I am a powerful servant for Him.

Ron: I'm like a little boy performing on life's stage. I imagine spotting Jesus's face in the crowd. He looks at me with love and pride; I look at Him with gratitude and joy for having created me.

May our Camino voices ring true and loud in heaven. We might seek to hear His voice, but oh, how He loves to hear ours!

The lyrics to this song ideally end this chapter on an especially good "note":

Listen to Our Hearts
by Steven Curtis Chapman

And listen to our hearts
Hear our spirits sing
A song of praise that flows
From those You have redeemed.
And we will use the words we know
To tell you what an awesome God You are.
But when words are not enough
To tell You of our love
Just listen to our hearts.[39]

Join me as Our Camino encounters a new imagery. It is Jesus extending His steady hand in support of every scary, wobbly ride through our life. Along our Camino on this next stretch of trail, we might even recognize a "Godcidence" or two.

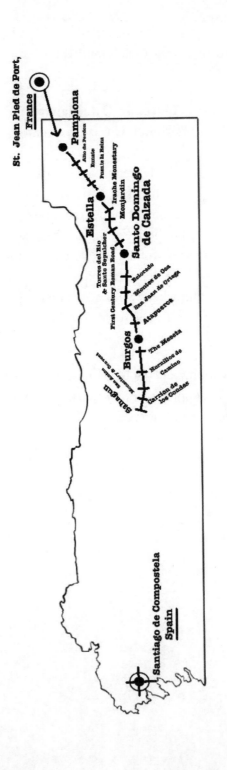

St. Jean Pied de Port, France

Pamplona

Alto de Perdon

Euate

Puente la Reina

Irache Monastery

Monjardin

Estella

Torres del Rio & Santo Sepulcher

First Century Roman Road

Santo Domingo de Calzada

Belorado

Montes de Oca

San Juan de Ortega

Atapuerca

Burgos

The Meseta

Hornillos de Camino

Carrion de los Condes

Sahagun

Santiago de Compostela Spain

Chapter 11

GODCIDENCE

Definition—Godcidence: "A circumstance that looks like a coincidence, but is obviously a 'God thing.'"

Lorraine D. Nunley

"Sometimes I just look up, smile and say, 'I know that was you, God.'"

Unknown

The Camino

Camino pilgrims who share their experiences along this ancient trail widely agree to a common discovery. They face three powerful challenges: the first third of the distance is physical; the second third is emotional; and the final leg of the trail is spiritual.

With a little more than three hundred kilometers (185 miles) of exhausting climbs behind, the trail offers a relief from the Pyrenees Mountains and the steep, rock-strewn trail. Now begins the Meseta, a level, monotonous, high plateau terrain. For many, this begins pilgrims' emotionally charged Camino. Simple life occurrences that would normally be perceived as unimportant now tearfully strike at the heart. Simple personal belongings now carry poignant memories. Simple encounters with others are now the source of little dramas that ambush the sentiments of unsuspecting pilgrims. Most ironic is the setting for this emotional stage—the Meseta's serenity for the next 126 kilometers (78 miles)!

Regardless of its vast expanses of flatland, the Meseta is *not* without fascination. The highlights include a legend attributed to Napoleon's troops at Hornillos del Camino; the fourteenth- and fifteenth-century healing miracles at St. Anton monastery and convent; the delight found at an albergue run by singing nuns in Carrion de los Condes; and Sahgun, the geographic center of the Camino. Each are uniquely captivating.

The Meseta

The Meseta, Spanish for "tablelands," is either a welcomed easier section of walking trail or dreaded for its long, monotonous terrain. The geography is as exciting as America's Midwest and comprises forty percent of the land in Spain. The Camino traverses the northern end from Burgos to Astorga, a total distance of 215 kilometers (133 miles). This flat-as-a-pancake land undulates gently between four hundred meters (1,300 feet) and a thousand meters (3,200 feet). Mile after long mile stretches ahead with only wheat, barley, and shepherd's fields.

What some pilgrims claim as boring is found as a gift by others who craved long periods of reflective thinking free from fear of an ugly stumble and fall.

Some notable characters are linked to the Meseta. The story of Don Quixote de la Mancha was inspired by the southern region of this tableland. Two highly revered saints, St. Theresa of Avila and St. John of the Cross found deep communion with God in this famous Spanish landscape.

Hornillos de Camino

Hornillos, meaning "small oven," is a quaint, little town with but one small fountain, Fuente de Gallo, with a rooster atop. Small as this sleepy town is, the legend of Napoleon[40] and his soldiers makes it noteworthy. During the Spanish War for Independence, his soldiers stopped in Hornillos for food and supplies. All of the town's people were at the local Catholic mass. The hungry soldiers saw this as their opportune time to steal and kill all the hens and roosters for a feast. Their plan was to smuggle their booty out of town in the soldiers' drums. However, when the people realized the thievery had occurred, they confronted the soldiers at the fountain square. The soldiers refused to admit to the stealing. The legend continues that the women in the town prayed to St. Anthony, patron saint of lost items, to intercede. At that moment, a miracle occurred. One rooster began to crow while in the drum. A coincidence? The guilty soldiers were caught, and the fountain with the rooster fixed over it was renamed to capture this legend of God's unusual means in answering prayers.

San Anton Monastery and Convent

After miles of level walking along farmlands, the abandoned ruins of San Anton capture attention with their two-story, sixteenth-century arch over the Camino. On one side is the monastery, and on the other the convent founded in 1146.

The history of the San Anton Monastery[41] and the miracles that occurred at this location of the relic of St. Anthony of Egypt make it awe-striking. A legend that likely occurred during the Middle Ages claims that a devoutly religious man brought his daughter to the church in fervent hope that she might be cured of burning blisters and an intense fiery sensation to all extremities—fingers, hands, toes, feet. Her suffering included loss of circulation, gangrene, maddening agony, even hallucinations. During his prayer time in the church, his daughter was miraculously healed. The disease, once common in western Europe, came to be called "St. Anthony's Fire."

For centuries an Antonine religious order resided there and became widely known for healing this gruesome, torturous ailment. They used a sacred symbol in their healing, a T-shaped cross with an upward curving horizontal cross beam. This symbol, named Tau[42] (pronounced like the word "how") by some accounts, means "love." It is respected for its power to ward off evil and bring protection. Others conjecture that the order was also skillful in performing amputations of areas where gangrene set in.

Sadly though, untreated victims of this heinous disease went mad. Some even speculate that the disease might have been present in the early New England colony in Salem, Massachusetts—an interesting thought to ponder considering that mysterious witchcraft was believed to have occurred there from victims thought to have gone mad.

Years later it was discovered that the source of this scourge was a fungus that grew in rye and some wheat flours. Today it is controlled by simple antibiotics.

Carrion de los Condes

One of the most soul-healing stays of the entire Camino is at the albergue of Santa Maria. After a long day's walk, the town's center of Carrion de los Condes cannot appear soon enough. Pilgrims pour in eagerly, shedding their gear and heavy backpacks. Unlike any albergue along the Camino, they are greeted by a religious order of Catholic nuns (Sisters) in their light grey and white, loose-fitted habits and veiled head pieces. However, it is the uncontainable joy that radiates from their faces that penetrates guests' impatient dispositions. While standing in a long cue waiting to check in, a plump sister approaches with a tray crowded with cups of warm tea and cookies. What a cherished gift for weary pilgrims! The sister's sunshine-warm smile and her aura of peace and love are disarming.

After being warmly welcomed and settled, the Sisters invite pilgrims to a sing-along. Crowded in the entry way, up a staircase, and spilling out into the adjoining room, pilgrims from all over the globe sit cozily squeezed together. Before them are three Sisters, one, a guitarist. They begin by inviting all to share their name and a reason why they are walking the Camino. Most respond in English, some have fellow pilgrims translate for them. What cannot be understood in their language, is piercingly understood from heart to heart. Many choke up in tears as they speak, others express that the reason to walk the Camino is unfolding with each new day, still others share that they felt an undeniable heart-tug from God. (This was true for me.)

If the rare opportunity to share intimately with other pilgrims isn't enough to bind the strangers, the singalong certainly does. Printed sheets of various folk songs in different languages are passed around. Forty to fifty people sing along loudly, undaunted by the quality of their voices nor the fear of mispronouncing the words. The overflowing peace and joy exuded by these sisters transforms weary pilgrims into a warmhearted Camino family bonded by a sense of God's love.

Sahagún[43]

Sahagún (pronounced "say agoon") is not only a city of medieval distinction, but its very location is significant. Before walking into town, the trail passes between two stone statues, roughly twenty feet tall, with a cement threshold connecting them. On one is carved Alphonse VI, the Brave (1065–1109). He went to war with his own brother, eventually winning the city. His motive was to promote and protect pilgrims on the Camino. The other statue is of Bernado de Seriedad, one of the founders of Sahagún. Engraved in the threshold are images representing the entire Camino journey.

Pilgrims brim with pride and excitement because this exact location pinpoints the geographic center of the Camino de Santiago. Countless pilgrims have a photo of themselves straddling the centerline of this monument. That's four hundred daunting kilometers (250 miles) completed through God's grace—and that same amount before them, in need of more of His grace.

My Camino

"Everything I need comes to me in the perfect place and time."

(Unknown)

This half of the Meseta served as an incubator for two deeply emotional reflections within me.

I plodded along on a blazing hot day. The southern sun was a heat lamp striking my left side. After several hours, I stopped at a pilgrim rest stop which provided a most welcome picnic table under a broad shade tree. I shed my backpack and joined some new pilgrim friends I'd met days ago. I pulled out a water bottle I'd been carrying for weeks now from my first days in Medjugorje. I'd grown partial to it, not only because it fit so comfortably in my side pocket, but I had it beside me when I prayed at all the holy shrines. This may sound irrational, but I had a sentimental liking to it.

While at the rest area, two Canadian couples arrived. As usual, we exchanged the popular questions and our answers. "What city are you from? Where did you start walking the trail? What called you to the Camino? What are you getting out of the Camino?"

After a lively exchange, I said my goodbyes, threw on my backpack, and started along the trail. About two miles out, while on a long, steady downslope, I dropped a trekking pole. Upon bending down, other gear spilled out of my pockets and from the upper pouch in my backpack. Some items rolled downward into a small ravine with tall grasses. I collected myself and continued down the long, steepening slope. The trail leveled off, and that was the first time I realized my water bottle was no longer in my pocket.

Not only had I grown attached to this thing, but I was at the start of the emotional section of the Camino, and my feelings were becoming super sensitive. The loss hit me. *I must find my water bottle.* So I walked the entire two miles up the incline hoping to find my water bottle. It was nowhere to be found. With anxiety welling inside I thought, *Don't give up; keep looking.* I began the descent *again* in another search, but to no avail.

It was time to confess my irrational preoccupation with this water bottle from Croatia. Time to surrender, to detach from a *thing*, and to disengage emotionally from this inanimate object.

Easier said than done. I walked along teary-eyed on this new stretch of dead-flat trail praying, "Lord, I know that I can only receive your full grace with arms that are empty. It's just a stupid . . . plastic . . . water bottle! I don't want to care about a 'thing.' I want to care only about You."

No sooner had I finished the prayer than my "blues" evaporated, and I felt free of the water bottle obsession. I trekked ahead a few more miles, feeling liberated, lighter in spirit. I recited Psalms and prayers of praise while living a victory of surrendering this "thing" for a hope of more of Him. As for the loss, I just offered it up as a small sacrifice to the One I wanted to follow with all my heart. It was a good feeling of victory over my old ways of preoccupation and selfishness over "things."

After another two hours, a new struggle reared its ugly head. With no water bottle I was parched, my tongue thickened, and it stuck to the roof of my mouth like it was glued there. I detected the early signs of dehydration—prickly, tingly skin, and a cold sweat. Each weary step was accompanied by a new, pounding headache aggravated under the relentless, baking sunlight.

I need water; I need some fast! An alarm was growing louder in my head as I looked ahead and behind. The only pilgrims in sight were miles ahead and before them were several miles before reaching the nearest town.

I confronted my panic with a simple prayer. "Lord, I don't want a 'thing' to be more important than you. But it was my water bottle, and I'm crazy thirsty. I'm in trouble. Please help me, Lord."

I stumbled along for a short mile or so staring down at my feet to avoid fixating on the distance before me. My stare at my boots was shaken by an inexplicable surprise. A short distance before me on this narrow gravely walking trail, a grey minivan was preceding the clay-colored dust cloud it was stirring behind it. The driver skidded noisily to an abrupt halt right beside me. The passenger window dropped, and a stubbly faced Spaniard leaned toward me holding out a plastic water bottle. And, yes, it was icy cold!

Not a single word was spoken. Our eyes met briefly as I exchanged my dumbfounded look with the man's big grin. The van pulled ahead leaving me standing in disbelief in billowing Camino dust.

I walked aglow with gratitude for my answered prayer. The miles before town shrunk. Just a comfortable mile or two from my new albergue, I chose a shady rest stop just outside town. To my surprise, the Canadian couple I had chatted with earlier in the day arrived twenty minutes later. One of the gentlemen approached me as a man on a mission.

"I saw that you left your water bottle back at the rest stop earlier in the day. Something inside me said you might like to have it back. I've refilled it for you." He smiled humbly as he held the bottle before me.

Utterly shocked, I received it. I could not contain the story of how sentimental the object had become for me, how losing it had disappointed me so, and how God had answered my prayers with the special delivery from the grey minivan. Even more puzzling, they encountered no minivan, no free bottle of water.

The Canadian listened politely to my gushing gratitude as I tried to relate that it was God's gift for him to return it to me. Then my new Canadian friend extended a profound gesture. He removed a canteen from a side pouch on his backpack. He looked me in the eyes, ever so kindly, and said as he held out his canteen, "Here, we drink as brothers."

I asked myself, *Did what just happen, really happen?* I prayed. I trusted. Then a God delivery of His faithfulness was transported in a grey minivan forbidden on this narrow walking path. And what perfect timing! Within minutes of a desperate prayer. I surrendered all sentimental attachment in preference to God's will. God's overwhelming generosity and compassion enveloped me. Coincidence?

No! I determined. This was a "Godcidence"—a circumstance that looks like a coincidence but is obviously a "God thing." God's timing was, and always is, perfect. This I came to believe in a deep way through these water bottle incidences.

Praise and gratitude to God renewed over and over again within me. I walked along basking in my surprise encounter with the divine. His presence was tangible in my spirit.

My revelry lasted but a few short miles when a new question stirred in me, "*Where is God while I'm searching bug-eyed for a Godcidence? Where is He while I'm hanging on a desperate prayer waiting for His answer?*"

The answer came just days later.

*   *   *

The Meseta has a spirit about it. Devoid of risky trail hazards, I continued walking God's creation carefree with my treasured water bottle at my side. Only while lost in my daydreams did I encounter a little wobble induced by the weight of my backpack. Looking back, I believe it was during one of those side-to-side stumbles that God shed light on my question: *Where are you, Lord, while I'm hanging on a desperate prayer waiting for an answer?*

I was a little boy, about eight years old. I had just recovered from surgery for an appendix that had burst. It was painful, and I remember that it took a long time to get the infection arrested. "You get well, and we'll get you a brand new bike," my parents promised. Talk about motivation! Wow, my first bicycle!

By that late spring, I was back to full strength. Dad took me down to a local bike store and told me to pick out any bicycle I wanted. I chose a candy-apple-red Schwinn with polished chrome fenders and plastic streamers dangling off the backs of the handlebar grips. I couldn't wait to clothespin baseball cards from the frame to the spokes to create a racket, alerting all as I sped down sidewalks, "Cool kid on a fast bike coming!"

My challenge was that I didn't know how to ride yet. My friends learned while I was recovering from surgery, and I was not the free-spirit-terror they had become as experienced bike riders.

I started with the training wheels. This was only a teaser to what thrill would be in store if I could only learn to ride like my big-shot friends.

I recall hopping on my shiny twenty-six-incher while struggling to sit erect. Dad put his hand on the back of the seat, wrapping his arm around my back, and placed his other hand atop my hand, fiercely clutching the handlebar grip like a life preserver.

We were off. Dad ran alongside while I tried, with all my will, to keep the whole process working simultaneously. I watched the front wheel, concentrated on the pedals going front to back, stole quick glances at where I was headed. I had so many things to coordinate. Through each trial run, Dad raced alongside.

The recollection became so real and the details so vivid as I relived the feel of my dad's hand gripping the back of my seat, his stubbly, bearded chin on my cheek, and the smell of his Brylcreemed hair and Old Spice aftershave lotion. I could swear I heard his dress loafers clomping along just beneath me as I pedaled along. Priceless!

I recall a moment when I caught some speed and then that devilish front wheel zigzagged into an unpredictable, uncontrollable wobble. Turn one way, then too much, then the other, no, too much. Back and forth. My eyes bugged out and I was all goose-bumpy and scared. *I'm gonna fall. Pain is coming.* "Daddy help meeeeeeeeee!"

I could hear again Dad's little chuckle and reassurance, "I got ya. I got ya." I was in my father's steady hands. One hand steadied me from behind; one helped guide me along the right path.

There was a lesson for me in this memory and an answer to this question:

Where is God when I'm hanging on a desperate prayer?

The answer: He is holding me. Just as my dad helped me navigate through my wobbly bike ride, I am forever in my heavenly Father's steady hand. It's no coincidence that I've survived all the wobbly rides throughout my adult life. God was and is right alongside me and holding me. It took the perfectly timed, surprising gift of a bottle of water and the memory of my cherished first bike ride to imprint these truths in me.

Our Camino

"Those who leave everything in God's hand will eventually see God's hand in everything."

Unknown

Once we embrace the belief that God is everywhere, we grow in the awareness that His graces are everywhere. The lyrics of the popular song "Awesome God," by Rich Mullins, ring true in our hearts: "His wisdom, power and love—our God is an awesome God!" [44] This truth eddies in the depths of our souls. As we watch for His grace, a string of random incidents can be seen to have occurred for a purpose, and the purpose brings profound insight and wisdom into our lives. Some might still dismiss them as "coincidences." I would not agree because God's hand can be undeniably recognized in each event leading to the grand revelation. The precious "Ah ha" moment energizes our faith because, undeniably, God's blessings were present all along.

God used a lost water bottle to shake me out of my tiny world of petty wants into the big world with God in the middle of perfect incidences. This was a Godcidence. What makes them so unique, so precious, so worth our attention?

- It's all about their discovery and the moment of awareness that God walks with me.
- Each of the incidents are blessings, even in disguise. God intervenes on my behalf.
- The incidents make sense; they have a purpose. God guides me in His wisdom.
- Every incident and person involved leads to God's heart. God loves me.

Entertain a wildly creative notion. What if our cell phones had an app called "Godcidence"? What if we could simply tap the "Godcidence" app and up would pop a treasure map of our current life journey? God-cidences past and present would be labeled. X marks the spot: a glimpse of God's heart and mind is here! A unique concept, true, but let's enter this notion further.

Let's imagine that we want to use the app, but where do we go to get a good wifi signal? Where do we look for divine "wifi hot spots"?

My 11 Divine "Wifi Hot Spots" for Godcidences

1. *God in goodness shown through others.* A group of volunteers are helping at a homeless shelter. The plugged toilet overflows. It is a dirty, disgusting, and immensely humbling task, and no one seems brave enough to take on the job at hand. A long, awkward moment ensues. Surprisingly, someone cheerfully steps forward, selflessly accepting the task. His example not only surprises all around him, but it embodies the spirit of what it means to "serve others sacrificially." Those on mission trips, in ministry, and in charitable service projects commonly witness Godcidence experiences in those around them.

2. *God in dreams.* God spoke to heroes of our faith during their dreams. Isaiah, Joseph (father of Jesus), and Peter the apostle are just some who experienced a desperately needed answer to their prayers during a dream. Today, many attest that they received an answer to their prayers during a vivid dream. They awake knowing in their heart-of-hearts that the message pointed them in a God-honoring direction. The fact that the dream occurred precisely when it did suggests that a Godcidence has occurred.

3. *God in whispers.* Scriptures point to listening within us to that "still small voice" (1 Kings 19:12, KJV). Elijah the prophet sought God, but He was not present in the wind, the earthquake, or the fire. He heard God in a "still small voice." That voice is not limited to Elijah. Many people make claims that God spoke to them. Of course, it is rarely claimed one actually hears an audible voice. Still, a message comes to them which is perfectly aligned with

truths about God. These "God whispers" often occur during intimate moments in prayer, through a comment someone makes, or
even in some word or line read. We're not imagining things. God
does speak to us. These Godcidences are little whispers that point
us toward His perfect will.

4. *God in nature.* Gaze upon a sunset, a secluded lake away from the
crowds, a moonlit night, a mountain landscape, or the vastness
of an ocean. The beauty of creation mirrors our Creator. They
cleanse the busyness in our mind, the troubles of our heart, and
relax our body. With less clutter to distract us, God's messages can
flood our consciousness.

5. *God in His forgiveness of us.* Perhaps it's our ego, our pride, or stubbornness. Most are reluctant to admit their faults, their hurtful
mistakes, and their sins. But as we face this truth about ourselves,
we can be truly free. Peace replaces tension, joy replaces despair,
and freedom casts away Satan's prison of old, deadly habits.
When we get right with God, we see Him through new eyes of
faith. We see how God has orchestrated care for us, even in our
sinfulness. We see Godcidences of His mercy.

6. *God in affirmations.* Sometimes God speaks an uplifting message
deep in our souls. On occasion someone will pass along a sin-
cere, encouraging affirmation of our goodness. These are little
gifts from God that delight and strengthen us for the journey
ahead. God may also use us to deliver His perfectly timed affirmation of another. Our words may be the strength someone
needs, perhaps even the answer to someone's prayer. We'll hear
some say, "That was just what I needed to hear!" Whether we're
the receiver or deliverer of affirmations, these Godcidences are
empowering.

7. *God in silence.* Prayer is a conversation with God. We can't hear Him
if we do all the talking. Silence graciously invites intimacy with
Him. It creates intentional space for listening in a humble posture

to receive whatever messages He wishes us to receive. Silence is an atmosphere where Godcidences often blossom within us.

8. *God in surprises.* God has His way of breaking through the impossible in our life. Here's one example: You're called upon to make an emergency, cross-country trip to help a very sick family member. Vacation time at work is unavailable. There is no money in the bank account. No one nearby can fulfill your other home obligations. You feel guilt for not being able to help a loved family member who needs *you.* You shoot up a desperate prayer. Within days, surprises spring up. Someone cancelled their vacation time and now your earlier vacation request is possible. A rebate check comes in the mail. Just that day, the airlines offer a discount travel promotion. A neighbor offers to cover responsibilities at home. Out of the blue, a refund check arrives for an overpayment that was made. No one knew the dollar amount needed for travel. However, the surprise refund check not only completes the funds needed for the trip, but for the exact dollar amount. This string of events is perfect in timing and details. Godcidences come in surprises.

9. *God in miracles.* The medical analysis is grim. The condition is terminal, and the doctors' advice is to "get your arrangements in order—nothing more can be done." Hospice is called and the condition is monitored. Constant tears, anxiety, and soul searching overwhelm you. All anyone can do is pray. In the days ahead, little things begin to change. Pain subsides, appetite improves, skin color looks healthier, and each day more and more mobility, even long walks are possible. Doctors run new tests looking for signs of their death notice diagnosis. The new lab results reveal the impossible: the condition is inexplicably gone. Coincidence? Not a chance! This miraculous chain of events points undeniably to the presence of Godcidences.

10. *God in our suffering.* It is impossible to experience life without a share of suffering. Sickness, death, financial collapse, crippling

stress, depression, failures, or broken relationships can and do come along. These are unavoidable and heartbreaking. Scriptures abound with the stories of God's intervention during suffering and He is present in our life's suffering today. When we take our attention off ourselves, we can awaken to God's love to us as shown through others. These expressions surround us as Godcidences to sustain us through our trials.

11. *God in the face of the poor.* Who of us have not been either poor in spirit, poor financially, or just poor enough to fear our future? Yet Jesus said "blessed are the poor." What's so blessed about poverty, about being needy, about being weak? Look into the face of a beggar, a homeless man or woman, a person who admits he's bankrupt without God in his life. Look into the face of these "blessed" and see a clear truth: "We are nothing without God." This declaration of dependence puts us in right relationship with "Jehovah Jireh," God, our Provider. Whether we're looking at the face of the poor on the street or in the mirror, all that we have is a gift from Him. Through the lens of meekness we see all gifts provided to us from above. What are we to make of these discoveries?

They're Godcidences demonstrating how abundantly He provides.

*   *   *

Countless Scripture references speak to the many strange and wonderful ways God orchestrates the delivery of His graces. The eerie arrival of them could be lucky breaks or coincidences. However, my friends Mike and Nicole have a story that makes no claim of coincidences. They said yes to God, and God provided one miraculous event after another as a steady stream of His blessings. They experienced a shocking number of miraculous events in the perfect time with the perfect answers. Their Godcidence story is embodied in this Scripture, "What no eye has seen, nor ear heard, nor has the heart of man imagined, what God has prepared for those who love him" (1 Cor. 2:9).

What family could prepare to grow from a household of six to ten in just three short months?

"Things have a way of falling into their proper places, at the right time, and in a special way. God orchestrates events as we align our plans to His call."

Adrian Pantonical

*   *   *

Faith, the oldest of the girls, gleamed a playful glance across a monstrous dining table seating seven adorable little girls, a mom, dad, and grandma. At the opposite end was her target, one of her new sisters. Faith poked a playful finger in the direction of one foster sister and declared, "I remember the first day *you* moved in. I thought you were a little brat." The accused one's facial expression revealed delight and pride that the special moment put her in the spotlight. Faith's statement could be considered harsh, but the grins and giddy giggles from all the girls showed no hint of hurt or resentment was intended or received.

Faith continued, "Mom spent the day preparing the room for you. The bunk bed was set up and Mom had put all the bed linen on the top bunk, thinking that's where you would want to be. But noooo," Faith playfully recounted, "You wanted the bottom bunk; Mom had to climb up and pull everything off the top bunk that she just made, and start the bed making all over again." She ended her story with a little shoulder shrug and a grin. The accused nine-year-old's smiley, giggly face ducked behind her finger barricade to hide her guilt and her grin. An aura of giddy joy erupted among all the girls in a barrage of delightful banter.

All seven young cuties ages two to sixteen beamed with pride, chuckles, and impatient excitement to share their perspective of growing into such a big, special, God-honoring family. Each story captured a snapshot of God's grace.

I asked, "When did this foster idea start?"

"It actually was a mission begun many years earlier," Nicole began. "Mike and I discussed being foster parents even before we were married. It was something we promised each other would happen some day in the future."

However, the genesis of this desire came during Nicole's childhood. She was a young girl when a neighbor couple took in a foster child. Nicole fondly remembered how impressed she was that the couple's "yes" saved her new playmate from a life of abuse and neglect. She saw the miracle of hope in her younger friend's life. Nicole spoke with conviction, "In my heart, God planted the desire for me to do the same thing one day."

The calling surfaced again in her early adult years and remained during courting and marriage to Mike. In a fourteen-year span after the wedding, there was a twelve-year-old and twin nine-year-old girls. Mike and Nicole agreed, "It was the perfect time for us to foster."

They went on to share, "We only wanted one. It had to be a girl. And we didn't want babies. We were beyond the diaper thing and all the night feedings, bottles, and toddler challenges. We prayed as a family. "This was going to be a God thing," Mike insisted, "we needed to be sure that our girls saw that the changes in our family, even their sacrifices, were to bring another child to God." With the family solidly in support, they began the foster parent paperwork.

It is said, "If you want to make God laugh, tell Him your plans." Heaven was about to echo with laughter.

Nine months later, the Department of Children and Family Services (DCFS) called on a day following the twins' birthday getaway at the Wisconsin Dells. Looking back, Mike asserted, "It was a really crazy perfect time in our family life for this."

The agent started, "Mike and Nicole, we have a placement that we believe would be ideal for your family. Two sisters—a six-month-old and eighteen-month-old needing an emergency placement."

"Two?" Mike exclaimed. "It was such a surprise. And I wasn't sure I was ready for one, let alone two. Plus, they were babies! It was a total shock."

Nicole added, "Fostering was already in our hearts. And they were sisters," her voice sparkled on the last word. "I couldn't break them up. What a 'coincidence' that we completed the foster classes at the exact time of the youngest baby's birth," she laughed.

The day the two girls arrived was still vivid. Their sisters recalled, "We were peeking from behind curtains when the DCFS van pulled in the drive. When we first caught sight of them we were bouncing up and down like cheerleaders as the two little ones were brought into the house."

Once inside, there was a startling discovery: both girls looked like Mike and Nicole's biological children. The resemblance of all five was freakishly similar.

Mike thought, "Five kids and three adults, that's a big enough family." Turned out God's plan was bigger. It was only three months into the family's new transition when startling news came via another DCFS phone call.

"Mike and Nicole, I'd like you both to seriously think over something. Your new girls actually have two older sisters. Their mother is lost in a drug addiction, and these two girls need a home immediately. We don't want to split them up. An aunt agreed to take all four of them, but we believe your family would be the healthiest option. Talk it over and get back to me by tomorrow. Coincidentally, one of the girls is nine years old, same age as your twins."

There was a serious family discussion that led all to believe that God's hand was in this new twist. "We were all completely surprised! But the real sacrifice would be on our three oldest." Mike explained, "Our three biological children would need to share 'mom and dad time' with the four new girls. They would need to make sacrifices to help with all the extra work Nicole and I would face."

Nicole added, "Turned out there really wasn't uncertainty in any of us. This was all from God; it was His calling for our family." Mike nodded in complete agreement.

"Life was a little crazy at first," Nicole continued, "there are now seven kids, my mom who lives with us, and Mike, the steady, logical one. Add to this hysteria, I homeschool the five oldest. So yeah, it gets crazy here."

Just how mysterious is the will of God was apparent as Mike and Nicole shared their journey toward adoption. This included a search for the biological father of the children. They discovered the biological father of the oldest foster girl. "This young guy had no idea he even fathered a child," Mike explained. In his mid-twenties he was contacted with the news, "You are the biological father of a twelve-year-old girl." As he reeled from the shock, Mike and Nicole reached out to him. They told him he could have supervised visits to meet his daughter, and they also asked him to consider consent for her adoption.

Nicole shared, "It was a little scary at first, for all of us. But we still believed this whole adventure was a God thing. The first visits were awkward, but little by little the guy found comfort in our home with all the kids. Surprisingly, he was touched by seeing the whole family so happy. We learned he never really knew what family life could be. His childhood was a mess."

"Would you like to go to church with the family?" we offered.

"Not a churchgoer, but I'll give it a try. More time with my daughter," he responded.

Enthusiasm grew in Mike's voice, "So the next Sunday we headed to church, all ten of us, and this new young guy. Here we're doing our God calling with all these kids, and God begins a work in this man's heart. He was riveted to the message. He prayed. He listened to every word of the sermon."

Nicole added, "And not just that Sunday, but Sunday after Sunday. He insisted on sitting in the very front row right before the pastor. I could read it in his face—his heart was moved. Later one night, he called me, troubled. He heard the story of Jesus, but he had led a pretty bad life. He didn't feel worthy of God, nor of the beautiful family his daughter lived with now. He sobbed on the phone."

Nicole beamed, "I shared with him the salvation promise of Jesus. Over the phone he gave his life to Christ."

Mike excitedly interrupted, "And not just him, but the grandparents asked for a visit. They came to the house for family time, and they got so into it they came to church. They totally listened to the sermon and took part in all the church activities afterward. The grandpa's heart was undeniably touched. We invited them back to the house. They were loving it—kids running around, all the happy noise, and a family meal with us. God was working in them, right in the middle of our doing the God thing for these kids."

Nicole added with conviction, "God blessed us with Mike's good job, income, and kids who love the Lord. We know He was using us to save kids from a life of abuse, of neglect, of ignorance of God's love and mercy." A reflective pause came before she added, "We know God called us to save these kids for Him. He surprised us with little graces every day. That's how God is. He is faithful."

As the interview ended, the kids wanted to perform a little piano recital. Each played a small piece to the raucous applause of their sisters. The love they held for one another was palpable. It was pure. It was innocent. Then Faith, the oldest and most experienced, sat at the piano bench with her six beaming-with-pride sisters, giving a look that read, "Wait 'til you hear this!"

Our tears were uncontrollable as she played the song, "Amazing Grace."

Final Reflection on Godcidences and God's Steady Hand

Our Abba, our heavenly daddy, hears our every cry. He cares deeply for us. He counts our every tear. He loves us. He loves you. He does. There is no ache in our heart that He doesn't know. We need only to cry out to Him like a child, "Daddy, help meeeee!"

Our heavenly Dad places his strong arm around us to brace us up, and His other grasps our hand to help us steer through life in righteous directions. We might even sense the sound of His shoes running alongside us. If God had an aftershave fragrance, I'd guess it'd be named "Mercy." What a sweet fragrance!

It's so easy to get consumed in the pleasure of life's ride and lose control. After all, God's creations are made for our pleasure. However, when we let them become centerpieces of too much of our time, attention, and desire—then we're headed for an uncontrollable crash.

Fortunately for us, we share a faith in a God who cares for us in the crash. No other religion worships a God of compassion for the sinful. Check it out. None do. Only our God offers that kind of hope.

Some find themselves in a life crash even when they've led a kind and loving life. It isn't fair. It isn't right. Yet their life is in shambles.

How do we navigate through life's obstacle course of stress and fears?

Just this: we grasp the handlebars of faith with all our might. He cares for us. And He will always care for us. Always.

Godcidences are fingerprints of God's grace. His mighty arms surround us. His steady hand rests upon ours.

> "Stop trying to take control of life. It gets in the way of divine intervention."
>
> Cheryl Richardson

*   *   *

Walk this short stretch of Camino with me and discover a new enigma: growing in grace requires moving from stuffed lives to starved ones.

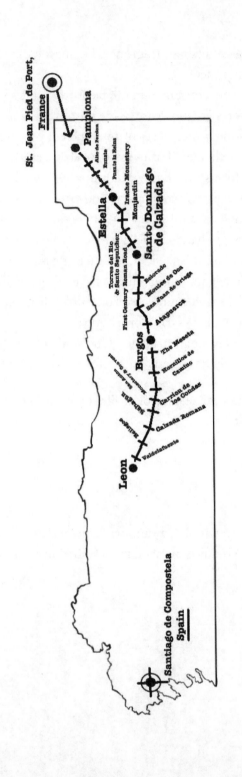

Chapter 12

FROM STUFFED TO STARVED

"The key to Christian living is a thirst and hunger for God. And one of the main reasons people do not understand or experience the sovereignty of grace and the way it works through the awakening of sovereign joy is that their hunger and thirst for God is so small."

John Piper

The Camino

The pilgrim cannot exhaust the historical captivations and natural beauty on the Camino. This is true for these next forty-two kilometers (twenty-six miles). The trail from Calzadillas de los Hermanillos to Leòn follows the Meseta, the Spanish tablelands. Four highlights bear special attention: the Calzada Romana, meeting Elvis in Reliegos, the Roman wall in Valdelafuente, and the magnificent Cathedral of Leòn with its festive town square.

Calzada Romana[45]

The Roman Empire created marvels that still exist today. On the Camino, one such awe-striking example is Calzada Romana, the longest stretch of the Roman Road located in Spain.

How the Calzada Romana[46] was built dumbfounds those who are privileged to walk it today. The construction involved digging a trench roughly 1.5 meters (five feet) deep and installing a series of base layers as a foundation. Heavy boulders and finer gravel strata form the base. The sand base allowed placement of additional large boulders, tightly fitted to form the road surface. This road stretches hundreds of miles and was traveled upon by Emperor Caesar Augustus. Warring Christians and Muslims also used the road, as well as the famed Charlemagne. Its existence twenty centuries later serves as a testimony to the countless years of slave labor it took to construct a road of such length and durability.

Camino pilgrims traveling the Calzada Romana cannot help but feel a personal connection with the past and be overcome with awe of the Roman Empire's might and the far-reaching effects it had throughout Europe and beyond.

Reliegos

This sleepy little village is easy to pass through without fanfare or notable stops, but La Torre snack bar is a must-see stop on the Camino. Why? Elvis is here! Pilgrims can't miss the small, brightly painted blue building with wild designs adorning it. Inside, the walls and ceiling are completely covered with what appears to be graffiti. However, it is pilgrims' inspirational messages, slogans, song lyrics, sketches, and poems that cover nearly every inch inside and are written for future pilgrims.

The mind cannot begin to take in the plethora of pilgrims' inspiration captured on the walls and ceiling. If this isn't attention-getting enough, the proprietor is. This slender man grins behind the counter, wearing a black beret. He begins singing Elvis songs and does a little jailhouse-rock dancing. His animated personality and effervescent, engaging demeanor are wonderful diversions to a day of long, boring Meseta walking. Before leaving, Elvis invites his visitors to take markers and leave their own messages on the ceiling or wall.

Valdelafuente

This small town has remnants of the old Roman wall.[47] The oldest sections of the wall were begun in the first century; others were constructed in the third century. The remaining structures surrounding Valdelafuente add deeper admiration for the Roman Empire. These walls are five meters (more than sixteen feet) wide, stand eight meters (twenty-six feet) high, and stretch 2,117 meters (a little less than 7,000 feet—nearly a mile and a half) in length! They were all hand-built by slave laborers who brought in the boulders, cobblestone, and mortar. Characteristic of some thirteenth- and fourteenth-century sections, narrow slit-like openings a meter wide and two meters tall (roughly three by six feet) provide a space for archers to shoot with relative safety from enemy attack.

The lowly pilgrim gazes with amazement at this example of the Roman Empire's formidable strength and pervasive control during the early centuries.

León

Like Valdelafuente, León has bragging rights to the ancient Roman wall. This city's name is a derivative of the term "legion," from a time Rome's legions were encamped there. León also proudly claims identity to the Spanish word for "lion." The sources of strength behind this city's name only adds fascination for this star attraction on the Camino.

There is a spiderweb of short, disconnected streets that meet at the town's central structure, Cathedral of León,[48] also known as "House of Light." It is an inspiring French-Gothic architectural wonder dating back to the early 1300s. Situated in the center of a large town square with broad expanses of open sidewalks, its spires and columns stretch thirty meters (one hundred feet) and covers 1,800 square meters (roughly 19,300 square feet). The sheer size is jaw-dropping.

The cathedral's notoriety comes from all the stained glass, which many claim rivals the famous Cathedral of Chartres, eighty kilometers (fifty miles) southwest of Paris. The Cathedral of León proudly displays

770 stained glass windows, soaring twelve meters (forty feet) in height, making it an architectural jewel. The glass artistically captures sacred moments in the Christian Scriptures and the saints' lives. The cathedral's high, curved, arching ceilings are washed in soft red and yellow as sunlight filters through the glass. Visitors first sit in rapt amazement of this towering magnificence only to experience something much deeper—a holy peace unique to this place of worship.

It is no surprise that the cathedral is the town square. Happy, festive pilgrims stream through narrow side streets to crowd as near to this towering gothic structure as they can. Robust laughter and wine-induced, raucous storytelling overflows from countless outdoor cafes and bars. By nightfall, pilgrims and local townspeople transform Leòn's central square into a party as they revel in the artistry of exquisite food, great wine, and abundant, jovial conversation. It is an experience that buoys the soul.

My Camino

"If you're not hungry for God, you're probably full of yourself."

Unknown

The Camino is now a long, level stretch, delightful for those who like to get their heads in the clouds and revel in God's thoughts and insights. No fear now of stumbling on large stones that were common earlier on the Camino. This brought a freedom to my walking and my thinking. I began to recall the fun I was having on my Camino. Walking the Spanish countryside, meeting such good-hearted people as the bishop and his wife, and oddly enough my time with Elvis at his cafe. His performance echoed back to the memory of our firstborn son who was quite a gifted performer. He performed the role of Elvis/Pharaoh in the play *Joseph and the Amazing Technicolor Dreamcoat*. The sting of missing him in my life surfaced. How I wished he could receive the blessings the Camino brings. The thought had a lingering effect.

I committed to pray for "my Elvis" all the way to Santiago, and this resolve grew into a desire to dedicate the journey to him.

Sometime later in the day a pilgrim friend shared a Facebook entry. It captivated my reflection time. It read, "I don't get a little bit out of prayer. I don't get a little bit out of church. And . . . I don't get a little bit out of God."

Not even getting a little bit out of prayer, church, or God sounds like a popular complaint amongst our youth and even some of our adult friends. Does this ring true for you? I know I've heard this all too often from those falling away from their Christian faith life.

As I reflected upon this statement and the dilemma of those close to me who have turned away from prayer, church, and even God, suddenly the complaints came roaring back to describe . . . me! I had to confess, "As a young adult, this was my attitude too!" I was finishing college, starting a career, and blazing a new life direction. Prayer, church, and God were nice things, but I had them on a shelf for when I needed them, like seasoning on a spice rack or a tool on a workbench. I knew where they were, but I didn't really need them to keep all *my* plans moving forward. "God, I can do it all by myself . . . thankyouverymuch."

I reflected upon the season of life when I harbored attitudes of not getting even a little out of a faith life. Today on the Camino I saw those days in a new light, best illustrated by a memory of Christmases at my parents' home.

Holidays at home were always a love feast. My precious little Italian mama always loved us with food. She did not cook just one meal; she cooked four, which included turkey, ham, spaghetti, and lasagna. Each was a favorite of a family member. The tablecloth was invisible because of all the huge dishes covering it. The meal launched with a confusion of knives and forks hitting plates, monstrous platters hovering over other monstrous platters, and the barking of "Pass the sweet potatoes!" Because there were four completely different meals, we were expected—dare I say, required—to taste at least a little from each. And this was only the first course.

Then came the stuffed artichokes. Ma cooked artichokes like they were made back in Italy. They were like ambrosia! No matter how much you'd already eaten, an artichoke the size of Mohammed Ali's fist was irresistible. In short order it was time to lounge in armchairs, open a notch in our belts, and relax. There was a pause in the eating before another mouth-watering invite, "Cannolis!" My sweet mama loved us with all the favorites until we were nothing short of stuffed.

Why this gluttonous story? It reminds me of that time in my life when I allowed myself to be stuffed with . . . uh . . . myself. I was cutting a path toward my life's direction and the thought of adding any time for prayer, church, or God was like considering a double Whopper burger right after one of Ma's big meals. I had no room for God because I stuffed myself with me, myself, and I.

Life has a way of taking surprising turns that are outside of our plans. This was true for me. Infertility, the death of my father, and personal challenges presented themselves. Each of these widened an unhealed hole in my heart that I tried to stuff with anything but God. Some would call this their "God-shaped hole." Now I was looking at my own God-shaped hole. It was time for a choice. More of me or more of God?

I realized the truth and chose God. If I stopped filling that God-hole with other things, I would become starved for Him. This is the hunger I welcomed. Only God fills a God-hole, and I wanted my God-hole stuffed!

Even more interesting is the rest of that Facebook page message. "I don't get a little bit out of prayer, church, or God, because of what there is to lose: ego, greed, depression, insecurity, fear of death. These are ugly qualities we lose, which is ultimately . . . gain!"

There it is. The riches we gain in prayer, church, and God are not little; they are huge!

The message on Facebook rang so true in my life this Camino day. I don't get a little bit out of prayer—I get a lot! A lot of intimate conversation with God who loves me. I don't get a little out of church—I get a lot! A fountain of blessings with fellow believers striving to grow in the knowledge and service of Christ. And I don't get a little out of

God—I get a lot! An abundance of His saving grace in this world and in eternity. Yes, all that I get brings me more than a sense of fulfillment; it brings joy.

So what am I stuffing myself with that hinders me from hungering for Him?

Me, myself, and I.

When I sense that I am getting so little out of my relationship with our Heavenly Father, it is always because of me, not Him. He hungers to grow a deeper, more intimate relationship with me, in fact, with all of us. Here's the enigma.

Being stuffed with the world leaves no room for Christ.

To be stuffed with Christ comes by starving the world right out of myself.

I thank God for the hunger pangs for Him on that day's Camino journey.

Our Camino

"Man is a hungry being. But he is hungry for God. Behind all hunger of our life is God. All desire is finally a desire for Him."

Alexander Schmenann

Repeat after me. "Hi, my name is _____, and I'm a happiness junkie." All aspects of our life are driven by the desire to be happy. Our work, our leisure, our choice of foods, our friends, and how we spend our time are all responses to what makes us happy. Being happy is not a bad thing. It's a natural part of living in the gift of His Creation. It is good, until our happiness cravings grow more important than the Giver of gifts.

I confess, when things in my life are available, I cannot resist stuffing myself with more and more of them. Is this true for you?

Are not these truths for all of us along our Camino?

Happiness is temporary, but this truth is easily forgotten.

It's been said, "Don't get too excited when things are going well. And don't despair when things are going badly. Nothing stays the same for long." Life rides through ups and downs like a roller coaster. We need only beg God for the faith to endure.

Why? Because things are temporary. Friends move, dream jobs are lost, money doesn't buy everything, nor is there ever enough. Good things don't last, or the pleasure of our favorite good things loses its zing and becomes just another thing we take for granted. Life deals some hurtful blows. We worry and stress when difficult things invade our lives.

So we might ask ourselves, "Where is God while our Camino roars on this roller-coaster ride between happiness highs? Why doesn't He just stop us? After all, God can do anything, right?"

Interestingly, St. Augustine, early doctor of the Christian faith, gave us this theological insight as to whether God can do anything. His teaching would suggest a strong, "no." First and foremost, God cannot stop loving us. No sin can stop God's mercy. That's a given. Furthermore, God will not take away His gift of free will, even when our choices for happy things are placed above a choice to follow Him. This is why we can stuff ourselves with things that will eventually harm us, perhaps even destroy us. God always honors our free will.

Some might also argue, "Yes, but doesn't God want us to be happy?" I'm not convinced that happiness is God's priority for our lives. Our free will can lead us to choose to be happy, to choose an attitude about life to help us maintain our happiness. But His hopes for us hold a greater gift than happiness. Jesus said, "These things I have spoken to you, that my joy may be in you, and that your joy may be full" (John 15:11). It is not happiness that Jesus desires for us; it is joy! That's a big difference for our Camino.

While happiness can, for a while, make us smile on the outside, joy is God's undeserved lasting favor deep in our soul. Not sure of the difference? Ask a prisoner of alcoholism who begged God for help and was set free. Talk to someone whose answer to prayer saved them from financial doom. Hear the testimony of someone who surrendered their life to Christ and is now born again. Listen to someone surprised by hope after a pleading, desperate prayer when life was hopeless. In all these, joy abounds.

As perplexing as it is, many have found joy while in miserable places like an abusive marriage, a hospice bed, bankruptcy, or a demanding job. Still others can claim joy while caring for a wayward child, serving an irrational boss, or strained by unemployment. Joy can be found in the worst of circumstances. How?

Joyful people embrace the truth of their happiness addiction. They surrender the drive for happiness and have replaced it with starvation for Him. This leads to a freedom where they know deep within that "God loves me." They can freely claim "I love God, and He is all I need." In that freedom, joy flourishes.

This relationship transcends any happy thing in this life. Wealth, power, and the esteem of people will, at best, bring temporary happiness. They will not bring us joy. Only in our hunger, no, our starvation, for Him can we confess the sorry truth of who we are and humbly confess:

"Hi, my name is _____, and I'm a happiness junkie."

This is a truth that can set us free to receive: His joy in us, a joy that can make us full.

*   *   *

Being starved for God was certainly true for Stan. His faith Camino followed a roller-coaster path through multiple "stuffed to starved" life challenges. In the end, his life hunger for happiness proved to be his hunger for God. Stan's faith journey from heartache to joy is an overwhelmingly inspiring message. Hear it in his own words:

Although I was only three years old at the time, life in 1945 Communist Yugoslavia was always scary. My earliest childhood memories are of our family prayers begging God for help. My mom, younger brother, and I were always cautious. Dad, on the other hand, was more courageous about his faith and was not afraid to speak up against what he called the "godless Communists."

Terror came one night. We were all awakened by a heavy pounding on the front door and fierce shouting. I shook uncontrollably as I watched Dad taken away by uniformed Communist soldiers. It took decades before we met an eyewitness who told us what happened. Dad, along with dozens of others, was taken to a forest, stripped naked, bound hand and foot, shot, and thrown into a fifteen-meter (fifty-foot) vertical cave. Their crime? They would not deny their faith and surrender to Communist ways.

Mom prayed and cried, prayed and cried. Now labeled as a Communist resistant, her job had been taken away. How would we survive? Anyone helping those who refused to give up their faith for Communism would suffer. We begged for God's help.

A couple nights after Dad's arrest, Mom, my brother, and I escaped to the Croatian border to live with one of mom's sisters. God heard our prayers! My aunt was so kind and generous. In fact, the entire community knew of our plight and helped us. The parish priest was especially good to us. We lived in that village for eight years, I attended school there, and became an altar server for the parish priest. His compassion for our little family touched me, but I admired him most for fearlessly opposing the Communists.

At age eleven, I arrived at church to serve at mass for this favorite priest. I stood frozen in shock as I discovered his bullet-ridden body behind the church. The Communists had silenced one more.

Because I would not deny my own faith in God, I was forced out of my village school to attend a Communist boarding school. As a way to honor my father's courage, I refused Communist teachings. This cost me beatings and public ridicule. Through the next four years, my family begged and begged for God to save us.

When I was fifteen, Mom surprised my brother and me with an escape to America. She had secretly saved money and planned ship passage for all three of us. I remember the unusually rough and stormy Atlantic voyage. We arrived in New York City sick, exhausted, and with only five dollars between us. We were starving, poor immigrants with nothing but the train tickets we already had purchased for Chicago where our sponsor would pick us up to live in her home.

A taxi driver agreed to take us to the train station for the little money we had. The train dropped us off in Chicago two days later, even more starved and weak. Our sponsor met us at the station. The moment we met her, none of our suffering mattered; we had escaped from the Communists. God answered our prayers! We had begged for freedom, and now we would live as Americans. We would be free! Or so we thought.

We soon discovered that our sponsor would provide us with only a one-bedroom rental, no more. Our fear and the threats of the Communists were replaced by this hard-hearted, verbally and emotionally abusive woman. She berated us and treated us as intruders in many ways. For example, she refused to allow us to use her table for homework or to watch her television, which was a new American sensation. We were allowed to hear it in the background, but she never let us watch it.

Her cruelty led us to beg God for help. My mom, brother, and I all worked sixteen-hour days, saving every last penny until we were finally able to afford our own apartment. We were free!

For the next several years God richly blessed us. We were so, so happy. I attended St. Mel High School where the Christian Brothers, a religious order of men, taught. They were exceedingly kind and generously helped our family. Only with their help were we able to survive.

At the same time, my athletic abilities skyrocketed. As a freshman I made the varsity soccer team, and we won the national championship. I excelled on track and boxing teams. My intellect was recognized, and I won academic star performer awards. Track scholarships came, as well as acceptance to the University of Illinois on a full scholarship for dentistry. I graduated top of the class. Shortly thereafter, I married Camille and soon after that, our first son arrived. Love, life, and happiness were brimming.

I was then accepted into US Navy Officers' Training. This provided unparalleled career opportunities. As a naval officer during the Vietnam War, I served on battleships and aircraft carriers by performing oral surgery and doing facial reconstruction, a highly skilled and sought-after medical ability. Life could not have been happier. Making it even richer, my prayer life was strong and I held the treasure of the closest relationship I had experienced with the Lord in my life thus far. I was living a dream life.

Then heartbreak struck.

Our second child, our little girl Jeanine, suffered a prolonged spell without oxygen during birth. She was left with severe brain injury. As time went on, it became clear she would never talk, feed herself, or care for herself in any way and would need twenty-four-hour care. We again begged and begged God to help. With all this trauma, I resigned from the Navy. My life was speeding in new directions. All I could do was pray. Only God could help us. Only God could help me.

God answered our prayers through the birth of our second son, Richard. His little life brought healing and new hope to our family. Sadly, that period of relief would evaporate eighteen months later.

While playing a league soccer game, I collapsed. After being rushed to the hospital, doctors discovered a life-threatening infection in the lining of my left lung, which needed to be removed immediately. While recovering, I received word that my mom was on her deathbed. Doctors wouldn't release me to go see her. But this was my mom who gave her life for her sons—for me! I could not allow her to pass without my love and care. So under the cover of darkness, I removed my IVs and respiratory hoses, dressed, and traveled to Mom's hospital room to share some of her final life moments with her. My brother and I prayed and begged God's mercy for our mother. As night wore on, my strength was failing me and I was rushed back to my hospital bed. It proved to be one of my life's bitterest regrets. I missed my mom's passing by a few short minutes.

In the weeks following, my health began to recover and my hopes returned as our little family began to find a normal life once again. Or so we hoped. Within the year we discovered that Camille had breast cancer. I witnessed my wife bravely fight her cancer for two-and-a-half years. When she was in her final days, our little Richard fell deathly ill. I rushed him to the hospital to learn that he had life-threatening viral spinal meningitis. He was given critical care while I was sandwiched between pleading to God for both my wife's and our son's lives. "I beg you, Lord. Don't take both of them at the same time."

It was nothing short of miraculous that days passed and our son's condition improved. His fever left, and he regained some strength. All the while, Camille was slipping away. She pleaded to hold our toddler again. Even though Richard was out of grave health danger, doctors didn't advise taking him out of hospital care. It was a risk, but how could I deny my wife's final wish? Again under cover of night, I prepared our son for a quick departure to see his mother for the last time. Joy and heartache clutched me as I witnessed my wife cuddle and rock our son for a few brief minutes.

Because Richard was still weak, I bundled him up and rushed him safely back to his hospital bed. While there, I received a call that my wife just passed. The now familiar heart-stabbing regret flooded me. I had missed a second love's passing without being there for them. In deep despair, I begged God to help me.

Help cascaded in. Even as life overwhelmed me with raising the two boys and arranging care for our special-needs daughter, I managed to pull together my oral surgical practice. God's care was abundant, and the practice became highly successful and lucrative. However, the business side of the practice was proving too great for me to handle. I turned that part of the business over to a reputable investment group. I trusted them.

This proved to be a devastating mistake. It was discovered that the investment partners absconded with the funds of many of their clients, including mine. I was penniless! Again, I got on my knees and begged God, "Help me! Won't you help me?"

I'll never forget the night following this news. Despair was strangling me and every terrible thing that had happened to me from childhood until then was crushing me. It was a dark, dark place. I remember thinking that life for everyone would be better if I just ended mine. I sat on the couch fixated on a 45mm on the coffee table before me. I stared at it and thought and thought and thought. A sweet voice shook me. It was Richard's voice, "Daddy! Daddy!" He was having a bad dream. While comforting him, I believe God gave me new courage to live.

I struggled as a single dad to care for my kids and be part of their school activities. In time I met Carmen, a widow, whose children attended the same school as my mine. She offered to help with my sons on occasion. She was deeply spiritual and encouraging. In time, the friendship grew into romance. Within a few short years, Carmen and I married and blended our families. Raising a family of five children was an adjustment, but a family we became.

Gratefully, my surgical practice was creeping out of financial crisis. A happy life with promise filled our new life together. God held a prominent place in our family and married life. Years passed and my situation improved to the point where I could retire. I was determined to buy a medical trailer, park it in a poor barrio in Mexico, and do free dental work for the poorest of poor. This was my dream life.

The dream didn't last long. I ran into heart complications and my arteries were stinted three times. I survived the treatments and thankfully came back in full strength. I was convinced God had more for me to do. I poured myself into our children's and grandchildren's lives. My life was rich in faith and love. This was to last but three short years.

Doctors discovered that I had a nine-centimeter-sized tumor in my abdomen. During a surgery, doctors discovered one hundred additional small tumors. Some success with a daily chemotherapy pill for leukemia was my last-chance option. I was back on my knees begging and begging God for my life. Again He was merciful.

I began to live a simpler, yet slower life. But live I did. I returned to the medical trailer, helped others, and enjoyed the strength God provided. Two years later, doctors found a new cancer in my lung. Peace could only come on my knees. I prayed my all-too-familiar pleading prayers. I knew that surrender to His will was my only option. I moved forward with round after round of chemotherapy and a radiation treatment that almost killed me. Like a cat with nine lives, I again regained more and more strength.

Today I live with what God has provided. I accept what is and surrender to whatever His will is for me. As I've reflected upon the gift of my life, some truths have been born in me.

First, God is faithful. Through every trauma and life-threatening trial, God was always there, even when I couldn't feel His presence. He was there to lead me to the next step.

Second, all the trials in my life made me stronger in love for those around me.

Finally, people tell me, "You're always smiling. You seem so happy." I must admit, people do see me as a happy person, and it pleases me to be perceived that way. But to know my story is to know the gift in my life is something far greater than happiness; it is life in Him. He is the only source of joy in my life today.

"To be filled with the Spirit, we must be emptied of self."

Unknown

* * *

Our Camino through stuffed and starved challenges is not without the power of the Holy Spirit. At Pentecost, the Spirit presented Himself as a strong wind. Walk this next stretch of Camino where we meet pilgrims who carry a power of His presence with them. It is unmistakably holy and their departure leaves a backdraft—dare I say, a Holy Spirit backdraft.

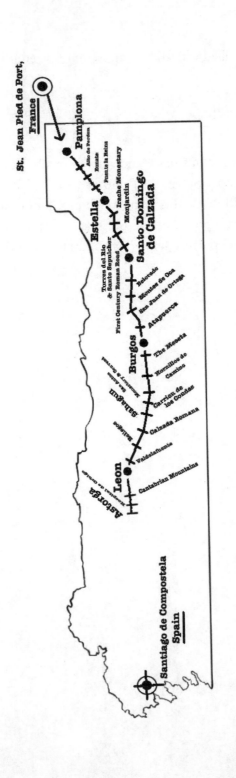

Chapter 13

HOLY SPIRIT'S BACKDRAFT

"You might as well try to see without eyes, hear without ears, or breathe without lungs, as to try to live the Christian life without the Holy Spirit."

D. L. Moody

The Camino

Spanning between Leòn and Rabanal del Camino for seventy-one kilometers (forty-four miles), are breathtaking, snow-capped mountains. These create a stunning background for some fascinating local history. Pilgrims journey beside captivating sites where medieval romance and chivalrous battle occurred. Remnants of Roman artifacts leave onlookers mesmerized. Even before reaching the city of Astorga, anticipation builds. Trailside fruit and snack bars, fringing the route, are managed by some unusual personalities. Indulge in a short rest and conversation with the owner and an unexpected slice of life wisdom may await. Within the city are many historical and cultural treasures worth exploring.

Cantabrian Mountains

The Cantabrian mountain range parallels the Camino from east to west for 360 kilometers (roughly two hundred miles). Along this stretch of The Way, the range stretches further south fifty kilometers (thirty miles) away. With an elevation of two thousand meters (6,500 feet) coupled with being so close, the Cantabrians tower over the pilgrim. God's majestic creation is truly stunning to behold. Their beauty lies in the rugged, blue-gray peaks set in stark contrast to the stunningly white, snow-capped ridgeline. Awe-inspiring!

Hospital de Òrbigo

It was July 10, 1434 when the noble knight Don Suero took up the challenge to defend his honor in the ancient town of Hospital de Òrbigo.[49] After being rejected by a fair maiden, he locked his neck in an iron collar[50] until he completed his personal mission. He challenged to joust any knight daring to pass him across the arched bridge over the River Òrbigo. To restore his honor to the fair maiden, Don Suero needed to defeat every knight's attempt to cross the river for a month, as well as win at least three hundred lances. Knights all across Europe took up the challenge. Knight after knight met their doom under Suero's brave determination and jousting expertise. He collected the quota of lances and was celebrated for regaining his honor and thereby freeing himself of the iron collar.

One legend claims that during one of his final contests, Don Suero was wounded. Yet, he was still determined to complete the defense of his honor until the end. Collecting the three hundred lances was only part of his mission. He had committed to walking the rest of the Camino pilgrimage to the Cathedral of Santiago. Another legend claims that as he traveled, the wounded knight carried for inspiration a blue ribbon from the lady for whom he fought. Interestingly, some legends claim the lady had a change of heart and left a message of her love for Don Suero inscribed on the ribbon.[51]

This ancient love story is credited as Cervantes' inspiration for his book *Don Quixote*. Of course, the bridge still stands today, in the undisturbed setting where the medieval jousting tournament took place. A pilgrim needs only a moment's pause to imagine the gallantry displayed there in order to win a love's hand. It is no wonder that the bridge has been renamed "Paso Honroso," that is, "Passage of Honor."

Astorga

It is not unusual to find trailside vendors selling light snacks and fruits to exhausted pilgrims. For several years now, one noteworthy vendor has gained great attention, and for good reason. David, a young man in his early thirties, completed the Camino himself and afterward determined to give his life in service for pilgrims along The Way.

Located just before the small city of Astorga, David mans a fruit cart parked along the dusty trail. He is unique because he sleeps in a makeshift tent alongside the farm's storage barn in order to afford more supplies for the pilgrims who visit. A small shed alongside the trail with a canvas covering allows pilgrims to escape the sun's rays.

When David spots a new pilgrim nearing, he runs to his cart and rings the bell hanging from it. In a quick about-face, he runs wide armed to welcome the approaching pilgrim. After determining their country of origin, he throws one hand on their shoulder. Then he looks caringly into their eyes. His sparkling blue eyes hold an authentic interest in them. He makes each pilgrim feel so important, so cared for with his gentle questions, often in the pilgrim's native language. "Are you good, friend? Are your feet OK? Have you eaten? Please, come find refreshment. You need to rest a bit. Please, sit here for a while. Rest. Can I bring something to you? Here, I just cooked this my meal. Please eat, I'll make another." All refuse to take his meal.

Typically, dozens of pilgrims sit alongside the shed and under the shade trees surrounding his trailside stand. David welcomes one pilgrim after another and settles each in a restful spot. If a pilgrim makes it to the cart before his warm welcome, it is common for the new arrival to lift a piece of fruit or snack and call out, "How much?"

David's standard response follows, "Take it. I don't care about the money. It's not important."

This amazes all within earshot, not only because it flies in the face of anything resembling good business, but they realize that coming from him, it's entirely believable. This is who David is. He holds no sign of attachment to anything—comfort, security, or material stuff. Pilgrims use a small donation box to reward their host, but David lives free of money concerns. His sole mission is to serve others. The beauty and simplicity is contagious. The pilgrim can't leave without the nagging epiphany: Wow! To be free like David!

Astorga—City Life

This city of 12,000 people features lively city life and is enriched by centuries-old artifacts. Astorga was an important Roman city due to its location 870 meters (2,850 feet) above the surrounding countryside. Its location and altitude made it valuable as a military command and observation center. Remnants of the old Roman Road, along with its ancient Puerto Romano,[52] "Roman Door," still stand along with sections of the first-century Roman Wall. This served as a bunker to defend the city's valuable market square.

Astorga enjoys a bustling, mid-sized, commercial center. Its location has been popular throughout the centuries as a hub city of sorts. Multiple Camino trails from different directions converge here. The city's open plaza is surrounded by small shops and restaurants, making it a delightful meeting place for resident families and pilgrims as well.

Some noteworthy history came from Astorga. When Francis of Assisi walked the Camino in the eleventh century, it is believed he made a stop here. Walking the Camino has a universal reputation, claimed by pilgrims, to liberate one's soul of needless burdens and thereby free the pilgrim to experience God more intimately. One can only wonder if the saint from Assisi may have experienced these blessings along his Camino pilgrimage that empowered his spiritual legacy.

Another Astorga boast is the Museum of Ways, designed by famed architect, Antoni Gaudi. This intriguing, towering, castle-like structure houses a unique collection of art and sculptures of the apostle of the Camino, St. James. Two of Gaudi's magnificent architectural designs are bookends for a different Camino trail. His influences in Astorga in the west are connected by the Catalan Camino trail that begins on the far eastern end of Spain in Barcelona. For the pilgrim beginning the Catalan Way, a sight to behold is Gaudi's architectural jewel of all Europe: Sagrada Familia.[53] This Catholic basilica has eighteen towers that stand 170 meters (550 feet) high and are made of stone carvings representing the stories of the Bible. Sagrada Familia's construction has been ongoing for 150 years, with hopes of completion in 2026.

My Camino

"We do not have the words which perfectly describe the Spirit . . . it is a voice that one feels, more than one hears."

Boyd Packer

It was one thing to see the Cantabrian Mountains, but it was far more intriguing to my Camino to experience their breezes eddying before me and raising the trail's clay dust like incense. These intermittent blasts got me thinking about nature's breezes. Lake and ocean breezes have a distinct quality and fragrance. Mountain breezes, however, are quite different. There's something of lightness in mountain air—a chilly, clean purity. They often quietly stiffen and then slip away for short periods, only to reappear in the next stretch of the journey. These little zephyrs provide intermittent embraces of the mountain peaks. *What a great gift, Lord!* I thought.

God sparked my imagination about the nature and movement of these mountain breezes. They are like the nature and movement of the Holy Spirit in my life. When I am open to receive the gift of His presence, it is always a sensation of movement, lightness, and something unmistakably pure. The experience is nothing short of joyfully holy. Just as these mountain breezes delight me, so too, Spirit Winds enter my life with God's insight and wisdom.

I encountered the presence of the Holy Spirit alive and moving in my life through these mountain breezes and was humbled. I needed only to be open to the gift swirling about me to recognize it. While I walked, I recalled times when a "coincidence" occurred that solved a problem I was having. I reflected upon how truths swirled into my spirit before I was about to make a really stupid decision. I remembered events of grace that occurred at perfect moments to save me from what could have been hurtful. Each new step along The Way carried recollections of event after event in which the Spirit gusted into my life.

Perhaps it is no coincidence that while stirring these Spirit-filled thoughts, I happened upon two pilgrims carrying a popular belief about the Spirit. When I meet other pilgrims along The Way, almost without exception we ask one another. "So why are you doing the Camino?" I typically wait for those I've just met to offer their reasons first. Motivations for walking a 790-kilometer (five-hundred-mile) pilgrimage commonly include such things as health, a physical challenge, to experience a different culture, to see Spain up close, and sometimes, "because my wife wanted to do this."

Then I give my response, "I had an intimate moment in my prayer time. It was then that I knew God wanted me to walk the Camino. 'Have faith,' He told me."

I have observed varying degrees of comfort and acceptance with that response. The two pilgrims I met that day responded with, "Well, I'm spiritual; I'm not religious." I've heard this often enough to notice something common about how this is said. Many announce this as a proud badge of their new faith. On this day, these words rattled in contrast with my insight about mountain breezes as movements of the Holy Spirit. *Lord, how should I respond to the "I'm spiritual; I'm not religious" thinkers?*

I came to these realizations. First, those who attest to this always recite it in that order. It is a line of thinking that credits themselves with some type of belief. They believe in a "spirit." When I've gotten into a dialogue over this, I often find we have common experiences. I share a life event when goodness, which I identify as the Spirit, surprised me at the perfect time after a prayer. The "not religious" believers agree that my experience was from the Spirit, however, many go on to explain their interpretation of these occurrences. They claim, "The event has nothing to do with prayer or God. It just happens."

As far as the "being religious" part goes, they shun the experiences they've had at church and view it as a lot of "blah, blah, blah." They claim, "Religion and church don't connect with my life."

I hear some validity in their perspective, sad to say.

These people all have something in common in their message. It's this: "I'm in control. And I'll take God my way." Listening to their explanation implied this belief system, "I'll take God when I want Him, how I want Him, and in the way I want to believe Him." It strikes me as walking a buffet line. "I'll take God this way, not too much of this, a lot more of that, and maybe none of that. Yep. God, my way."

My Camino reflection teetered between my imagination with mountain-born Spirit winds and the "I'm spiritual; I'm not religious" popular belief. I saw something in my life that was common in both frames of thought. Unfortunately, I was not proud of what I saw.

The Holy Spirit is present to me only by the degree of control that I surrender to Him. The more open I am to the Spirit's movement, the more room opens in my heart to experience His grace. Over the years I have weaned myself of the faith-filled-buffet line. My Camino, on this day, revealed a new truth in me: I am not spiritual enough, or even religious enough. But that's OK. It is enough that I am His, moment by moment.

I pray that's enough for you, as well.

Our Camino

"There is no better evangelist in the world than the Holy Spirit."

D. L. Moody

The Holy Spirit and a backdraft? What's the connection?

Plenty—when it comes to describing how the Holy Spirit empowers us to do His work. Here's some background.

The dictionary defines a backdraft as follows: "A backdraft is a dramatic event caused by a fire, resulting from rapid reintroduction of oxygen to combustion in an oxygen-depleted environment."[54]

The simple science behind fires is that three elements are necessary: heat, fuel, and oxygen. Interviews with firefighters describe that when a room or building is ripe for a backdraft, the fumes and combustibles in the structure are gasping for oxygen. When a window or door opens, oxygen is sucked into the area like a jet engine revving up. Almost immediately, the rapid gush of oxygen feeds the fire. This ignites an explosion propelling everything and everyone out. This is what is known as a backdraft.

Now consider what the Scriptures tell us about Pentecost. At Jesus's ascension into heaven, He prepares His apostles for the Pentecost experience: "you will receive power when the Holy Spirit has come upon you, and you will be my witnesses in Jerusalem and in all Judea and Samaria, and to the end of the earth" (Acts 1:8).

It is a fair assumption that before Pentecost, the apostles did not have power, at least not the mighty power the Holy Spirit brings. They also had not begun evangelizing the world, at least not yet. The apostles were chosen to be "fuel" to start Christ's new church.

Let's consider the Pentecost event:

When the day of Pentecost arrived, they were all together in one place. And suddenly there came from heaven a sound like a mighty rushing wind, and it filled the entire house where they were sitting. And divided tongues as of fire appeared to them and rested on each one of them. And they were all filled with the Holy Spirit and began to speak in other tongues as the Spirit gave them utterance. (Acts 2:1–4)

Here is the connection. The apostles were assembled in prayer for fifty days (Pentecost means fiftieth) after the resurrection of Christ, Easter Sunday. With that much prayer, that gathering in the Upper Room was ripe for a spiritual explosion. They were promised the Holy Spirit and He delivered. Imagine this—a heaven-born jet stream coming from far above the mountaintops, streaking through the entire house. That's the oxygen. The Holy Spirit placing tongues of fire upon each apostle? That's the heat. Can you picture it?

A Holy Spirit backdraft!

As fuel for Christ's new church, the apostles were propelled from this backdraft by a power they never held before. They were promised a mission, and now they were on fire to spread it "to the end of the earth."

Holy Spirit backdrafts can and do occur during our Camino. By my personal observations, truly spiritual people have an aura about them. They possess a peace and presence that is much like the pure freshness of mountain breezes. In conversations, they are keenly present to us and what's being shared. It's obvious in their riveted eye contact. They are supremely good listeners. Also, they are characteristically nonjudgmental, compassionate, and authentically affirming. Above all, they're Christ-centered, prayerful people. David, the vendor in The Camino section of this chapter, possesses many of these qualities.

Encountering such spirit-filled people draws us into their Holy Spirit backdraft. Many are steal-your-breath-away captivating to be around. In a way, we become like that building gasping for oxygen. We are gasping for the Holy Spirit to breathe His fire on us.

How can this happen for us?

We start by being open to Spirit-filled believers we encounter in everyday life. They breathe heaven's oxygen and fire. We need only to offer ourselves as fuel for the Spirit's mission for us. Consider this: spiritually potent people might be guided by God's will to ignite a Holy Spirit backdraft in us. They might be the flame to ignite the power in our Camino.

*   *   *

I experienced a treasured Holy Spirit backdraft in the town of Hospital de Òrbigo. It presented itself in a surprise encounter with a fellow pilgrim, Werner, a young man from Cape Town, South Africa. Here's how the Spirit brought it about.

Some fellow pilgrims and I stopped at a small cafe for lunch while waiting for the albergues to open for the day. We sat on a sunny patio enjoying the view of the famed medieval bridge over the Òrbigo River. While seated there, my walking companions decided to head for a different albergue, leaving me with Werner, who was biking from Leòn to Santiago.

Surprisingly, we were the only two left on the patio. Werner was in his early thirties, a big man, and baby-faced with a gentle soul. After some general get-to-know-you pleasantries, I began to notice a spiritual nature in my new Camino acquaintance. Werner asked question after question about me, about my life, and what God was doing on my Camino. He was present to me body, mind, and spirit. He truly cared about me. This touched me deep inside.

The tables turned, and as I probed Werner, his recent heartache and reason for his Camino surfaced. His eyes reddened and welled over with tears as he shared that his father had committed suicide. In his thick accent, he began, "I loved me Papa, me daddy. It tore me up for these past two years." He went on to share the details, the confusion, the lost time he endured. I was absorbed in his tearful story and soon recognized he was a wounded, little boy in a big boy's body. In those very moments, the Holy Spirit was so present, nearly tangible. Almost uncannily, mountain breezes, or what my imagination would call "Spirit winds," swirled around us on that little cafe patio. Coincidence? Or God? Godcidence?

Werner shared a variation of a Camino tradition he was following. Since the ninth century, pilgrims have carried a small stone from home to represent a burden they wish to lay at the foot of Cruz de Ferro, the Iron Cross. Pilgrims refer to this as their "burden stone."

Werner shared how he was following his calling on the Camino. Because he was biking for only eight days, he chose to carry eight stones.

"I will cast one stone each day. On me first day while leaving Cape Town, I cast me first stone." He choked on tears, as did I, and continued. "I determined to begin me Camino by surrendering the heartache of losing me daddy. I didn't want to carry the memory of how he died, how I missed his love, and how I missed him." He gained composure and added, "So I cast away me first stone, number eight, in me hometown to release myself of me loss of me Papa, yea, me daddy. I place a stone each day on the trail to mark God's deliverance from me burdens. I call them 'celebration stones.' Each stone is a celebration of God's care for me, not burdens I've carried." With a robust smile full of beaming hope he added, "By the time I reach Santiago, I will be free!"

At that very moment a mountain breeze churned among us. Goosebumps surfaced on me and the hair on the back of my neck stood at attention. Breathless, I thought, *a Spirit wind.* Werner added, "Willie, I've come to see that it is not getting through suffering that's important. It is celebrating what God has done to bring us through the suffering." In this we were one in mind and spirit in our life experiences.

Werner added, "Today I cast what I call excess baggage." He chuckled, "I carry around too much weight (he rubbed his big frame) and too much emotional baggage. Today that is the 'celebration stone' I cast. God will free me. I'm convinced."

Completely stunned, I realized that I was sitting in the vortex of Spirit winds, overwhelmingly blessed and dumbfounded. Werner added, "You know, Willie, I was riding through and looking for a place to have lunch; I was starved. I rode right past this place. Rode right through the town for a couple kilometers [a mile or so]. Then I had a little moment when the Holy Spirit told me to ride back to this place. Now I know why. He had this," pointing a finger to both of us, "planned for my day."

Even my heartfelt "Amen!" held no expectation for what happened next.

Werner, the gentle giant, rose from his chair, and walked to my side of the table. Towering over me he gently asked, "Willie, can we pray together?"

What a setting God had chosen! I stood in Werner's shadow as we leaned together in prayerful celebration of all God's care for us through our every life trial. We were two pilgrims trying to fight the good fight of faith. How appropriate that this occurred alongside Paso Honroso, the "Passage of Honor" in this little medieval town known for where a brave knight fought his good fight for honor and love.

Then off rode Werner, leaving me in the Holy Spirit's backdraft!

"Let no one come to you without leaving better and happier. Be the living expression of God's kindness—kindness in your face, kindness in your eyes, kindness in your smile."

St. Mother Theresa of Calcutta

*   *   *

We pray for many reasons. Often it's for relief from trials, answers to the big life questions, direction, and help in desperate situations. These burdens are heavy crosses that have a weight and wait to them.

Walk the Camino with me to Cruz de Ferro as I shoulder prayers for those suffering under the "wait of the beam."

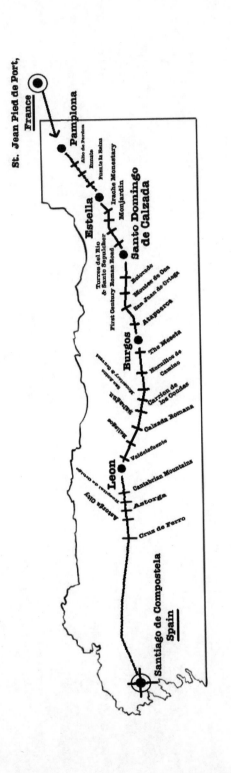

Chapter 14

WAIT OF THE BEAM

"Hope is like the sun, which, as we journey towards it, casts the shadows of our burdens behind us."

Samuel Smiles

The Camino

Cruz de Ferro is a Camino jewel and for good reasons. Anchored in historical significance, Cruz de Ferro also serves as a shrine where pilgrims' heavy burdens and even heavier hearts are buoyed.

Cruz de Ferro—The Iron Cross[55]

The historical origin of this not-to-be-missed spot on the Camino adds to the fascination of this shrine. The focal point: a wooden pole standing roughly five meters (sixteen-plus feet) high, anchored in an impressive mound of small stones about half its height. Affixed atop is a Christian cross made of iron. It is unique in its raw simplicity, and at the same time its origin is claimed by many faiths.

Some claim the Romans marked the location for the god Mercury. Others claim it is a marker by the ancient Celts who set a stone there to mark the location as a memorial or place of offering. Still other sources claim that the pole was placed on the trail to direct pilgrims through the tall snows in these mountains. Many credit Gaucelmo, a hermit in the area, with mounting the mast in the stones back in the eleventh century. Regardless of the different claims, the pole gained a Christian distinction when the iron cross was attached at its top.

It is tradition for pilgrims to carry a stone to place at the foot of the cross. Some collect a stone on the trail just before arriving, while many others carry one all the way from home. For some on The Way, their stone represents their gratitude for their life—their journey. Others who walk the Camino leave a stone in hope of forgiveness for some sin in their life. Still others believe that their stone represents some heavy burden in their life, therefore, the name "burden stones."

Cruz de Ferro holds a spiritual presence. Out of respect for other pilgrims' display of reverence, most who arrive observe a respectful silence to allow some privacy for the kneeling pilgrims at the foot of the cross, some of whom may be sobbing deeply. Other arrivals stand or sit at a short distance from the mound in stunned silence. A minority of pilgrims climb to the mast as tourists eager for a photo opportunity in complete oblivion of the spiritual importance surrounding the shrine. Regardless, it is rare for anyone to visit the Iron Cross without being changed, in some way, by a presence there, or even simply by the reverence and emotion of fellow pilgrims.

My Camino

"Hope is being able to see the light, despite all the darkness."

Desmond Tutu

Before leaving for the Camino, I shared about the tradition of the burden stone with close friends and family and asked if they would like me to carry a specific one-word burden prayer for them. I prayed for each person and their prayer word every day along my Camino. My list of more than eighty one-word prayers comprised heartrending needs including infertility, cancer struggles, broken relationships, and life-threatening diseases. All were terribly heavy burdens. It was my honor to carry these burdens to Cruz de Ferro and surrender them at the foot of the cross.

Fast forward to that morning in the town of Rabanal del Camino. I emerged from my albergue to a gift left by nature during the night—a heavy, two-inch blanket of snow. This is not unusual for an altitude of 1,150 meters (3,700 feet). The Camino trail blazed ahead through gorgeous wildflowers, shrubs, scrub pines, and flowering heather shrouded under a brilliant white snow cover. With large, gently falling snowflakes still dancing earthward, it was like walking in a snow globe.

The pretty, snowy trail was a stark contrast to the heavy, low-lying, smoky-grey cloud cover pressing down overhead. Fear struck as I caught sight of the trail's horizon. Yikes! Off in the distance was the ridgeline of Cruz de Ferro. *How will I manage a three-hundred meter* (1,150 feet) *climb over seven kilometers* (a little over four miles)? Staring at the elevation before me, I swallowed a gulp of chilly air and shivered a bit, frightened by an even more intimidating challenge. A snowstorm was apparent in the dark clouds hanging over the upcoming mountain peaks. I gulped a new thought: *Have faith, Willie. You have eighty-some burden prayers you're carrying for loved ones back home.*

Slippery step after slippery step, I made my way upward. It was not the snowy trail or the temperature that kept my attention. It was the dark, heavy cloud cover that weighed on my spirit. I am not sure which prompted a short depressive episode during the walk. *Is it the low-hanging dark cloud cover or the weight of the burdens some carry?*

Drifting into this thought came the lyrics to one of my favorite songs, "God's Own Fool" by Michael Card:

So come lose your life for a carpenter's son.

For a madman who died for a dream.

And you'll have the faith His first followers had.

And you'll feel the weight of the beam.[56]

My boots, now more like snowshoes, slip-sloshed through the snowy mush with these lyrics recycling in my mind. I prayed, "Lord, each person on my prayer list carries such heavy crosses, their beams of burden. The lyrics 'weight of the beam' testifies to only half of their suffering. How some endure for years under the '*wait* of the beam' until You answer them! It sounds like a double burden—the beam's weight and the wait time under it."

Biting snow and pelting sleet stung my face. The gloomy cloud cover that hovered a short distance overhead continued to weigh down my spirit. The weather was the perfect backdrop for the burdens I prayed for along the ascent. Immersed in each story behind their prayers, I felt their hopelessness. I cried for them. I prayed deeply for them, hour after hour.

My reflection came to a dramatic halt with my first sight of the monument. Cruz de Ferro creates an exhilarating first impression. Roughly one hundred meters (three hundred feet) away, I spotted the rusty, iron medieval shape of the cross high in the air. The cross is fixed to a wooden pole standing roughly five meters (sixteen feet) high. At its base, the mountain of stones is built up about three meters (almost ten feet) from the trail's base. This gave me a chill. Millions of pilgrims over the centuries have placed their burden stones here. A Godly insight glimpsed; *we must all carry our crosses, our beams in life.* This was made clear by the sight of Cruz de Ferro before me. It was certainly true for those on my prayer list. And it was certainly true for me. As I stood transfixed upon the sight, a new revelation surfaced. *The weight and wait of these beams are not meant for us to carry alone, but to surrender at the foot of the cross.*

I trudged up history's story of pain to the cross's base. *Oh, if these stones could tell their stories!* I wriggled my knees into the rubble of snowy stones, all in a myriad of shapes and sizes, some with messages written on them. I held out to the cross my own burden stone. It was a stone that had sat on my desk for years, and written on it was the one-word burden I had chosen for my Camino. When I held up the stone, my word suddenly held an echo of divine irony. I walked this Camino with the word "hope" painted on my burden stone. How I desired more hope to be found at many levels of my life!

The irony struck me.

I was carrying eighty-some names with their burdens, but my single word "hope" was the answer for all of us! We don't have to carry our burdens alone. We have hope in the One who can carry it for us! We don't have to fight to forgive ourselves. We can hope in the One who forgives everyone of everything. We don't have to have all our lives' answers decided. We have hope in the One who has plans to prosper and not harm us (Jeremiah 29:11).

The charcoal-colored sky hung suspended over me. This time, I gave it no mind. I was here to pray my heart out by reading and rereading the names and burden prayers of all I carried with me these past 480 kilometers (three hundred-plus miles). Each person's face came to mind, their life's heartache, their dear faith, their love for me, their hunger for God's mercy. I prayed for each of us to see some sign of hope.

My prayers ended. *What do you want me to take away from this, Lord? What might you offer me to remember your gift of hope in a memorable way? You gave us the rainbow as a message in the sky to remember your promise. What message can I bring back from here to help others find hope? For me to keep my hope in You?*

Upon finishing my prayer, the dark clouds ever-so-slowly began to strain apart, revealing glimpses of a brilliant white sun. *What? Really?* Far above the blanket of darkness, the azure sky and that gorgeous sun pierced the mound of the cross. It was such a stark contrast to the day of gloominess. The warmth filled my chilled body. It was almost surreal.

I stood there watching, suddenly enlightened. *The sun is God's hope. It is always shining, just as the sun always shines on Earth. Somewhere on the planet, there is sunshine. The dark clouds, like my life burdens, screen the light as they drift into my life unwelcomed. Their dark and rolling heaviness presses down on me. These have stretched over my horizon for days, weeks, months, and at times, for years. I wait and wait. Will the darkness of carrying this burden ever break? Where are you, Lord, in the cloudy darkness?*

God had a lesson for my Camino that day in the simple moments when the sun's breakthrough served as a shining message of hope. Like God's love and care for me, it is always just above me. I need not fret over my burdens or the gloom that covers over my life. It is only a temporary cloud cover. Hope is still shining and will break through again and again. All I need to do is "have faith." Just as I stood to leave the cross, the sun burst through the dark clouds. Heaven's flood lamp of "Son light" illuminated the monument and me.

I stood there, sunbathed in hope.

I was tempted to think this was a gift only for me on the Camino. But I prayed, "I have hope in you, Lord, that I will see, for my whole life, every sun-filled sky and think of it as Your sign that You are always there. I hope I never forget."

Our Camino

"And hope, if it had a scent, would smell like spring rain, like something new and alive."

Jennifer Rush

"It's hopeless." These are two, heavy-hearted words we often hear on our Camino. We hear them from a desperate friend, a family loved one, and on occasion we say them ourselves. The burdens we carry feel impossible and endless. We can't find a way to escape the cycle of despair or the staggering weight of these beams. Addiction, abuse, monstrous debt, wounded relationships, persistent infidelity, overbearing employers, infertility, life-threatening disease, and so many other heartbreaks leave us wounded and trapped without hope.

For some burdens, professional help is the best option. Therapy unties the long history of how an invisible burden has woven its way in and throughout life. Medical help is needed for physical ailments.

For less extreme situations, disciplines for life can lighten the load of our burden stones as we weather the wait.

Eight Ways to Nurture Hope

1. Pray.

Whether we call it prayer or just a good talk with the God of the universe, it's where everything begins. Get alone with Him. Imagine Him sitting right beside you and tell Him everything. Yes, get all the anger, impatience, and all the "it's not fair" frustrations off your chest. Lay it all on Him. Be honest. Feel free to cry it all out with Him. He can take it. Are we not His children? He knows us better than we know ourselves. He longs for us just to share it all with Him.

2. Hope that vs. Hope in.

Catch the words used by those praying for hope. Oftentimes these prayers start like this:"I hope that my loved one gets this new job," or "I hope that the doctor finds the cure for my health problem," or "I hope that I find more money to pay my bills." In this prayer language, we are telling God what we want Him to do. We hope that our solution is granted. Of course, we should always tell God our needs, but we should be careful not to cross over the line by dictating how.

Consider posturing a hope prayer in a fundamentally different and humble way. For the believer, it is not a "hope that"; it is a "hope in." Our hope is in Christ. Regardless of the burden and regardless of how long it's carried, our "hope central" must be the faith we have in the One who carries us, burdens and all.

Hope that	vs.	Hope in
"I hope that my health problem is found."		"I hope in Jesus, the healer."
"I hope that I interview well for the job."		"I hope in Jesus, mighty counselor."
"I hope that I have enough money for the bills."		"I hope in Jesus, my provider."

A "hope that" prayer is situational, and based upon our predefined notion of what hope will, must, and/or should be for a particular situation. In contrast, a "hope in" prayer is relational. It anchors us in the One who knows and provides His perfect hope precisely in His perfect timing and in His perfect ways.

3. Study your history with God.

When we take a long, hard look back on our lives, we see events that went surprisingly well. Other events may have been difficult, but we survived and even rose above the struggle. Yet other recollections may cause us to shake our heads and ask, "How did I ever survive that?" If we're honest, we see that God was there all along. Our lives are woven through difficult events that are filled with joy, trials that are near-disasters, and bitter failures that are turned into good. Why? Because our God is faithful. Study His track record in your life from past to present and you'll see reason to "hope in" Him during current and future challenges. His history of faithfulness is reason for our hope.

4. Be open to something different.

The hope we seek might be gift wrapped right in front of us, camouflaged in the ordinary of our lives. We don't see it or accept it because it looks different than the answer we expected. And so we prayerfully wait and wait under the weight of our beams for what we believe are the only answers to our hopelessness.

This kind of thinking gives God little permission to lead us to His answers for new hope. Many claim they have received His blessing in disguise. His gift of hope also comes in disguise, many times in different gift wrapping.

Hope doesn't come the way you *think*. Hope comes the *way* you think.

5. Anticipate strength born of the struggle.

The "wait of the beam" is never easy. We pray under these crosses for days, weeks, months, and sometimes for years. We beg, *Where are you, Lord?*

Must we "wait" so long under the "weight" of such burdens? Why? Why must we suffer? And for so long?

We don't know the mind of God. We may never know the whys. So what can sustain us during the wait? Encourage us? Make the wait worth it?

His grace.

Scripture is filled with descriptions of how His grace under the weight and within the wait can sustain and encourage us. The graces born of the struggle are embedded in Scripture. Here are a few.

Jesus says, "Come to me, all who labor and are heavy laden, and I will give you rest" (Matt. 11:28). Paul reminds us that we are called to "rejoice in our sufferings, knowing that suffering produces endurance, and endurance produces character, and character produces hope" (Rom. 5:3–4). Then there's Peter's challenge to see that our suffering refines our faith, like gold is purified in refiner's fire (1 Peter 1:7).

These and many other Scriptures point to the truth: our burdens can forge us into better people, stronger in character and charity. Conversely, our burdens can leave us bitter and angry, often alienating us from others.

Be assured, our present burdens are temporary. They are the fertile fields where our faith grows and actually flourishes on God's timetable. One day they will be lifted, and we'll be freed. Here's the challenge for our Camino while we wait for new hope: Which "me" do I want to be when the burden is lifted? Stronger and wiser, or weakened and resentful?

6. Let yourself be loved.

When life's burdens become so heavy, many retreat from friends and loved ones for a variety of reasons. They don't want to burden others with their problems. They "just don't want to talk about it." Some might not feel lovable, or even likable in the place they're in. The Evil One loves to slide us into isolation and bring us into his neighborhood of despair. Fight the pride inside and reach out to others. Talk to friends and loved ones. Let yourself be loved, even when feeling unlovable. Love is a powerful antidote for hopelessness.

7. Hang on to "right now."

When a person with heavy burdens shares their story, it all too often concludes with, "It's hopeless." This is their view of reality, and when some well-meaning listener says, "just go and pray more," it does little to buoy their hope. What encouragement might we offer them?

I have found a two-word phrase that serves two unique purposes. It validates the burdened one—truly hearing and deeply understanding them. At the same time, the same two-word phrase points toward hope.

The phrase? "Right now."

Consider how these two words refresh the following messages:

"I will never be free from this addiction. It's hopeless . . . right now."

"I will never get out from all this debt. It's hopeless . . . right now."

"The divorce tore my heart out. I'll never marry again . . . right now."

Yes, these two words apply to many situations our Camino does and will face. Why? Because "right now" we need to be really understood for the weight we are carrying. At the same time, we also need to know the "wait" is only in the present. Our hope lies just before us. We might not see it "right now." We need only to be reminded that *what is,* is not forever. Hold firmly to the belief that new hope is ahead. Right now.

8. Don't quit.

At times, our Camino may travel under heavy, dark cloud cover. The gloom just above and around shouts, "It's hopeless!" We need to be reminded that above the darkness is the brilliant sun light fighting to break through the misery. Our faithfulness in prayer pierces the darkness, pierces hopelessness. Such prayerfulness places us on the predawn of being sunbathed in hope. Don't give up. Consider the prophet Isaiah's words: "But they who wait for the LORD shall renew their strength; they shall mount up with wings like eagles . . . they shall walk and not faint" (Isaiah 40:31).

Our hope is *in* Him.

*   *   *

Waiting on the Lord is far beyond a casual belief for the prayer life of Father Tom, nor was it casual for the 152 others aboard Trans World Airlines (TWA) Flight 847 when it was hijacked in Athens, Greece on June 14, 1985, by Shiite Muslim terrorists from Lebanon. These terrorists demanded the release of seven hundred Lebanese prisoners held in Israeli camps. What an international stand-off! Breathlessly, the entire world prayed and waited and waited and waited for God's hand to intervene. I was privileged to interview and then compose Fr. Tom's gripping faith walk story:

I grew up on Chicago's South Side in St. Cajetan Parish. It was an all-Irish neighborhood, and everything revolved around church, the church school, and my large family and friends there. As a kid, I had a growing desire to become a priest. I was certain of it, but of course I tested it out by asking the Lord, "If you don't want me to be a priest, show me." He didn't show any signs of stopping me, so the desire kept growing. On top of that, I've never been one to play with doubt. I just trust in God's will and move ahead. That's how I was raised, and it's how I've always lived my life.

After my ordination and over many years, I served as pastor at several parishes. My longest stay was at a church in St. Charles, Illinois. I enjoyed being a priest, and the people were so supportive. Life felt easy, certain. I was forty-nine years old in 1985 when I agreed to go on a pilgrimage to the Holy Land in Israel. Afterward, we took a boat to Greece for another tour, and from there we were to fly to Rome. I remember boarding the plane, feeling so at ease dressed in my comfortable casual shirt and khaki-colored pants. Life felt so free, beautiful, and so peaceful. Little did I know that something as simple as the color of my pants would bring me to the brink of death in just a few hours ahead.

Fifteen minutes after taking off from Athens, two crazed passengers ran from the very back of the plane to the cockpit area screaming something in Arabic. This abruptly reversed my mood. *What is going on here?* When one of the two screamers held up a hand grenade and pulled the pin, we knew. Our plane was being hijacked. Both men kept shouting commands in Arabic, making it clear they meant business. When they waved their automatic pistols overhead for all to see, we clearly knew they meant *serious* business. Our senses were on high alert. They broke into the captain's cabin, shouting even more loudly and frantically. All 153 on board sat frozen, breathless, with our hearts beating like the drumline in a parade. One thing was clear: the flight crew was no longer in charge, and terror would direct the next twenty-one hours from Athens to Beirut, Lebanon, then to Algiers, and then back again to Beirut.

Inside the plane, the intensity of our situation was heightened by the two air pirates continuing to shout commands in Arabic, none of which we understood. We were all Americans, and none of us understood Arabic. This infuriated the hijackers further. Wide-eyed and trembling, we desperately searched for what they wanted us to do so they would not kill us. Turned out, they wanted our passports. Without delay, we found them and surrendered them. Then they gestured for all of us to bend our heads forward and place our hands on the backs of our heads. Craning my neck and spine was excruciating to maintain. We later called this our "847 position." Little did we know this would be our posture for three full days before landing back at the hijackers' final destination, Beirut.

There was no question that these thugs (as I call them) were to be feared. They proved it as we sat on the runway waiting for refueling. The pilot pleaded for more fuel and made it clear that the hijackers had threatened to start killing the passengers—one every five minutes. Clearance was not granted, which enraged our Arabic madmen. Hearing their shouting excited our pulsing nerves. They meant business, and were about to show the world they were dead serious.

First they pistol-beat the pilot and the first officer. They chose passengers who did not keep their heads down and brutally beat them right before us. This notched up our fears that were already near peak.

For some the horror was strangulating, making it almost impossible to breathe. After searching through passports, the hijackers found three military men—two naval guys and one Army Reserve Major, whom they savagely beat with an armrest torn from a chair. We heard this poor man utter, "One American must die." He groaned in agony in hopes that the beatings might not spread to others onboard.

Their demand for fuel was not met. But these were desperate men and they weren't turning back. They opened the door to the plane and sunlight filled the head of the plane. The Army Reservist was positioned in front of the open door. They placed the pistol to his head, still screaming their demands for fuel. Mercifully, the fuel came, and he was released.

We then flew to Algiers, again demanding fuel. It was granted, thereby making a return flight to Beirut possible. They had their reasons for such a crazy flight plan, but they were not to be shared with us.

I was curiously struck by the fact that almost everything happened in the middle of the night. It occurred to me that Judas left Jesus and went into the night when he did his deed of darkness and betrayal. This biblical connection came with the intense terror of landing back in Beirut. The hijackers would not allow the pilot to use the landing lights for our final approach. The pilot made the descent by feel and instruments only. He called over the speakers, "Put a pillow over your head. We're coming in hot!"

The plane was in a turbulent nosedive, wings bouncing madly up and down, and the engines roaring like a rocket as it strained to decrease speed. I looked out the window and saw what I guessed were a row of trucks. They were some 1,100 meters (roughly 1,200 yards) ahead—blocking the runway. The pilot's voice shouted overhead, "I'm bringing this baby in. Keep your heads down!"

The plane jerked and bounced while violently rocking from side to side. The ferocious noise and speed subsided to a casual cruising speed. Miraculously, we were safe . . . again!

However, the agony and torture would resume, during an ordeal all on board witnessed firsthand.

If terror within a person had a decibel level, what happened next would be ear-splitting. We had no sooner landed in Beirut when the most horrific brutality occurred. After scouring through the passports, they singled out a US Navy diver, Robert Stethem, at first mistaking him for a Marine. Turns out, they passionately hated the Marines. They dragged him out of his seat to the front of the plane and tied his hands. Here began a steady, merciless stream of savage beatings. They violently pounded his head and in a crazed hysteria beat him savagely, broke his ribs, and kicked in his knees. So ghastly! I cannot erase the blood-chilling screams and moans of that brave, twenty-three-year-old man. Then our hearts almost quit beating. They opened the cockpit door and held Robert Stethem up for those outside, as well as all of us, to see. The sight of the gun pointed at him stole our breath; the gunshot was even more terrifying. The climax came as many of us could feel and hear the thud of his body hitting the tarmac.

Lord, have mercy.

I could not pray fast enough or sincerely enough. I couldn't stop wondering, *Who's next? What if I'm next?* I'm sure we all feared the same beating and death.

To my surprise, a hijacker confronted me. His heavy, wiry, jet-black beard and mad-eyed stare drilled through me. I was shocked. After all, I was sitting obediently with my hands laced behind my head. *I was being obedient. Why me?* He screamed just inches from my face, "You Marine! You Marine!"

I still couldn't understand why he singled me out. *What made him think I was a Marine?* He pointed to my khaki pants. I understood. He thought these were part of a Marine uniform because of their khaki color.

He tapped his automatic pistol to my chest and gritted, "You *Marine!*"

"No! No!" I insisted. He kept tapping the gun's barrel on my chest, threatening me. *Am I about to get the same beating Robert got?* Goosebumps raced like electricity up and down my spine.

"No! I'm a priest. A priest!"

He looked at me confused, even disbelieving.

I uttered the first thing that came to mind and demonstrated making the sign of the cross while saying, "In nomine Patris, et Filii, et Spiritus Sanctus." It is Latin for, "In the name of the Father, the Son, and the Holy Spirit." This, I hoped, would identify me as a priest and as no real threat.

This crazed lunatic's eyes drilled into me just inches from my face as I sat silent, waiting in tension for what he would do. The wait was deafening; I think I stopped breathing. I too waited . . . and waited . . . and waited. I felt the crushing burden of whether I was going to live or die. A prayer flashed through me: *Lord, I hope in a couple minutes I see your face.*

Puzzled, and yet satisfied by my defense, my would-be assassin just turned and walked away. My life was spared.

Soon after, they released nineteen women and children along with some passengers with desperate health issues. I was one of the forty-nine who would continue in this nightmare for another fourteen days.

Now was the time to exit the plane. Every new plan was led by shouting, frantic hurry, and urgency. It was about three o'clock in the morning when we were hurriedly exited through the rear of the plane onto waiting trucks. Also there to escort us were a dozen or so armed gunmen with two straps of bullets crossing their chest—screaming and directing us. Some would occasionally fire rounds from their assault rifles with flames like flares coming from the barrel point. It was a stark contrast to the still darkness hovering overhead.

We were divided into small groups and placed in local residents' homes. We had no idea where we were—that was their plan. We slept in their available beds or on the floor anywhere. They provided meals for us and surprisingly, they were eager to converse with us. It seemed like we were somewhat of a novelty to them. Some homeowners were actually pleasant and accommodating—a far different attitude from our hijackers.

We would remain in a house for only two to three days, then in the middle of the night, be briskly awakened, told to grab our belongings, and moved to a waiting van to take us to our next residence.

One man who had surrendered his home confronted me with a challenging question. He tapped his pistol to my chest. "Why Americans no love children?"

I answered, "Americans love children."

He pressed harder, "No! Americans no love children. They only have two or three children in their family. Muslims have ten or twelve. No! Americans no love children!"

There was no convincing him otherwise. Thankfully, he put the pistol aside, ending his interrogation.

Days into staying at these homes, I was allowed to hold prayer services, including Scripture reading, and open prayers for all to beg God's intervention. Our faith, or rather, our renewed faith, hope, and love filled our little worship space.

We all knew there was a good chance we were going to die. All we could do was wait. Wait to see what would happen. Wait to see if we would ever get out. We prayed and waited for God's hand to come.

It was day seventeen into our hostage ordeal when something dramatic happened. Without explanation, we were hastily roused and told to gather our belongings. Imagine our surprise when all forty-nine of us were reunited at the Beirut airport!

In no time, we were flown to a military base in Germany. We had been freed! *Praise God!* I'll never forget our welcome home. In disbelief, we walked across the tarmac into the airport. There stood a few hundred military personnel holding signs welcoming us. One by one we met and shook hands with Vice-President George H. W. Bush. What a proud moment to be an American! Tears streamed down our cheeks as we were reunited with loved ones flown in to greet us. My sister stood in the crowd, beaming with joy and gratitude to see me. But she was not as grateful as I was to see her again. I was free!

I have often reflected upon my seventeen days of hell on earth. It occurred to me how many moments I was calm. It didn't make sense, but I was. Of course, the most drastic events were unnerving. But I still can't deny how many times calm came over me and so many of us between the dramas. I'd like to believe our nation was on its knees praying for us, begging and waiting for God's perfect plan to be revealed. The calm we felt must have come from others' prayers for us.

If anyone were to ask, "Father Tom, what did God teach you during those intense days? What life lesson did you learn about how to face the possibility of life or death?" I would give them this simple answer. "Live your faith every day you have. You have no idea what will happen tomorrow."

*   *   *

Humbling. What wisdom born under the "wait" of the heavy beam he carried! A wait carried with hope in Him.

Join me on the Camino to learn about "junkyard-dog-like kindness." Sound unusual? You haven't met Christina.

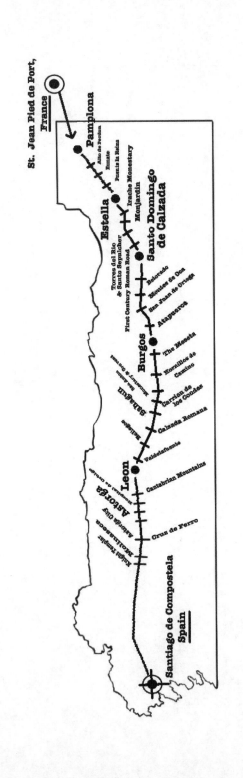

Chapter 15

JUNKYARD-DOG-LIKE KINDNESS

"There is nothing more beautiful than someone who goes out of their way to make life beautiful for others."

Mandy Hale

The Camino

After the mountaintop comes the valley.

One would think walking downhill would be less strenuous on the body and the legs. Not true. From Cruz de Ferro, at an elevation higher than the Pyrenees (a brutal nine hundred meters—a little less than three thousand feet), the trail descends to the town of Molinaseca. The walk is more than twenty kilometers (roughly 12.5 miles) and many stretches have a grade of six percent. Startling and even more challenging is one wickedly steep stretch of trail that is a little more than a 16 percent downhill grade. The composition of the trail compounds the challenge as it is abundantly covered with loose, golfball-to-softball-sized jagged rocks. A layer of light snow cover adds further challenge. Some sections of the Camino snake downhill on slippery slabs of slate. In other places, the trail hugs the hillside with a sheer drop-off of hundreds of kilometers. Utmost care is needed.

Eventually this stretch of the Camino drops into Molinaseca, a small, but busy town. It is a popular spot for pilgrims to rest their weary, often trembling, legs and feet from the strenuous punishment they just endured. This delightful town was born of the Camino in the thirteenth century.

Knights Templar[57]

From here, the valley dips another one hundred meters (325 feet) to a spectacular view of Ponferrada, home to the Castle of the Knights Templar. This commanding structure is perched atop a fifty-meter (160-foot) pinnacle located at the center of town. The Knights Templar left an indelible mark on the history of the Camino. Beginning in the early tenth century, this group of men, trained and skilled in military prowess, sacrificed their lives for a noble cause: to protect pilgrims on The Way. Thanks to these Templars, even the wealthy could take the pilgrimage in safety. Up until that time, travelers carried all their heavy coinage along the 790-kilometer (five hundred-mile) trail with excruciating effort. However, because the Templars were so trustworthy, the rich deposited their wealth with them. The Knights gave them a receipt of deposit and a note indicating the balance in supply. The well-to-do could now travel less encumbered to a town ahead, show their Templar ledger, and make a withdrawal. This accelerated fame and respect for the Knights Templar, and they were later credited with the first mobile banking system.

The Knights grew exponentially in number and reached into many European countries with large representation in France under King Philip, also known as Philip the Beautiful. Philip was reportedly handsome and vain, but threatened by the Knights' reputation and following. Philip had borrowed money from the Knights that he could not repay, so he crafted a plan: destroy the reputation and lives of the Knights. To that end, on October 12, 1307, King Philip sent sealed orders to all lawmaking officials in the country. It was under penalty of death to open or reveal the contents before the next day.

On Friday, October 13, the contents were revealed and spelled out, in shocking detail, the king's wild accusations of heinous crimes committed by the Knights Templar: homosexuality, sodomy, defecating on the cross, sorcery, and other wild claims. Immediately, the Knights were arrested, and Philip ordered them all burned to death. Their smoking corpses and stench filled the countryside.

This was not enough to eliminate the Knights' legacy. Philip sought a public confession of guilt by the Knights. Two Grand Master Templars were imprisoned and beaten daily in hopes of an admission of guilt. The torture continued for seven long years. In their weakness, the last two Master Templars admitted to the crimes, even though untrue, in order to halt the abuse. Taken before the Cathedral of Notre Dame and crowds of onlookers, the two were told to publicly admit that the Knights were guilty of the charges set before them.

However, it was Philip who suffered the final shame by the master knight's testimony: "I acknowledge, to my eternal shame, that I have committed the greatest of crimes. I made the contrary declaration to the truth only to suspend the excessive pains of torture. The life offered me on such infamous terms I abandon without regret."

King Philip's plot exploded to his own complete shame for what nobility, in its finest hour, revealed. In seething anger, he had these last two Knights Templar burned alive over a slow, smoldering fire to extend their agonizing death, and the death of a two-hundred-year history of chivalry and honor. It is no wonder that Friday the 13th's ominous reputation lingers today.

My Camino

"Ah kindness. What a simple way to tell another struggling soul that there is love to be found in the world."

Alison Malee

After the straining climb to the top of Cruz de Ferro, my legs were spent. This made walking down the steep mountain into the town of Molinaseca painful and terrifying for me. Navigation around the irregularly shaped and heavily scattered rocks made the walk even more laborious. If this was not bad enough, the trail was still covered in a thin blanket of snow hiding the directional yellow arrows.

Sometimes my boot placement was a poor choice, causing my foot to skid down and away. I felt like I was practicing a dance routine that included the splits. *Thank God for my poles.* I clung to them all the way. Each step was an adventure, a prayerful hope, a miracle of safety.

I was still just under 1,500 meters (nearly a mile) in elevation overlooking the Spanish countryside. It was nothing short of breathtaking. A random, crazy thought crossed my mind: *I am so overwhelmingly happy right now. No—make that joyful!* God's creation in a grand splendor stretched before me for twenty kilometers (twelve miles) until I approached Molinaseca.

With my poles now too heavy to lift, I dragged myself to my chosen albergue on the outskirts of town. This place has a strong reputation for its cleanliness and delicious home cooking. I picked up my pace as sooty-grey cloud cover thickened just overhead. I passed albergue after albergue in order to arrive at the town's second-to-last available place for a bunk and meal. The next town was five or six kilometers (3.5 miles) ahead.

Drenched in sweat, chilled, and with muscles like warm gelatin, I collapsed under the roof of the large entrance foyer. I lay there resting a while to catch some strength, anything to revive me. I pictured my guardian angel lying on the tile floor panting in rhythm with me. My mind's eye saw him raise one eyebrow and respond to the crazy hike we just endured. I imagined him saying, "Really, Willie? Really? You're killing me here."

I pried my sweaty back from the tile, got my wobbly legs under me, and shuffled to the registration desk. The couple I had been walking with logged in just minutes before me. I was next. *"Una cama por la noche, por favor"* ("I'd like a bed for the night, please").

"No, es completa!" ("No, we're complete—full!") was the response. The couple right before me had gotten the last two beds in the place. I was directed to the very last albergue in town, fifty meters (roughly 150 feet) up the road.

I dredged up my very last ounce of strength and humility. What a crushing blow! The letdown was even more difficult to accept when I entered the door. This albergue resembled an old college fraternity house. I stood paralyzed by the sight of the grimy, dark-colored walls damaged by years of neglect, dim lighting, densely packed double bunks, and dirty tile floors throughout. It was overbooked with noisy, young twenty-something-year-olds. They were just enjoying themselves, but it gave me no rest. The shower stall was less than a meter square (roughly two feet by two feet). I could hardly raise my arms. Worse yet, the water temperature was chilly at best. Then the crushing news: they did not serve meals here. If I wanted a meal, I had to return to the albergue that had just denied me a bed.

Upon heading out, the gloomy sky pressed down heavier, and chilly winds began to gust. I walked past the imaginary scene where the guardian angel conversation occurred. When I arrived, I was painfully startled by the contrast between the two places. Here the freshly painted, butter-yellow walls and polished tile floors were inviting. People spoke in polite whispers in respect for pilgrims' need for rest. It was spacious, brightly lit, and toasty warm.

I gulped down an "it wasn't meant to be" attitude and went back to the registration desk. *"Me gustaría comprar una comida para esta noche"* ("I would like to buy a meal for tonight"). The manager replayed, even more firmly, his same response of an hour earlier, *"No, es completa"* ("No, we're complete—full!").

I was beside myself. *What should I do?* I was desperate for rest. My body ached for food. *I need to think this through.* I asked if I could buy a beverage and sit in the dining hall. I would use the time to write my blog entry for the day and recuperate. Just as I finished an hour later, a gusty, bone-shivering rainstorm overtook the place. Raindrops fell so hard they spanked the sidewalk and overhead roof like firecrackers. Temperatures dropped ten degrees and I shivered uncontrollably.

What should I do? No dinner? There's nowhere nearby for me to go. The nearest place was miles away.

It appeared that there were only three people who ran the place. Two were men who scurried around, preparing the long dining tables for the pilgrims' meal. Long white table coverings, wine glasses, dinnerware, large white bowls for soup, and baskets of fresh warm bread were strategically set. I stood there looking on like an uninvited observer to a banquet.

I tried asking the other manager if there was any way he could please let me have a place for dinner. His reply was an emphatic, *"No! Es completa"* ("No! It's complete. Done.").

I stood in the foyer near a beverage bar just outside the dining area. I stared through the windows at the rain's crazy downpour. *What do I do? I could continue the one-kilometer walk back to town, but now I'm dressed in shorts and sandals. Not good for such a walk. I could run back to my dump of an albergue and eat the granola bar in my pack and drink water, thereby calling it quits for the night. Ugh, no dinner after such a hard day in the snow. Such an unpleasant thought, especially because my legs ache so terribly.*

As I stood alongside the bar, my mind wrestled between the storm and the dinner settings prepared inside, and the smell of home-cooked soup. Oh, the thought! *Warm, delicious soup.* I caught a manager and again asked if I might be allowed to buy a dinner to eat just outside the dining hall under the canopied patio. Once again, the man's aggravated reply, *"No! No es posible"* ("No! No, it is not possible."). With that, the man placed his hands on my shoulders, slowly turned my body toward the town, and pointed the way.

I was crushed.

Then from nowhere, a lady who was working in the kitchen near the bar came out. She approached me with a question, *"Cuantas personas?"* ("How many people?").

I replied, *"Solamente uno"* ("Only one").

She cheerfully called out to one of the managers, *"Una mas!"* ("One more!").

Precisely here, a Spanish drama erupted. A loud and lively vocal sparring match pierced the lazy air. Repeated attempts on her part were confronted with the argument, "*No. Es completa!*" Next, the other man with the "*No!*" answers joined the fray. All the while I stood sheepishly dumbstruck, just a couple arm's lengths nearby.

The three stood in a circle, faces clenched in defiance, the men stabbing emphatic index fingers downward to emphasize their stand, "*No! Es completa.*" The fury continued several unnerving minutes. Each volley of argument was met with this lady's raised, defiant index finger stabbing the air overhead insisting, "*Una mas! Una mas! Una mas! Uuuunaaa maaaas!*"

The men responded with a long argument, all in Spanish, none of which I understood. They bullishly resisted with their sharp staccato, "*No. Es completa!*" The argument grew louder and fiercer until it came to a rolling boil. Not even knowing what they were saying, I knew I was the source of their argument. The backdrop for this drama was dozens of pilgrims staring on. Awkward!

After three solid minutes of blustery debate, they abruptly silenced. It was as if they were prize fighters who just recognized the bell had rung—time to go back to their corner of the ring. The two men huddled and discussed something. *Was it a new strategy to use against this woman?* She turned from them and busied herself with something behind the bar.

Here's where the God moment awakened. Slyly, she stole a glance at the two men, then shot a quick look back to me, gave me a wink, and lifted her index finger as if to suggest, "Just wait."

A short moment later, these three Spaniards launched into a fully recharged argument. All three were shouting at one another. Both men kept shouting, "*No completa! NO, NO!*" She countered fiercely and repeatedly over their voices, "*Una mas. So ... la ... men ... te ... una. U ... NA ... MAS!*" (One more. Only one. One more!").

Somewhere in the middle of this donnybrook, she shot me another quick wink, and raised her index finger to assure me to keep waiting. Then snapping back to military readiness, she launched her defiant barrage in my defense. It was abundantly clear that this woman was administering a stinging tongue lashing. It was effective. The men stood silent and lost for words to use in rebuttal. Surreptitiously, she shot me another assuring look. The lobby, crowded with stunned pilgrims, stood agape, incredulous of the Spanish drama.

The climax came when she raised her voice in a display much like an attorney making his final argument in court. She stood on perched tippy-toes with a gritty determined expression and stabbed her index finger in the air at both men. She barked away at them, almost as if to shame them, intimidate them.

During her closing argument, of sorts, there was a fury of language peppered with *"Una mas! Una mas! Solamente, una mas! Mira al hombre!"* ("One more! One more! Only one more! Look at the man!"). The men paused. They looked at me as if seeing me for the first time. Silence seized them. They looked at each other, defeat on their faces. In a short moment, they shrugged their shoulders and politely walked toward me.

Graciously, one man motioned with one broad sweep of his arm with an open palm, politely said *"Señor, aqui"* ("Sir, here"), and escorted me to the dining area with the background sound of the thundering rainstorm playing outdoors.

There I discovered why the two men were so adamant against the lady's demand and my request. There was plenty of room in the hall, but they had already fully completed all the table settings. To add me, number thirty-three, would mean lifting thirty-two place settings at the table, and resituating the white table covering down to the end in order to accommodate one more place. Then they needed to reset all the din-nerware—again. The meal would be delayed in the process. It proved to be a great deal of extra work and inconvenience, something they did not want to do, nor want as a precedence for future pilgrims.

The meal was exquisite. It rejuvenated my body, but it was the defense, in compassion for me, that rejuvenated my spirit. I was grateful to my core.

After the meal, I found the lady and learned her name: Christina. I wanted to thank her. I extended my hand, then grasped hers with both of mine. I said, in exceptionally poor Spanish, *"Señora, muchas gracias. Yo necesito por algun misericordia. Tu fue Jesus para me eso noches. Dios te bendiga,*

Señora" ("Ma'am, I am so thankful. I needed some mercy, some kindness. You were Jesus for me this night"). Real Spanish speakers would laugh at my attempt, but the message hit its mark. I added, *"Dios te bendiga, Señora"* ("God bless you, Ma'am").

Christina sweetly replied, *"De nada."* ("It's nothing"). We both parted a little teary-eyed.

As I replayed that event in my mind over and over again, I was struck by many layers of life lessons. For one, I don't recall anyone, myself included, who was ever so tenacious about doing such a kindness for another. I've been with people who have tried to gently convince someone to be more compassionate, kind, or a bit more lenient with someone in need. The default approach is a humble, gentle persuasion.

But *never* before had I witnessed anyone so intensely argumentative about extending kindness to another—or to me! It was a fierce intensity that insisted kindness be granted. Christina fought for me in a way a junkyard dog would protect its yard. She fought for me. Why? After all, I hadn't asked her for it. I hadn't groveled or begged. I wondered, *Maybe the sight of me moved her to kindness? Maybe it was the Holy Spirit's call upon her? Or was she living out a modern-day call in a woman's order of the Knight Templar?*

Regardless of the source, Christina had a fire inside, a heart burning with compassion. She persisted for kindness. She was unwavering for kindness. She fought like a junkyard dog to ensure a kindness for me. Not one time, not twice, but three rounds of fierce arguments. She was a shield against selfishness and insensitivity. Christina, a petite, Spanish firebrand, stood in the gap and stabbed a single finger into the faces of two strong, flint-jawed men and pointed at their self-righteousness and injustice. And kindness won.

Christina reminded me of the same righteous anger Jesus displayed while cleansing the temple in Matthew's gospel. He demonstrated how righteous anger is needed. Evil needs to be confronted. And Christina confronted a wrong, and then unabashedly took on the evil and championed the fight for me.

My Camino was challenged. *For what would I fight like a junkyard dog?* Kindness is a good starting point.

Our Camino

"Have you ever noticed how much of Christ's life was spent in doing kind things?"

Henry Drummond

Let's take a look at the Beatitudes:

Blessed are the poor in spirit, for theirs is the kingdom of heaven.

Blessed are those who mourn, for they shall be comforted.

Blessed are the meek, for they shall inherit the earth.

Blessed are those who hunger and thirst for righteousness, for they shall be satisfied.

Blessed are the merciful, for they shall receive mercy.

Blessed are the pure in heart, for they shall see God.

Blessed are the peacemakers, for they shall be called sons of God.

Blessed are those who are persecuted for righteousness' sake, for theirs is the kingdom of heaven.

Blessed are you when others revile you and persecute you and utter all kinds of evil against you falsely on my account. Rejoice and be glad, for your reward is great in heaven, for so they persecuted the prophets who were before you. (Matt. 5:3–12)

Being comfortable has taken priority in our lives over living these beatitudes. Committing to fast from excess food or drink? Limiting screen time on TV or cell phone? Initiating a conversation with a street beggar? Giving attention to someone socially awkward? Lingering in a conversation with someone who is grieving a loss? These and many other similar situations take us away from being comfortable. It is human nature to run to the comfortable and minimize, if not avoid altogether, the uncomfortable.

After all, more comfort, more control, right? And control leads us to feel confident and powerful. Just as losing power and control leaves us feeling uncomfortable, gaining power and control makes us comfortable with who we are.

Being comfortable is a powerful driving force. But let's consider, is our comfort God's desire? Or His desire something higher, like the Beatitudes? Here's the rub: living these Jesus virtues lands us far from our comfort zone.

Being a *peacemaker* involves confronting evil talk and actions against others and is uncomfortable to do. It might even cost us friendships and family peace. Being *meek* involves fighting against self-pride and importance in order to live submissively. It might cost some ego status, leaving us feeling vulnerable. Comforting those who *mourn* when we don't know what to say is awkward when we're fearful of perhaps saying the wrong thing. It might cost some clumsy, tongue-tied moments before someone who is grief-stricken. Sacrificing inner peace to *fight for righteousness* may help the persecuted, but it comes with the possibility of being judged harshly.

Few of us find comfort in living out any of these beatitudes. Why? Because the costs are too great. This truth reveals how addicted we really are to being comfortable.

They may not be places we seek, but our Camino wanders into many uncomfortable tight spots, to be sure. We fear speaking up when it's "not our business to begin with." We avoid situations when "I'm just not good at those kinds of things." We encounter wrong things being done, but "If I say something, people will see me as weird." We think, "I'm sticking my neck out and making a fool of myself." These thoughts paralyze the inspiration to act. Why? Because we think "It's all on us to do."

But where's God? Where have we left Him?

In these incidents God is an observer; an overseer of what we do; a silent coach. We don't need God when we're doing only what is comfortable.

Get into God's comfort zone. Have more love than fear. Push beyond "on second thought" pauses. The apostle John assures us, "perfect love casts out fear" (1 John 4:18). This is a humble place where a righteous relationship admits God is God, we need Him, and we confess our dependence on His grace. It requires a selfless, reckless act to love like Jesus loves: fearlessly.

We need not fear living in an uncomfortable zone. Good, holy, and beatitude-minded people live in that neighborhood. It's where people like Christina live and fight like a junkyard dog for virtue.

May our dear Lord make us uncomfortable.

*   *   *

Angelo's outrageous experience of junkyard-dog-like kindness will inspire our Camino. In his own words, Angelo shares his faith walk which began in his birthplace, Bari, Italy, some fifty years ago:

> "A part of kindness consists of loving people more than they deserve."
>
> Joseph Joubert

I remember loving church as a little boy. My grandma took me to daily mass. I even remember being introduced to Padre Pìo, who just years ago was declared St. Padre Pìo. As a child I felt his holiness. I felt so at peace in church that I wanted to sleep there. I fondly remember having a little boy's pure love for God. I only wanted to be with Jesus.

All that was destroyed. At only age seven, I was sexually abused by a neighbor girl twice my age. I was so little; I didn't know what was happening. It felt good and so very wrong at the same time. It continued over a year. I was a little boy living the secret of shame and darkness. My innocence, gone. I knew it was wrong, but didn't know what to do about it. There was an evil spirit pulling me away from God. Too ashamed to tell my parents and too ashamed to tell a priest, I kept the darkness inside.

Over time, things changed in me. I became attracted to mischief in school and in town. In defiance of one of the nuns who taught me, I grabbed her head veil, yanking it off. The religious sisters at the time shaved their heads and wore their covered head piece as an outward sign of humility and a life of service to the Lord. I'm filled with shame for exposing the nun that way. But this was part and parcel of the hellion I was becoming.

My parents decided that immigration to the USA would offer an opportunity for a better life. We moved to Maywood, Illinois, and stayed with family. However, the children and neighborhood in this suburb of Chicago presented the wrong opportunities. Rival ethnic groups lured me into life on the streets. Fist-fighting, stealing, and a myriad of bad activities became my new childhood. It didn't take long before I realized that those who took me in and gave me protection were the meanest people I could have ever met. Considering how dark my past already was, life with these new friends was where I believed a bad boy like me belonged.

My parents saw the direction I was headed. They moved the family to Addison, a town miles from the gang life in Maywood. Even there, I found the wrong crowd.

Vito, the group leader, arranged fights with other kids who he saw as a threat to his tough-guy reputation. He often sent me to do this dirty work. I fought tough, mean, and could really finish off the other guy. Fight after fight I gained a sense of power, earning a "don't mess with me" reputation. I felt powerful, and I liked the feeling.

Then something changed me.

I was provoked to start a fight with one of the school's football players. He was a full year older. It didn't matter. After all, I was one of the baddest boys in the school. I remember grabbing him by his long hair, kicking him in the face, and whaling away on him with my fists. Somewhere mid-fight, I heard a strange voice. "If you do this, it'll never stop. You could kill someone."

I dropped my fists, covered my head, and allowed my opponent to whale away on me until the fight ended. I suddenly didn't want to fight anymore. My self-image as a bad boy was challenged.

I began using my tough-guy reputation to protect guys who were different—those who had personality quirks, liked to do well in school, or were maybe a little socially awkward. I felt for them. I enjoyed the fact that when I was around, no one messed with them.

That's when I met Ken. He was a good kid, he was smart, got good grades and all. He had a few habits that got other kids' attention. They picked on him only when I wasn't around. They say opposites attract and this was true for my friendship with Ken. He found me funny, a novelty with my Italian accent, and felt safe behind my strength and fighting spirit. Ken looked up to me and wanted me to look up to him too.

Word on the street was that there was a facility just miles from our homes where supply jeeps, trucks, and other equipment were stored. It was discovered that the area was high-fenced, and though the gate was locked, young male frames could slip through. The payoff? The open-air jeeps could be started by a push button on the dash. This was too irresistible for sixteen-year-olds craving a chance to drive.

Ken, Johnny, and I headed for mischief and slid ourselves into the facility grounds. There were the jeeps, ours for the taking. Because it was a late Sunday afternoon, we were unnoticed. Away the three of us went, each taking turns putting our terrible, new driver habits to work.

The darkest day of my life occurred that afternoon.

I was driving, Johnny was in the passenger seat, and Ken was centered in the backseat. In the open-air jeep, the wind blew through our hair as we raced along the roads within the yards. The road took a sharp corner and pitched strongly to one side.

Instantaneously, the jeep rolled over. Launched out of the vehicle, I hit the ground, skidded away from the overturning jeep, and was knocked unconscious. Johnny was tossed out as well. As we regained consciousness, the next sight horrified us, and flashes back to me even to this day.

Ken was lying on the pavement, with the wheel of the overturned jeep resting on his head. He was motionless, unresponsive. A Goliath of fear clutched me by the throat, squeezing life out of me. I couldn't breathe. Didn't know what to do. *What have I done?*

Johnny groaned to his feet. After his terror broke, we physically lifted the jeep from Ken's head. I knelt down and cradled his head in my lap. I kept shouting, "Ken! Ken! KEN!" Blood trickled from the sides of his ears. In my horror, I knew—Ken was dead.

I gotta do something! But I didn't know what. There were no homes nearby, no phones, no one that could help. To say I was terrified would be an understatement, especially with my history of fighting, stealing, and troublemaking with the police. I'm ashamed that I even considered trying to drag Ken's body through the gate and placing him by the road, making it appear that he was hit by a car. I couldn't do it.

Johnny and I swore to a story. We broke in, but Ken was driving. This would keep us out of terrible trouble, keep us out of jail. We spotted an older man doing maintenance. We told him of our friend and the need for an ambulance and police help. Within minutes, the emergency vehicles arrived.

Ken was taken away, pronounced dead at the scene of the accident. The police questioned us. Our stories jibed. We broke in to joyride the jeeps, Ken was driving at the time, and the jeep overturned, killing him. After lengthy questioning, the policeman accepted our story.

At this moment I was drowning in shame and guilt. I hated myself for the lies, hated myself for what I had done. The voice I heard during that fistfight returned, "Angelo, tell the truth."

Braced for the shame I would endure, the heartache of Ken's parents, and the strong possibility of prison, I stepped out of my guilt and called back to the policeman.

My head hung with bitter tears washing out of me. I confessed, "Officer, it wasn't Ken's fault. I was driving. It was all my fault." What screamed inside was the truth, *Ken didn't deserve this. I cannot dishonor Ken with a lie.*

The friend and I rode in the police car when the officer went to the door of Ken's home with the news. We sat in the back seat as the news was delivered. We could not hear, but the parents' reaction was clear enough. Their knees buckled as they staggered to the porch deck. Somewhere during their sobbing, they caught sight of us sitting in the back seat of the squad car. Shame and sorrow traumatized me.

The months ahead were filled with extended shame for what
I put my parents through, friends' anger toward me, court
appearances, and legal issues. The court ruling: accidental
death. I got five years' probation. This was nothing compared
to the notoriety that followed. The ugly details were shown
on major news networks. Everyone knew my fatal mistake.

The weeks and months following Ken's death left me paralyzed in fear—I couldn't talk to anyone. I lived muted by the
hardship I caused, with no interest or belief that my life would
or should ever return to normal—until a surprising request
came one year later.

Ken's mom was inquiring of me through my older brother.
She asked him, "Would you ask Angelo to come with us to the
cemetery?" It would be the anniversary day of Ken's death.

I'll never forget the feeling of lead in my feet as I saw their car roll
up our drive. I wanted to run. *How could I face them, face Ken's grave?*
We rode along silently. No one can speak when your breath's
been stolen. Fear and shame were burglars holding my heart.

The car rolled up within a short walking distance to the
gravesite, yet it felt like a nine-mile trek. The three of us stood
staring down at Ken's plot, his headstone. My head hung in
disgrace. Ken's mom and dad softly stepped alongside, each
put an arm around me.

They started praying. I had only enough strength to listen.
Words could not form, my voice, gone. Ken's mom softly continued, "Angelo, we know it was an accident. You didn't mean
to hurt Ken. We know you loved our son." Ken's dad added,
"We forgive you."

I was shaken. I couldn't believe what I was hearing. I deserved
their anger, hard questions, stinging memories. Any and all of
these would be just, my rightful punishment.

I was not given what I deserved.

I was given what I didn't deserve.

Kindness.

It was the sweetest and most generous gift. In that moment, it imprinted all the Beatitudes deep inside my heart. Meekness, comfort, righteousness, peacemaking, mercy, and purity of heart were all there. And, most amazingly, right beside Ken's grave.

It was generous kindness in its purest form: forgiveness.

As Ken's parents ended our visit, they closed in more tightly and affectionately around me. The tone of their voices was softer, with even more loving acceptance as I heard their final wish.

"Angelo, go on with your life."

"Amazing grace . . . how sweet the sound . . . that saved a wretch like me." These are words of the famous song "Amazing Grace." *Now I was the wretch that was saved. I was called to live free.*

Forty years have passed since Ken died. But God has worked a saving grace in me. I live my life with a mantra, "Please don't let Ken's life be in vain."

Today, Angelo fights like a junkyard dog so it doesn't. He fiercely defends the immigrant workers he employs. He demonstrates love and support for guests he serves at the homeless shelter. And if there is news of anyone whose heart has been broken, this compassionate Italian hugging machine will be found alongside to offer comfort. Angelo acts as a guard dog to ensure kindness is shown to those around him.

*   *   *

Have you considered this question: "What are you here for?" The next leg of the Camino captures an event that provokes possible answers.

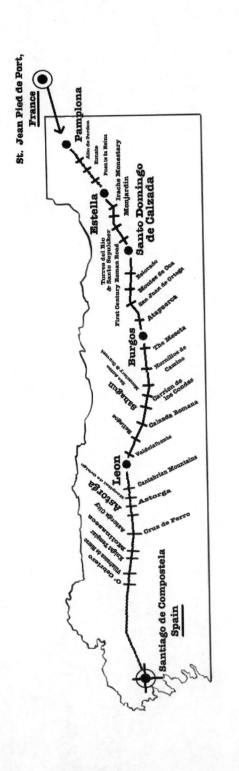

Chapter 16

WHAT ARE YOU HERE FOR?

"Everything you want is on the other side of fear."

Jack Canfield

The Camino

Two peaks bookend fifty kilometers (roughly thirty miles) of this stage of The Way. The magnificent Templar Castle in Ponferrada sits at 540 meters (1,770 feet). A mercifully gentle, level grade follows as the trail weaves westward through the delightful ancient city of Villafranca de Bierzo.

What a contrast occurs in the last seven kilometers (just over four miles)! The trail abruptly spikes seven hundred meters (three thousand feet)—that's two Washington Monuments, or three Eiffel Towers, stacked one atop the other. The climb rewards with views from the medieval mountain village of O'Cebreiro (pronounced "O thay bray air o"). This village has existed since the ninth century, as a place to assist pilgrims on their journey to Santiago. The town holds a profound respect for a miracle that occurred there.

Villafranca de Bierzo

History abounds in this little town. Quaint, narrow cobblestone roads pass under residents' balconies, which often display colorful flowers in window boxes. Archaeologists claim early man lived there. The Romans were known to have occupied it. But it is the Camino pilgrims that gave Villafranca importance.

The Church of St. James stands as a twelfth-century miniature of the church in Santiago. It has stunning arches and an astonishingly detailed wood-carved sanctuary. Of particular attention is the Puerta de Perdòn, "The Door of Forgiveness."[58] Over the centuries, many pilgrims walked the Camino as penance for a grave sin committed and carried their remorse each day on their Camino. At Puerta de Perdòn, pilgrims beg God's forgiveness and His grace before continuing on to the Cathedral of Santiago.

The fifteenth-century castle Palacio de los Marqueses is captivating with its rounded turrets and military lookouts. It is easy to imagine knights roaming the grounds and even guarding the castle from above.

Further exciting the pilgrim's imagination of the medieval life is the famed Calle Agua, or Water Street. Houses alongside the river prominently display shields decorated with coats of arms from centuries-past inhabitants. Long ago, townspeople stood on their balconies and cheered pilgrims on The Way as they passed through.

Today, the walk through Villafranca de Bierzo still enlivens the spirit of hundreds of years ago when this town and its townspeople welcomed and cared for passing pilgrims.

O'Cebriero

The ascent is brutally exhausting, and pilgrims are eager to grab a bunk here and revel in the mountain panorama. Most find themselves dumbstruck by the commanding view of the sweeping mountainscape stretching to the horizon. One sits speechless at the warm butter-yellow-, gold-, and tangerine-colored sunsets and sunrises. This setting serves as a theatre for God's creation at play.

A treasured historical event occurred in the town's small church, Santa Maria la Real,[59] tucked right along the Camino trail. The church sits alongside the portion of the trail that roller-coasters steeply up and down through hill and valley. During the fourteenth century, a pilgrim chose to brave a fierce snowstorm on this treacherous trail to get to a mass service. When he arrived at the church, he was met by a visiting monk who chided him sternly, "You could have been killed. You could have fallen down the mountainside, or been lost in snow where no one could find you." Then the monk added, "No one else is here. What are you here for?"

Local history captures his simple response: "I am here for Jesus."

How could the monk refuse? He agreed to celebrate the mass for this one congregant.

During the most sacred moment of the mass, a miracle occurred. The celebrant elevated the bread wafer, the host. Before their eyes the host transformed into human skin, relaxed, and folded over the monk's knuckles. He placed it upon the paten, a silver, plate-like vessel used during the mass. Completely stunned, the priest elevated the chalice, also made of silver, only to find that the wine had been transformed into human blood. It was reported that when this happened, another miracle occurred involving the statue of Mary holding the Christ child, situated on the wall alongside the altar. Both men witnessed Mary's head turning toward this heavenly sign.

The humble peasant was there for Jesus, and his faith was rewarded by Jesus being fully there for him.

Some seven centuries later in this little, ancient church is a side chapel with the statue. In a glass case set nearby is a striking red velvet display holding the silver paten and chalice. To think, these two vessels held what some Christians believe was the transfigured body and blood of Christ!

My Camino

"You have to say, 'I'm forgiven' again and again until it becomes the story of your life."

Cheryl Strayed

It was shortly after noon when the trail skirted an ancient country church. *Oh, yes! Time for a brief stop and perhaps a noon pilgrim mass.* I wanted to stop in to pray for those who had entrusted me with their burden words, and if possible, attend mass. I also had some things to get off my chest with our Father. I needed time on my knees.

I slipped into the small chapel only to see that the service had already begun. I tried, oh . . . so . . . hard to be inconspicuous. That's not easy with walking sticks tapping the old Spanish tile and an eight-and-a-half kilo (nineteen-pound) backpack. The wooden pews were crowded tightly with kneelers, which made it impossible to clank my way in unnoticed. First my backpack straps rattled on the bench, then my poles screeched across the floor. Regardless, I was finally able to settle in a spot in the last pew.

Unlike every church I'd attended on the Camino, the locals here did not seem welcoming. *How peculiar!* In fact, I was getting disgusted looks and unwelcome glances. *This is sooo odd*, I thought. After settling in, I noticed how beautiful the altar looked. It was crafted with an exquisite wood grain. *Okay. Altars can be made with whatever.* But also odd was that a woman was speaking—in Spanish, mind you—at length, and from the pulpit. This also was not customary in a Catholic service. After her speech, of which I understood *not one word*, the priest walked down from behind the gorgeous wood altar to sprinkle holy water. *Yes, a pilgrim blessing! I certainly need one!*

An epiphany erupted. The sprinkling was not intended for the altar, nor for any pilgrim. The holy water was for a blessing over a wood coffin! And the deceased within it! *Lord, forgive me!* I had crashed a funeral service!

No wonder I was unwelcome. Needless to say, I slunk out as silently as a clunky pilgrim could.

It was a classic "Willie being Willie" moment. I had honorable intentions for being there. I simply wanted time with the Lord. However, I hadn't paid attention to the details or how others might perceive my actions. My thoughts quickly became self-shaming for not paying attention and for any pain I might have caused the grieving in that chapel. *I'm sorry, Lord!* I continued beating myself up and couldn't find a way to forgive myself for my actions. This is typical of me—though I never deliberately intend to offend, many times I just miss the details. And I do wild things like crash a funeral service, on rare occasions. I repeatedly poured through my litany of apologies and made my confession for being "an idiot."

Suddenly, I sensed our Father speaking to my heart. "Willie. Enough. I understand. I hear your regret. I forgive you!"

My thoughts derailed. I realized sometimes I head to places thinking I know what I'm there for, but come to realize that what I'm there for is not as good as what God has me there for. I was not there to crash a funeral. I believe God had me there to really see myself more deeply—my faults, my weakness, and my struggles with self-forgiveness.

Forgiveness is not dependent upon me. It is dependent upon my acceptance of His forgiveness.

I felt the Holy Spirit's encouragement. *What are you here for, Willie?*

I am here for Jesus. I'm here for His love. I'm here for His forgiveness. Not my self-forgiveness, but *His* forgiveness.

Our Camino

"How many times do we pay for one mistake? The answer is thousands of times. The human is the only animal on earth that pays a thousand times for the same mistake. The rest of the animals pay once for every mistake they make. But not us. We have a powerful memory. We make a mistake, we judge ourselves, we find ourselves guilty, and we punish ourselves.

If justice exists, then that was enough; we don't need to do it again. But every time we remember, we judge ourselves again, we are guilty again and we punish ourselves again, and again, and again."

Don Miguel Ruiz

What are we here for? It's one of those bigger-than-life types of questions. Variations of the same question come when people say, "I'm trying to find myself" or "I don't know what I want to do in my life." Most of us wrestle with our life's purpose at benchmark events such as when choosing a career, changing a career, retiring, and many times in between. The question is a heavy-stakes mystery. What *are* we here for?

What are *you* here for?

Here is Jesus's answer:

You shall love the Lord your God with all your heart and with all your soul and with all your mind. This is the great and first commandment. And a second is like it: You shall love your neighbor as yourself. (Matt. 22:37–39)

Our Camino may be enlightened by our attention to one small word captured in these Scripture verses: *all.*

As believers, we are called to love God. But the Scripture calls us to love with our "all." No thing or person can we love more. Nothing in our soul can compete with the love we have for Him. Neither can any knowledge that gives us confidence or brings us security vie with the love we have for Him. He wants all our love. All of it.

Can we claim we're "all in" right now? Probably not. But that is where our Camino may provide the answer to what we are here for. Is there anyone or anything we love in our life more than our Lord? What in our soul has undue attachment? What frequents our mind? Are there any attachments in our life greater than God? What unforgiveness might be keeping us at arm's length from Him? What is keeping us from being "all in"?

It starts with being honest about these things. Determining to loosen the grasp on other loves in our lives allows us a stronger grasp for love for Him. We cannot fully embrace His love and our false loves. It takes letting go. It takes growing our love more and more. It takes our all.

St. Mother Theresa of Calcutta advised us on how to grow more in love with Him. "Give God permission,"[60] she encouraged. Give Him permission to do what He wants for and in us. The only limits on where and how we can grow in faith come from the limits we put on God's redeeming work in our life. God gave us free will. It's our choice to cooperate with Him. The greater the permission, the greater is the power to transform us. So how do we control freaks give God more permission?

Whatever the next opportunity to love Him or to love others may be, give it an effort greater than you have given in the past. Not sure how to do that? Jesus is still the Good Teacher, so ask Him how to love more, bigger, better. He will. After all, He is the model of sacrificial love. We need only give Him permission to take us beyond our comfort zone. This is where our love will grow, by degrees, until He has our all.

But what should we do when our "all in" effort fails? Backfires? What if we blow it?

Ask for God's forgiveness. Accept it. And when we find ourselves brewing over the mistakes and striving to forgive ourselves, what we're really doing is assuming God's role as Judge, Forgiver. That's a scary thought. God is merciful whereas we, even on our best days, are by no means as quick to forgive.

Father Mike Schmitz offers this sound reminder: "God knows me more than I know myself. God loves me more than I love myself."[61]

May I add: God forgives me more than I forgive myself. He forgives us as Judge and Forgiver and sees us as His loved sinners. We might not be quick to see loved and sinner as compatible. But God does. So when our Camino is sinking in the quagmire of our futile self-forgiveness, it is pride slithering through our thinking.

"I can't face God with what I've done. I'm too ashamed."

"What if God asks me to confess what I've done to another and ask their forgiveness?"

"What I did was so terrible. So unforgiveable."

"I'm only human. Everyone makes mistakes."

We don't have the power to deliver ourselves from sin, and our pride may be keeping us from the only true source of forgiveness. That's right. We might be our own worst enemy, keeping us from forgiveness.

Here's the good news: once we confess our sins and pride to God, He forgives us. The guilt ends there. All of it?

Yes, all of it. All is forgiven. The horrid, the despicable, the most damaging "all" is forgiven. With forgiveness comes the greatest gift, a healing of our troubled soul and freedom—a new, life-giving freedom.

When it comes to forgiveness, I am thankful I'm not God, and that you're not God either.

*   *   *

"Whatever you've done before, accept it and let it go. You are not perfect. You are capable of making mistakes. Stop hiding from the shadows of the past. Don't be trapped in darkness of shattered memories. Let the light pass through and shine upon you."

Juan Lucio

Few knew the man behind the man in Ed. He was a husband, father, hardworking pipefitter, and provider—a regular "working Joe." Few knew the war hero he was and his battle with "self-unforgiveness" born out of war. This is Ed's, or rather, Lieutenant Colonel Ed's, faith walk story as was shared with me in his own words:

> December 7, 1941, was a defining day for me. Pearl Harbor propelled me toward becoming the man I dreamed of being— a fighter pilot serving my country. I was a senior in high school when the news broke. All of us guys went home for lunch, determined to enlist that afternoon. I had had some early training in flying prop planes, doing crop dusting over farm fields. (Times were freer back then.) By age eighteen, I was good. Stunts, dives, and low flyovers. I'm a little ashamed to admit it, but I regularly scared the bejesus out of poor, dumbstruck farmers staring at my antics from cornfields below.
>
> "Ma, my country needs me. I'm a flyer. That's what I'm meant to do," I argued.
>
> My mother would have no part of it. "The war will be here months from now. Get back to school and finish that diploma first," she insisted.
>
> Mom won.
>
> Just a few months later, I was at the recruiting station and off to basic training. The Marines Flying Squadron became my life. I earned my Wings of Gold and was promoted to Second Lieutenant. This was what I was here for—to train, to serve, and to protect my country. This was what God had made me for! I was certain of it, as any nineteen-year-old could be.
>
> The Marines remained my life for the next thirty-one years. When the Vietnam War broke out, I received a call to return to active duty. I was promoted to Lieutenant Colonel. My wife asked me what I was going to do. "I'm a fighter pilot. It's what I'm here for. To protect my country. She needs me."

The decision cost me my marriage.

After Vietnam I came home, got back into my career as a pipefitter, married a wonderful woman, and had four great kids.

During my years as a Marine, I had flown Corsair jets for three campaigns—World War II, the Korean War, and the Vietnam War. The four thousand flight hours and 150 combat missions came with high military honors—two Distinguished Flying Crosses, the Bronze Star, Purple Heart, eight air medals, and the Cross of Gallantry.

I was just a tough ol' bird.

When Desert Storm broke out, I volunteered to fly fighters again, an unprecedented fourth campaign. How could I not volunteer? I am here for my country whenever she needs me. First Lady Barbara Bush wrote a note of fond appreciation and, on behalf of the president, declined my offer. I continued with civilian life as best I could. It was tough, yes, and not without heartache.

*   *   *

It was blatantly clear to family and close friends that the effects of war raged within Ed. They knew PTSD (post-traumatic stress disorder) was his demon due to all too many war memories. Sadly, they coped as best they could with episodes of it. At age eighty-nine, the depths of this warrior surfaced in what appeared to be his nearing end of life. While in a nursing home, he caught an infection that overtook his frail health and weakened body. He regularly spoke with disjointed, sometimes jibberish-like rambling. Soon after a bout of "crazy talk," his faculties would surprisingly reappear and he could converse in a lucid, clear way again. This would last a few minutes, then he'd grow weak and return to some wild story from his past.

It was in one of those moments that the tough ol' war hero privately shared a heartbreaking confession with me. I remember it in detail.

Ed's eyes were glazed, staring. He seemed to be seeking a familiar face, although I was the only one in the room. He did not recognize me or know where he was. I later realized his face was searching for a safe place to share his burden, his shame held for decades.

He began reliving his story. "We were flying a combat mission in enemy Korea. I was part of a division flying Corsair jets. Our flight leader picked the target on the east side of the mountain range. I challenged him, 'Sir, in due respect. I've studied the maps. I'm convinced the target is five miles west.'

"I could have been court marshaled. I was a major at the time when our leader barked back at me, 'If you're so damn smart, you lead.'

"So, I did." Major Ed's face sprang to life. "I took the point and led the squadron west over that mountain range. There it was. I was right! The airfield and base—hidden for far too long. We caught the enemy asleep in an early dawn raid. Total surprise. A complete bomb and rocket run! Oh, baby! Dozens and dozens of enemy soldiers were running back to base. I came in with fifty calibers flaming. Mowed 'em down. They fell like bowling pins. Dat, dat, dat, dat, dat, dat, dat. Round after round I shot 'em. The snow was covered with blood. They didn't have a chance. Killed 'em all. Nothing left. Nada. Nothing. Zilch!"

There was a long, deafeningly silent pause. Lieutenant Colonel Ed stared up at the ceiling. He stared at something important, something only he could see. Then his eyes, nose, and lips corkscrewed into a sour facial expression. Bitterness, shame, and agony replaced the excitement of the war moment he just shared. Torment seeped to the surface. I could only watch; words were impossible to find and useless.

Spellbound, I saw Ed refocus and stare in my direction. His face was fixed on someone's face before him—clearly not on mine.

He propped himself up from his bed on his frail arms and pleaded, "Please forgive me. God forgive me. I did what I was there for. A fighter pilot. But I killed all those people. I *killed* them! *I* killed them! Please forgive me. I can't forgive myself. I've tried. I've tried for years. But I killed so many people in the war. Forgive me! Forgive me!"

A deep well of bitter anguish erupted with tears, his sobbing reverberating in the room. Leaning on one elbow and with one hand hiding his face, his body shook as wails escaped from deep within his soul. He was a trapped animal straining to escape the torture. Long minutes went by before he dropped his hand revealing his bloodshot eyes. He fixed me with a pleading stare that begged for escape from his personal hell.

My mind raced for the right words. Only one certain thought came. I have no authority to forgive sin, but I could point Ed to the Forgiver of all sin. I offered a gentle assurance, "God will forgive you, Ed. Trust in His mercy. He will forgive you. He will. He will. He will!"

Ed's wide-eyed stare lost its strength as he slumped back down, his head now resting on his pillow. He quickly grew sleepy and closed his eyes. Peace, if but for the moment, settled upon him.

God only knows if Lieutenant Colonel Ed ever accepted forgiveness from Him and release from his futile self-forgiveness. We can only hope and pray. In the days after this private confession, Ed slipped into dementia for the final years of his life. After fighting three wars for our freedom, we can only pray the war within his memory, his heart, and his soul found peace in God's forgiveness.

> "Forgiveness is giving up the hope that the past could have been any different. It's accepting the past for what it was and using it in this moment in time to help yourself move forward."
>
> Unknown

*   *   *

Ever been a contestant on "Satan Jeopardy"? Never heard of it? Walk this next stage of the Camino and you'll learn how the devil games us.

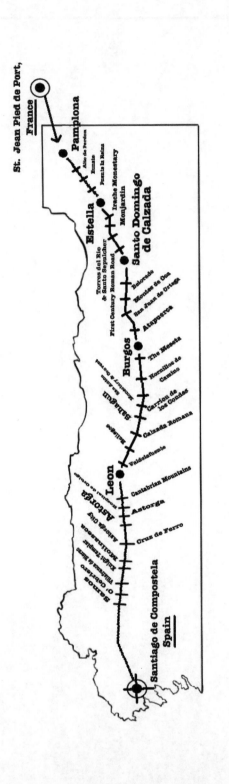

St. Jean Pied de Port, France

Pamplona

Alto de Pardon
Euncie
Puente la Reina

Estella

Torres del Rio & Santo Sepulcher
First Century Roman Road
Monjardin
Irache Monestary

Santo Domingo de Calzada

Belorado
Montes de Oca
San Juan de Ortega
Atapuerca

Burgos

The Meseta
Hornillos de Camino
Carrion de los Condes
Calzada Romana
Valdelafuente

Sahagún
Mansilla
San Miguel & Spital

Leon

Cantabrian Mountains
Astorga
Astorga City
Templar Castle
Cruz de Ferro

Astorga

Molinaseca
Villafranca del Bierzo
O' Cebriero
Samos

Santiago de Compostela
Spain

Chapter 17

SATAN JEOPARDY!

"Pray without ceasing, for Satan is preying without ceasing."

Unknown

The Camino

Delightful is the only adjective that can possibly describe the thirty kilometers (18.5 miles) from O'Cebreiro to Samos. The Way skirts panoramic views of patchy farm plots ranging from celery-colored to those deep and dark as pine needles. These plots and the little hamlets around them cling to the expanse of mountainsides rising to an elevation of 1,300 meters (4,260 feet).

The enchantment continues, especially at early morning. Because of the altitude, pilgrims are treated to what is known as "floating mountains." With the warmth of morning sunlight not at full strength, cloud cover hangs just beneath the mountain peaks at an elevation just below the trail. It is both eerie and captivating for the pilgrim to walk above the clouds—a rare experience. As the sunlight warms, the clouds strain apart to reveal the spectacular mountain valleys and luscious growth below.

Most of The Way for this distance follows farm after farm while occasionally slipping through small villages. Centuries-old grain cribs, each the size of a one-car garage, sit perched on concrete, stilt-like pillars about three meters (just under ten feet) high. The crib stands another three meters taller. This fascinating structure has a purpose. The open slats of the crib allow the grain to dry while preventing rodents from getting into the stored crop.

Over the next fifteen kilometers (roughly 9.5 miles) the trail commands an attention-getting, devilish descent of 530 meters (1,740 feet). This trek covers a distance of three kilometers (nearly two miles). Although steep, this distance is on hard-packed clay and loose stone with switchbacks, which helps the pilgrim manage the descent safely. Careful steps prevent slips and stumbles as the trail enters Triacastela, named after three castles that once commanded the area. They are long gone, but the quaint little farm village still graces The Way.

The pilgrims have a choice for this next section of The Way. They can take the shorter route along the highway to Sarria, or take the additional six-and-a-half kilometer (four-mile) alternate trail. The longer route follows quiet forests, gently rolling farmland, and a stop midway before Sarria in the town of Samos.

Samos

This ancient little hamlet with a population of two hundred is the better choice for those with stronger legs and enough time. The main attraction is the Benedictine monastery, which is one of the oldest and largest monasteries in all of Europe. It is mind-boggling to think this campus, nearly a city block in size, was established in the sixth century—nearly nine hundred years before Columbus discovered America! Thousands of monks lived there over the years, though only a handful do today. The monastery itself is an immense structure comprising four long dormitories built in a square-shaped configuration. Large, open-air corridors line the dormitories' exterior walls, which face an inner courtyard. The exterior walls are covered top to bottom with beautiful, artfully painted murals depicting events in the life of St. Benedict, founder of this religious order. The center courtyard contains a meticulously manicured, landscaped garden of small trees, breathtaking flowering shrubs, and a large central fountain.

Adjacent to the courtyard is the monastery's main church, adorned with intricately detailed sacred art, sculptures, and old-world craftsmanship of the altar and sanctuary. Alongside is enough seating for dozens of pious monks. Today, less than a dozen monks live and serve there. Pilgrims continue to find inspiration from these monks, who have dedicated their lives to prayer and service to the church. It is a rare treat to hear the monks chant the Gregorian prayers after the daily pilgrim mass. Beautiful!

My Camino

"Satan does not tempt us to make us do wrong things, he tempts us to make us lose what God has put into us through regeneration, namely the possibility of being of value to God."

Oswald Chambers

God's palette of warm yellow, gold, and white sunrise awoke the mountain horizon. I could not tear my eyes away as sunlight broke over the peaks. At an elevation of 1,300 meters (4,200 feet), the floating mountains were mesmerizing. Spring was erupting here in such soothing emerald greens. The guidebooks for the Camino claim that O'Cebreiro is distinctly similar to Celtic lands of Ireland and Scotland; if so, both own a piece of heaven on earth.

I felt the spiritual blessings of the holiness in O'Cebreiro while anticipating my arrival at another spiritual recharger—the centuries-old monastery in Samos. I pushed aside my foot and blister pains of the past days. After all, I was riding a spiritual high! No thirty-kilometer (18.5-mile) walk could distract my mission to receive even more spiritual insight. I was riding a spiritual wave, and I felt confidently filled with the Holy

Spirit. I swelled with pride for what I'd accomplished these hundreds of kilometers thus far. *This is exactly how my Camino was supposed to develop.*

This morning, for some reason, a memory of a past offense slithered into my thinking. It entered as a disturbing little recollection of particular people in my past. Up rose their hurtful words. I recalled the painful tone of their voices. Their harsh facial expressions. The loneliness I felt. The details of the old hurt sharpened, and grew more focused. I was reliving the ugly event in my mind and pain in my heart returned.

Then, almost seamlessly, an even more painful recollection slid in right behind the first. Again, details of this pain slowly dawned on me. Their selfish motives. Their hurtful words. Cruel actions. The dishonor and even disgrace I had felt grew clear in my memory. The scab of the old wound was torn off.

One old memory after another bubbled up like a lava bed of horrible old hurts. Each old anger, worry, injustice, and shame came back with all the unfounded blame. Making each recollection more dreadful was the length of time each event played in vivid detail. I relived each negative emotion kilometer after kilometer. I carried these past wounds painfully in my heart nearly the entire day, hour after dreadful hour.

How my spirits crashed from the high I had felt early that morning!

I prayed. "Lord, I am so close to Santiago. Days away. I only wanted thoughts of you. I wanted to stay on this morning's spiritual high. Why did You remind me of all these unpleasant memories?"

Precisely in the middle of my prayer, a redeeming truth overwhelmed me: God does not take us to relive old hurts! He does not take us to shame. Our Father does not take us to dishonor or disgrace. What had happened then?

A new truth confronted me. It was Satan! The Evil One! *Only the Evil One destroys! Only evil encourages despair! Only the Evil One steals joy!*

The epiphany burst like a champagne cork.

Satan was playing me! He was playing my old memories in order to darken my Camino. He was sapping the strength from my passion for Santiago. He was playing his role perfectly as the "Father of Lies, Prince of Darkness."[62]

I saw it clearly now. My overconfidence, tainted with a bit of pride, had created the opening for Satan's mischief. He had gamed me! One old hurt after another. My cooperation in recalling and feeling all those old events was his game's acceleration.

I could see what was happening. What a deceiver! As I thought through this, I allowed my creative juices to take over. I started to imagine something laughable. I envisioned my Camino day's experience in a wild way. Today I had become a contestant on the television show, *Jeopardy*. However, my imagined version of the game was a high-stakes competition for my soul. This was *Satan Jeopardy*!

Seeing it in this way made it possible for me to laugh at Satan's attempt to steal my joy. Here is how I saw it go: A category of old hurt would tempt me. I imagined myself falling for the temptation to relive events of that heartache. I'd say, "I'll take 'People Who Have Offended Me for $200.'" Offenses in my life of this kind would surface. Not long after exhausting my memory of all the pains in that category, I would be energized by emotions and the injustice involved. This enticed me to dwell on more and more pain and heartache. I would call for another category for $300, then $400, then $500.

Negativity incites a hunger for more negative thinking, more rehearsing of past hurts. Hurt upon hurt darkened my spirit within me when just that morning it had been bright and sunny.

Here's where my imagination went further. Other categories in Satan's game show would include:

* people who are arrogant and condescending toward me.
* old hurts and emotional scars.
* times someone stole or took credit for my ideas and benefited.
* loud, angry comments that disgraced me.
* times I was taken for granted.
* things I frequently worry about.

I played all the categories and raised the stakes with each replayed hurt. The emotion was so deep, so easy to relive. I was full-tilt into Satan's game. Crazy as it seemed, replaying the unjust, upsetting memories was hard to stop. The energy was dark and selfish, almost habit-forming. The more I dug into the details, the more hurt and negative emotion surfaced.

In hindsight, I recognized that nothing good came by reliving memories of old injustices. It only salted the wounds. The Deceiver stole my joy and re-broke my memories. And at what cost?

Wow! All for his stupid game, *Satan Jeopardy*!

I finally recognized where I had started this day and how my pure desires had drifted. I knew what I had to do. I asked forgiveness for my pride. I confessed my regret for even falling for the stupid game in the first place.

By God's grace and on this day, I beat Satan at his own game.

Our Camino

> "Be sober-minded, be watchful. Your adversary the devil prowls around like a roaring lion, seeking someone to devour."
> (1 Peter 5:8)

Satan Jeopardy! is real. The game is the product of my imagination, but Satan is real and his temptations put our souls in jeopardy. In John's gospel, Jesus calls Satan a "thief [who] comes only to steal and kill and destroy" (John 10:10). He tempted Jesus. Satan tempts us as well.

How does Satan manipulate us?

He lures.

He lies.

He disguises evil as good.

He promotes death.

He separates.

He divides.

He steals.

He works in darkness.

He destroys.

He shames.

He hates.

He deceives.

He wiles.

And he persists.

How can we avoid Satan's temptations?

Eleven Bare Truths about Temptation and How to Fight Them

1. *Temptation is a choice between sin and grace.* Temptation finds little resistance in a sinful soul. If we're not in a state of grace, we have to get there. How? We must face the truth of our sins and ask God's forgiveness. Confession leads to grace. The soul in the state of grace has greater power to fight temptation.

2. *Temptation is not a sin. Indulging the temptation is.* Temptations will bombard us at times, but we choose to sin or not sin. God gave us the gift of a free will. As we mature in faith, the greater expression of our love for Him is to surrender our will in order to follow His more perfect will for us. The tension is between what our will is and what God's will for us is. Sometimes it feels like a power struggle of the wills. However, the question for us isn't about willpower. The ultimate question is this: Whose will and whose power will we choose at the crossroads of sin and grace?

3. *Temptation is so tempting because it leads to the pleasure of sin.* Here's the tricky part. In most cases, pleasures in themselves are not sinful. We all have them. We also know the truth about who we are and our tendencies toward certain pleasures. It's the extremes, overindulgences, perversions, or godlike status we place on the pleasure that makes a pleasure sinful.

4. *Temptation slides us into sin; we don't fall.* Temptation comes in gentle persuasions and seemingly harmless invitations. Just a little won't hurt. But we all know it's never just a little. An unquenchable,

passionate obsession often starts with just a little. So what harm can just a little do? Any addict will tell us.

5. *Temptation is a test of our relationship with God.* How do we relate to God after temptation leads to sin? Is there remorse? Guilt? A desire to get right with Him again? Or is it business as usual? Do we believe we have no power to avoid temptation? That there's no use in trying not to sin? How we face temptation exposes what kind of relationship we want to have with God.

6. *Temptation grows stronger in wrong attitudes.* Our attitude might be inviting temptation. We use expressions like, "I can't help myself around sweets"; "I've always had a mouth on me and can't avoid using it"; or "I can't stop my thoughts when a pretty thing goes walking by." We sometimes invite even stronger temptation with attitudes like, "Well, that's how I'm wired; I've struggled with this my whole life." Even worse, at times we completely resign to a life of temptation with the falsehoods, "I ain't no saint, never will be," or sadder yet, "I'm not as bad as the next guy." Worse yet is the untruth, "That's just how God made me."

Really? God made us to sin? Think about that rationale for a minute.

We need to get real about our bad attitudes. They invite temptation without much resistance to sin. Is there anything in our attitudes that is holding the door open for the next temptation? We must close it.

7. *Temptation is Satan's game; don't toy with it.* Bishop Fulton Sheen, host of the famed 1950s television show *Life Is Worth Living*, said, "Temptation is not sin, but playing with temptation invites sin." At times we linger with a temptation, play with it, and entertain the possibility before plunging into the sin. What can we do instead? We can walk away. In some situations, it's even better if we run! Removing ourselves from temptation saves us from sin. We can run from Satan's game.

8. *Temptation thrives in our "bad neighborhoods."* We all have weakness in regard to temptations. Certain situations, places, even hanging around certain people can make it hard to resist the pleasure of sin when in such company. Those are the bad neighborhoods for us. An alcoholic knows better than to socialize in a tavern. Gluttons avoid buffet bars. Those trapped in lustful thoughts don't go to public beaches or community pools. Deep in our own truth, we know what our bad neighborhoods are. We just can't go there.

9. *Temptation withers through accountability.* We do this by finding an accountability partner, small group, or community who will help us fight through moments of temptation. They might share our same struggle or be someone we can call when tempted. Periodic check-ins during the week along with open and honest conversations about temptation battles help us win against urges. These are our good neighborhoods. Who wouldn't benefit from a good neighbor's voice when we're weak or needing affirmation to help us dodge temptation's storms? When we watch each other's backs, we watch temptation run.

10. *Temptation breeds in darkness.* We avoid the darkness of sin when we walk toward the light of Christ. Godly virtues lead us into His light. We must reflect upon what is true and what is noble, notice beauty in one another's goodness, and continually praise God for His blessings. When we develop these habits, virtues are born. Filling our mind with godly virtues provides a strong antidote for temptation's darkness. Let the apostle Paul's advice be our guide to grow us in virtue: "whatever is honorable, whatever is just, whatever is pure, whatever is lovely, whatever is commendable, if there is any excellence, if there is anything worthy of praise, think about these things" (Phil. 4:8).

11. *Temptation has no power in God's presence.* Scripture is God's truth, and living in truth is real power. Memorizing Scripture verses enables us to combat temptation. When Jesus was being tempted

in the desert, He fought Satan's lure by quoting Scripture: "It is written." Or even when we are in the heat of temptation we can pray just one word: "Jesus." It casts fear in Satan because "at the name of Jesus every knee should bow, in heaven and on earth and under the earth" (Phil 2:10).

*   *   *

Sometimes finding a way through temptation is like fighting our way through a forest fire. The blaze is all around us. It's fierce. It wants to consume us. My friend Paul is one who made it through the firestorms of life. He is a warrior who carries the scars of battles with Satan over addiction. Today he fights the good fight for the One who never left him and who walked with him through his own personal hell. This is Paul's faith walk story.

Hello, I'm Paul, and I'm an alcoholic.

It was hell on earth that I suffered. It had nothing to do with parental neglect or abuse, a trauma suffered, nor anything else. I didn't need to escape from some life hardship. I was the one who made the choices. But God used those choices to break me and then, praise Him, remake me.

My faith walk started in a good home. My parents were good people—Dad, a blue collar guy; Mom, a gentle, compassionate stay-at-homer. They cared for me and my sister and brother.

Many family parties were held at our home. Neither of my parents were big drinkers, but all the adults drank. Nothing crazy happened when they got together. I had always thought it was just normal, until I witnessed something that stole my curiosity and piqued an interest that has lasted my whole life.

I was about eight years old at the time. I had fallen asleep on the couch in our finished basement where the bar was. I could hear everyone upstairs talking and carrying on. Out of the corner of my eye I caught my aunt. She was sneaking around the bar drinking all the half-finished cocktails left behind—lots of them. My childhood inquisitiveness set in. *Why is she doing that? That's gross! How can that be fun?*

I indulged my curiosity at age thirteen by sneaking booze from my parents' liquor cabinet for my friends and me. We'd drink it then sneak into a local school dance. At that time, I discovered something better than the buzz I got from alcohol in this mischief. Others saw me as cool. Not only could I get drunk, but I was recognized for being a "bad boy." This added to my reputation. Being an athlete, a star baseball catcher, gave me status and admiration from my peers. Yeah, I was cool—a drinker and a bad boy. I was desired by girls and admired by guys.

By high school, my esteem grew. My baseball skills were impressive. I was recognized as an All-Star, All-State, All-Conference. My athletic physique, popularity, and baseball skills drew attention. Girls hung on me and even tough guys looked up to me. Liquid courage, booze, released my swagger. I liked being cool and drinking made it possible. It wasn't long before smoking marijuana strengthened the buzz, highlighted the daring bad-boy image, and spotlighted how cool I was.

I went on to a local college on a baseball scholarship. I was free now without my parents' watchful eye. I lived drunk, high, and lost in women. College life lasted one year. I moved back home and found a job as an apprentice machinist. I went to school during the day and worked third shift (evenings). The same mischief followed me after hours with work friends.

I met a gal who worked near my shop, fell in love, and married. I was making good money and had a home built. We had three great kids I'd do anything for. I was an all-in kind of dad.

Sporting events, travel hockey, school events—I was there. But the same pattern of mischief followed me to neighborhood life. I lived it up, party after party with couples and friends at each other's homes. I wanted it all. I'd do the work thing and the dad thing. But the thing I really wanted was to just get drunk, high, and do whatever sexy thing came along. Infidelity was an exciting added mischief, and I welcomed it.

This went on for years before a hard truth struck me. *I was sick and tired of being sick and tired.* I was lost in a lifestyle I didn't want anymore. I still don't know where that thought came from. My whole life I had always done what made me feel good. I snuck, hid, and lied my way into whatever I wanted. I couldn't figure out these new ideas. *Why wouldn't I want this lifestyle anymore?*

Coincidentally, another thought had gotten hold of me, an insight I had never had before. *I didn't like who I was. I didn't like me.* These thoughts became turning points in my battle with alcoholism. I wanted to stop. I didn't want alcohol to control me. I'd promise myself to go through the day sober. But by late afternoon, I couldn't stop myself. I was sooo good at hiding it and sneaking around for drinks. I was at war with this demon, but losing every battle.

I remember a time shortly after this self-discovery, I borrowed a friend's truck to buy building supplies at Home Depot. I couldn't resist stopping at a local tavern for a few. I was there hours later. Driving home, I ran a red light and was arrested. I spent the night in jail and was released the next morning. Even with the huge expenses of a DUI (driving under the influence) charge, I laughed as I walked out of the jail, finished the joint I had started the night before, and drove my friend's truck back to him.

So much for wanting to stop. The truth was that it was all about me. Always was.

A tug-of-war wrestled within me. I wanted to quit, but couldn't. I had spent years sneaking around to chug a little liquid courage before anything I needed to do. I needed harder and harder alcohol to make it. Everything revolved around it. Every temptation under the sun screamed for my attention. I couldn't stop. I couldn't.

I finally did the first courageous thing in my life. I checked into an outpatient treatment center. I learned about alcoholism, became accountable for the truth of my actions, and had a hard look at all my lies and deceptions. I saw me, and I didn't like it.

This started a lifetime of AA (Alcoholic Anonymous) meetings. For the first time, I was feeling what clean and sober meant. But it was too late for my marriage. Too many bad memories and unmet expectations dissolved the love we once had. She wanted out, and I was good with that.

The next couple of bachelor years brought me a freedom I had never experienced before. I was committed to the twelve-step program, and I was living it. For the first time in my life, I felt in control. I was doing life driven by my higher power.

My sober and confident lifestyle caught the eye of a beautiful woman who took an interest in me, adored my kids, and was willing to be in a committed relationship with me. It was irresistible. I moved in with her and entered her lifestyle, family and all. As nice as she was, I couldn't adjust to her demands and the control she exercised on my life, thoughts, and choices. Not that her ideas were bad, I just couldn't be me anymore. Our relationship was unhealthy, and I couldn't find the key to unlock how trapped I felt.

I fought back the only way I could. I slipped into old mischief. I began to sneak drinks and hide my buzz really well. Liquid courage gave me the false confidence to face the next anxious moment. Going to AA meetings went by the wayside as my old demon slithered back.

My art of hiding a quick drink failed on a Father's Day celebration. It was so much pressure with everyone drinking around me. I still felt strangled trying to perform up to my girlfriend's standards. I slipped back into a quick drink here, another, and another. This, along with a Valium I found, caused me to pass out. An ambulance took me to the emergency room where I was admitted. I regained consciousness in a hospital room. I sank to a new low of shame and guilt. I was toying with temptation, and I'd lost all I had fought for and won the past few years.

I returned to living with her again. I wanted to stay clean and sober. I worked crazy hard to regain her trust. My fall from sobriety meant demands and suspicion of my every action haunted me. Stress and pressure are devastating to an alcoholic's perseverance.

To prove my desire to make the relationship work, I chose a desperate plan. We were sharing an extra vehicle she owned, so I sold my car and used the cash to fund a Florida vacation with her and her adult daughter and boyfriend. My intention was, "Let's take time to relax, to enjoy each other, to make some good memories."

Shortly after arriving at the Daytona resort, the three started making expensive plans for the vacation. None of my wishes fit their liking. I felt disrespected, trapped, and lost again. While on the beach, I was asked to cater drinks to all three of them. This was my opportunity. I snuck one after another.

They never saw me drink, but my stumbles and slurred speech gave me away. I went back to the room and passed out, sound asleep. I awoke to find all my bags packed, my cash gone, and instructions to leave on a different flight.

I hated myself for what I'd done, for my disease, and how I'd cast away everything I learned in AA. I couldn't find a flight for a couple days. *Where was I to go? Where was I to sleep? Eat?* My shame was compounded by having to sleep on the beach a couple nights and pretending to be a guest at different hotels to shower and get by. My anguish cut deep as I caught sight of the three walking past me in the lobby, flint-jawed and angry. My dignity was gone. So much for being the cool guy. I felt like such a loser. A total loser.

I came home penniless, no vehicle, and homeless. My sister and brother fronted money for a few days at an extended-stay Holiday Inn. I was living in a snake pit of shame, replaying my mistake over and over again. I couldn't deny that I caused this all myself.

I didn't know what to do. I was on my last lifeline.

I called a friend—a believer. Within the next hour, my life was about to take a radical turn. My friend, his wife, and adult daughter invited me to live in their finished basement. He shared Scripture with me, was a consoling friend, and gave me back my dignity. He gave me a Bible, taught me how to read it, and gave me a basic lesson on who God was. I always knew there was a God, but I really didn't know Him in a personal way. Now I wanted to learn anything and everything about who Jesus is.

This friend and I prayed together and looked for new hope. The unconditional love I felt from this family was a love I never felt before from anyone. I had spent a lifetime experiencing, "I love you, if . . ." No one ever showed me, especially in my ugly sinfulness, "I love you, period. No conditions, no expectations, no demands. Just, I love you."

This friend took me to the door of faith.

However, I was the one who had to choose to knock on the door.

I'll never forget the night God became real to me. I was a baby Christian listening to a Christian radio broadcast. I could have sworn the message was about my sorry life, my failures, my sins. It got to me. There could be no more sneaking, no more hiding, and no more deception. I couldn't run from God anymore.

I phoned the show's helpline. A chaplain, a church counselor of sorts, took my call. I shared my story, all of it: the shame, the heartache, my failures. Then I did something I never did before—I agreed to get on my knees, right there on that basement floor. I begged Jesus into my life, not just as Savior but as Leader. I wanted Him to guide me. I surrendered my life to Him.

In the days following, I found a trail through the blazing inferno of my life and the ashes I left behind. By God's mercy, I moved out, got a car, and started rebuilding a new life. Today, I finally know how temptation gets me and I live a truth I learned in AA, "You only keep what you give back." So I sponsor struggling alcoholics and drive them to church and to meetings. I avoid temptation by volunteering at church. I fill lonely moments with Christian talk radio and music. I surround myself with good things. And I'm free. Free of all that nonsense.

I know now whose I am. I belong to Jesus, and I hear His voice over that old temptation telling me, "I love you, Paulie." There are no "ifs" or "only when" conditions to His love. Jesus loves me; that's the only buzz I need.

Yeah, my life is different. No, crazy better. In fact, new—
brand new.

"Hello, I'm Paul, and I'm a loved sinner."

But the Lord says, "Do not cling to events of the past or dwell on what
happened long ago. Watch for the new thing I am going to do. It is happening already—you can see it now! I will make a road through the wil-
derness and give you streams of water there" (see Isaiah 43:18–19).

*   *   *

Mercy? Misericordia? What's the difference? Read ahead and you will
feel the Spanish expression of the word in the life stories of those who
were lifted out of their misery by God's grace.

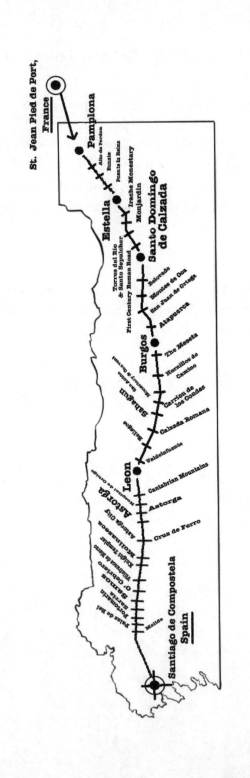

Chapter 18

MISERICORDIA

"God whispers to us in our pleasures, speaks in our conscience, but shouts in our pains: it is His megaphone to rouse a deaf world."

C.S. Lewis

The Camino

The journey from Samos to Melide covers seventy-seven kilometers (nearly forty-eight miles). It traverses interesting stops in Sarria, Alto Momientos, Portomarin, and Palas de Rei before arriving at delightful Melide.

The trail here is nothing short of enchanting. The pilgrim is sandwiched between a steady tree line and stone walls holding back antiquated farms and tiny hamlets. It follows large limestone stepping-stones and narrow foot bridges over gentle pools. Taking photos of babbling brooks and small waterfalls is irresistible. Some stretches skirt narrow streams hovered over by immense tree cover. If nature could embrace the soul, it would be here.

Further along, the undulating trail provides intermittent views of pasture, farms, and captivating little villages. The pilgrim shares the trail with farmers escorting milk cows—a déjà vu of farming methods hundreds of years old. While this is delightful, it brings with it the challenge of hop-skipping along the trail over manure plops!

A winding section cuts through a forest of chestnut trees that are easily a meter (three feet) in diameter. Knurly knots and the corkscrew twists of their bark are unique. Most of these trees are centuries old and completely cover the trail with the chestnuts they shed in fall.

Sarria

Sarria's popularity soars because of its geographic position on el Camino de Santiago. Why? Walking from Sarria to Santiago, the one hundred kilometers (sixty miles) officially qualifies one as a pilgrim on el Camino de Santiago. This respectable option shortens the Camino walking distance and time needed to reach Santiago, but still earns them the Compostela—the official certificate earned only by those pilgrims who walk the minimum one hundred kilometers.

The city itself pulses with energy. A flood of pilgrims enter Sarria, all eager to begin their Camino on fresh legs. New pilgrims from all over the world hold an excited, respectful eagerness to connect with seasoned pilgrims for advice.

Numerous outdoor restaurants, all excellent, crowd the Camino here. A narrow stretch of trail along the twelfth-century church of San Salvador and the remnant tower of the fourteenth-century Castle of Sarria inspire reflection on what life was like centuries ago in this historically and culturally rich city.

Portomarìn

Arriving at Portomarìn is no simple walk. Alto Momientos challenges the day's twenty-two-kilometer (roughly 13.5-mile) journey from Sarria. It requires a two-hundred-meter (650-foot) ascent over sixteen kilometers (ten miles). Not bad for a Camino morning. The toughest part is the descent of three hundred meters (nearly a thousand feet) over six kilometers (just under four miles). Toes bang the front of boots and knees jolt painfully.

Shortly after the difficult descent into town one more daunting challenge awaits: a long, stone staircase of nearly one hundred steps. Here is where the town's fascination rewards.

During medieval days there was a Roman bridge and town along the river. In 1962, the town decided to dam the river, creating a large reservoir. In preparation, historical buildings were dismantled piece by piece, salvaged, and reconstructed on the high riverbank immediately above the old town. However, some ancient buildings had to be abandoned, and succumbed to the new water reservoir. What treasures might be buried below?

From this precipice, forests and farms stretch out in a commanding panorama of the surrounding countryside. So rewarding!

Palas de Rei

Traveling to Palas de Rei, the pilgrim passes delightful little outdoor cafes and ancient churches. One in particular is worth a pause. Near the tiny village of Eixere is a small thirteenth-century chapel, built by the famed Knights Templar. It is a hand-hewn stone structure, the size of one large room. Medieval sacred art adorns the limestone walls. It is serviced by a man of the present-day Order of the Knights Templar, a claim validated by a photo of him in Templar garb. He stands prepared to collect a donation in exchange for a pilgrim credential stamp.

Pilgrim after pilgrim stream from the small church staring at their credential. To their shock, the stamp largely misses its mark, falling on other well-placed, artistically designed stamps collected miles and miles ago. By the sound of the stamp alone, the Templar sought to correct his misguided stamp by making multiple attempts anywhere his hand would fall. This spoils the overall appearance of the pilgrims'credential, once a fond artifact of their Camino.

Disappointing? Yes.

Unforgiveable? No.

The man is blind. What is endearing is the man's reverence for pilgrims. The tone of his voice is gentle, yet certain and reassuring. He seeks to help, or get someone to help with a pilgrim's problem. No wonder—he is one of the noble Knights Templar dedicating his life to God in service to pilgrims.

As one disgruntled pilgrim after another streamed from the chapel in front of me, I was the next pilgrim awaiting an encounter with the Templar. I engaged a friendly conversation with him. His gentleness and humility were tangible and had a deep impression on my heart. While preparing to add a stamp to my credential, I placed my hand gently on the Templar's to guide his stamp to its correct spot. The gesture was respectful and kind. The faithful Templar servant responded in a touching way and accepted the help in a spirit of humility and gratitude. Neither the Templar nor I could find words to speak.

The heart sees what the eyes cannot.

Melide[63]

The city holds a long place in history. Inhabitants date back to the Neolithic Era—the New Stone Age when stone tools, weaving baskets, and pottery were prevalent. Melide's popularity launched in the tenth century with the arrival of pilgrims from two Camino trails converging in the town—Camino Primitivo (the ancient, original trail) and Camino Frances (the popular trail taken by most pilgrims).

Melide boasts of a courageous historical moment during the nineteenth-century War for Independence with the invasion of Napoleon's troops. Few soldiers had weapons, but locals joined the fight alongside armed soldiers. Surprisingly, they carried only long sticks that appeared as weapons. This presented a false show of force against the enemy. Their bravery paid off. Napoleon's troops retreated.

Melide is well-experienced and equipped to serve the ailing pilgrim, both body and soul. Clinics offer medical advice for leg and foot pains. The fourteenth-century church of Sancti Spiritus holds magnificent sacred art and hosts a well-attended daily Pilgrim Mass.

My Camino

"We may feel like failures and wonder why God allows suffering. But as time passes we learn to look back and see how He worked things for good and how every trial drove us closer to Him."

Dr. David Jeremiah

A 790-kilometer walking pilgrimage will not escape some pain, blisters, or tendinitis. I had anticipated these and nursed them since Samos.

I could not deny the pain screaming for attention. My feet were crabby companions with their sharp, stabbing ache. Well-developed bulbous blisters, which had formed a week prior, were now stinging and throbbing. Each barked its tenderness with every step.

Upon closer examination, I suffered from blood-filled blisters on the tops of both middle toes and fluid-filled blisters on the seven other toes. *Praise God, one toe was spared!* Even the puncture and drain blister treatment provided little pain relief. I was shocked to see that two new blisters had even grown atop unhealed blisters. Yes, there were blisters on top of blisters! Adding to the painful ordeal was a pronounced and agonizing injury—an inflammation on the ball of my left foot, immediately behind my toes. Other ailments added to my pain parade including tendinitis in my knee and raging athlete's foot with its burning and itching. Then there was the onset of a chest cold with a hacking, productive cough. Making matters even worse, a surprising stabbing pain found a spot between my shoulder blades. It was muscle strain caused by carrying my overweight backpack all this distance. The decision to take that three-pound laptop plagued me here again. Ugh!

I was consumed with indecision. *Do I tough it out and hobble my way the last fifty-seven kilometers* (thirty-five miles) *to Santiago? It's only three more days. Can I make it three more days? Can I even walk that far? Or walk at all?*

My body and heart argued. First my body: *Listen to your pain. Stop!* Then my heart: *Don't quit! Be strong!* My dream had always been to walk the entire distance right up to the Cathedral of Santiago. This was my passion, and it was challenged by my fear of physically failing. *Could I do it?*

Gratefully, Melide had answers. This town has a respected clinic where my foot issues could be examined. If the news was grim, a bus stop across from my albergue could take me to Santiago. If I pushed forward from Melide and pain arrested my Camino mid-trail, I'd be stuck. *What could I do? Could anyone help me?*

I hobbled my way to the clinic. Each step was a piercing knife pain in the ball of my foot. I cried "ouch, Ouch, OUCH!" with each step. The clinician examined my foot, shook her head, and said apologetically, "I am sorry. Your Camino is *fin*" (Spanish for "ended"). She well knew how devastating such news can be to a pilgrim. It certainly tore my heart out. I was three days away. Just three! Because she could see the agony in my every step, she walked to a counter, and returned with a thick gel cushion for the ball of the foot. Wearing it reduced the sharp contact of the footstep, bringing comfort. I asked her to examine some medication I was carrying but hadn't taken for fear of possible side effects. She added, "These are a strong anti-inflammatory medicine with painkiller. They must be taken with food." Her face shed a new confidence. "They will help!"

"Gracias. Muchas gracias," I replied. I strained to my feet and hobbled toward the door. I felt sad but relieved by the trustworthy guidance. I hadn't taken a second step out of the clinic when the clinician caught me. "*Una momento*." Her face held compassionate understanding. "Sir, take the medicine, rest your foot, and see how it feels tomorrow. You might find enough improvement to be able to walk your Camino again, but very carefully. OK?"

Her voice reached my ears like a drop of honey to my lips. Hope. My Camino was in God's hands.

I left the clinic and gingerly hobbled to the nearby Sanctus Spiritus Church. To onlookers, I must have resembled a barefoot, burning-coal walker. "Oooh, ow ow ow!" I pain-danced my way, arriving for mass only a few minutes late. This was the place I needed to be—on my knees and begging direction.

Lord. What should I do? Should I take the bus and be safe? Do I remain in this little haven close to the clinic? Or do I try to walk a shorter distance at a slower pace? What if I do more of the Camino and the pain gets too intense? What if it gets so bad I can't go on at all? I only knew one thing: I was in misery.

Drifting into my evening prayer was this Scripture: "But he said to me, 'My grace is sufficient for you, for my power is made perfect in weakness.' Therefore I willingly boast of my weaknesses, so that the power of Christ may rest upon me" (2 Cor. 12:9).

Boast of weakness?

I just sat there after mass and prayed a desperate man's prayer. "I am weak, Lord, and I need you. You know my heart, and You well know how badly I want to finish this Camino. I am just three days, just three single days away. But I surrender it. I give the Camino back to you." I resigned to a fact: tomorrow I would leave for Santiago on foot or by bus. Those were my only choices.

Back in the albergue, I took the meds, and slipped into my bunk. That night I fell into the sleep of the dead. My body was spent.

The morning held a great surprise. Unthinkingly, I stepped out of bed to gather my belongings and repack my bag. I'd been standing for a while when it dawned on me: my foot pain was less—far less! It was now a two or three on the pain scale, a great improvement from the eight or nine the night before. I tested it. It was way better!

I walked around the halls. I stood on the foot with more weight and discovered I could walk with minor pain and only a little sensitivity.

A humbling truth awoke. _This was God's mercy._

I geared up and delicately slid back in my boots. Another test. _Yes!_ My foot was tender, but manageable. Hope sunrised in me, and His grace was present from my soles up. Out from that albergue, I took one step of faith after another. I was walking, but couldn't understand how it was possible, considering what I had felt the day before.

Hours and distance on the trail washed up questions. *What is happening? How can this possibly happen? And why should it happen for me? Where might the pain erupt again? And when?*

The answers didn't matter. But I did know this: this was my own "walking miracle."

God was powerfully present on my Camino. He walked with me, showing His presence over and over.

Later, I stopped at a little roadside cafe for lunch and to air out my badly injured feet. I selected a table just a few meters (about ten feet) from the trail. Here I watched pilgrim after pilgrim trudge through the gooey mud, dodging large stones and the eroded gully in the center of the trail.

A bright, tangerine-colored, three-wheeled cart rolled on the Camino before me, carrying a young adult male. He was every bit of sixty-eight kilograms (150 pounds). It was clear that he was paralyzed and struggling with other severe special needs. A man strained forward with a grasp on the front wheel handles. Two other men plowed in sync, one on each rear wheel handle. All three grunted ahead step after step, escorted by two women saddled under heavy backpacks with supplies.

I gaped at them, along with every other pilgrim on the road. *How could these five manage this? They were obviously middle-aged. Perhaps over sixty years! How?* The "why" was clear: to fulfill the wish of the paralyzed young man. What a life joy for him to witness the Camino trail—its beauty, its peace—and to be carried by those who undeniably loved him!

This was obviously a calling from God. No one would choose to strap human deadweight in a cart to walk a trail that holds risk for even the sure-footed pilgrim. No, the grit and determined look on the faces of these men and women left no room for misunderstanding. It was a labor of love so powerful that it will be forever branded in my memory. I stared as they struggled, wove, and slid their way through the muck.

Was it difficult? Fraught with potential injury? Miserably painful? Laborious?

Undeniably so. These people were on a mission to demonstrate Christ-like love: mercy.

I knew the Spanish root of the word "mercy" is *misericordia*. *Miseri* translates to "misery," the *cor* meaning "with," and *dia* meaning "God." *Misery with God*. That is, God enters into our misery and is present to us in it. The Divine is with me in my misery; the Divine is with all of us in our misery. Whatever heartache, pain, suffering, misery—God is there.

My imagination painted the gospel image of the four friends who lowered the paralyzed man through the roof to bring him to Jesus. I recalled how well the Scriptures described what happened between Jesus and the paralytic. I could imagine their faces. However, I never gave the four carriers in the gospel narrative any thought until this day.

Today, along with a few privileged pilgrims, I saw a reenactment of those four friends mentioned in the gospel. Instead of a man on a litter, it was a young man on a brilliant tangerine-colored, three-wheeled cart. Instead of a roof break-in, it was a muddy trek on the Camino.

Both held something eerily similar in my reflection: the loving expression on the faces of those who carry a man's misery. In studying these faces I saw mercy in action.

Misericordia. Misery with God present.

My ugly foot pain bore out a testimony of God with me in my misery. But I was awakened to another comforting thought. In countless ways, God has sent compassionate souls to carry me through my suffering. As I recall their faces, I see His. This humbles me.

Oh that some soul in misery may look into my face and see God's embrace!

"I don't think of all the misery, but of the beauty that still remains. . . . My advice is: Go outside, to the fields, enjoy nature and the sunshine, go and try to recapture happiness in yourself and in God. Think of all the beauty that's still left in and around you and be happy!"

Anne Frank

Our Camino

"Strength is born in the deep silence of long-suffering hearts; not amidst joy."

Felicia Hemans

Misericordia. Misery with God. His mercy.

My childhood story, "The Egg Money," illustrates the word for our Camino.

We lived in Brookfield, Illinois, a suburb of Chicago, in an old, two-story bungalow. These homes, constructed in the early 1900s, were built like Gibraltar. However, a half-century later, things were beginning to fall apart. On this late winter day, after days and days of heavy rain, a crisis surprised us in our own little bungalow.

My dad, mom, two younger sisters, and I, about age seven, awoke to a gagging stench. It drifted up through the floor, even reaching our second-floor bedrooms. Still in our pajamas, Dad led our way to the basement with my five-year-old sister and my baby sister slung on Mom's hip.

Perched on the bottom step of the staircase leading into the basement, we all stood before the shocking truth: a sewer backup. The five of us fought back vomit from the horrific, foul stench. The basement floor was under two inches of raw sewage, toilet tissue, and other debris. Disgusting! We kids were scared by a sight we knew nothing about, except that something bad had just happened. I was old enough to understand the look Mom and Dad had. They were scared.

We all returned upstairs and changed clothes while Dad got into old shoes and work clothes. I vividly recall Mom opening all the windows despite cold late winter temperatures to release the reeking odor, hoping ventilation would make it bearable.

Little boys cannot resist big events: fire trucks passing, the garbage truck in the alley, mail delivery, huge planes overhead. Today was no different for me. The basement stink could not keep me from stealing a glimpse of Dad wading through all the yuck, opening a floor drain, and shoving a garden hose into the hole in the floor. Hours later, nothing got better.

I heard Dad tell Mom about a guy he worked with who did plumbing on the side. He explained that he needed a sewer rodder and this man would have one. I sensed something even more serious on their faces when they discussed how they'd pay him for the service call.

Dad got on the black rotary-dial phone and called his coworker. He came right over. I stole peeks as the two men sloshed through "the stuff" while running a long steel cable through the floor drain. Both pushed, then pulled back, pushed the cable back in and out, over and over again. They strained together, sweated, gagged, and swore through the ugly task until a gush sound came. It worked! They were happy, so I guessed we could all be happy.

The two then began the gruesome job of clean-up. They used brooms to push everything to the floor drain. It worked. Soon they were using a garden hose to wash the residue from the walls and floor.

Dad kicked off his shoes and went back up to talk to Mom. He kept asking, "How we gonna pay him?" The conversation looked and sounded kind of scary. Their faces were tense. I didn't understand it. Then one said something I knew was serious.

"The egg money." In those days, Mom and Dad did not use a check-book. They cashed Dad's factory work check, which was not much. The cash paid for things: utilities, mortgage, and gasoline. Then they held back cash for groceries—*the egg money*. This cash was stored on a shelf in a far kitchen cabinet.

Dad took what was there and headed back to the basement.

I followed surreptitiously behind. Mom and my sisters were soon looking on as well. Dad thanked his plumber friend, pulled the egg money from his front pocket. He extended it to the man.

The man looked at the money, looked into my dad's face, then to Mom and us kids. Silence, a long silence followed. The plumber's eyes kept shifting from my dad's face to the money and back again toward Mom and us kids.

"Naw, Ray. No money. I was glad to help."

Mom started to cry and the girls shouted, "Why are you crying, Mommy?" I didn't understand it all, but I sensed something important was happening. Dad choked up a little, thanked him, and slid the cash back in his front right pocket. Yeah, the egg money.

Memories fade with time. But this one is seared in my mind, more than sixty years later. I can still see, feel, and recall the smell of our sewer-backup misery. But more than that, Dad's plumber friend was with us in our misery. *Or was he Jesus in disguise?*

"With" is a powerhouse word. It adds depth to our faith. It's a relational word: God in company with us. "With" is a commitment word: God committed to us. "With" is an affirmation word: God supports and encourages us.

"Misery" is a word that conjures up powerfully emotional experiences. Our Camino can't escape them—grief of the death of a loved one, the trap of addiction, financial crisis, abuse, serious life-threatening disease, loneliness, painful relationships, and depression. Heavy storms come and before long, all the misery in our lives eventually clogs the pipes and backs up, causing us misery.

We need only ask for misericordia. He will be with us in our misery! Not from a distance either. God kneels down and lifts us up out of the dirty, the scary, the painful, and even the stink our Camino may wander into.

He might come disguised like Dad's plumber friend, as a pusher of a cart holding a paralytic, a clinician helping weary pilgrims, or just maybe in a Godcidence as a friend able to help us during a desperate moment.

Misericordia will not cost you the egg money. On the contrary, it costs you nothing. Misericordia is free, and freeing.

*   *   *

Can an eighteen-month-old experience misericordia? Little Clara's faith walk will convict us to have faith for our Camino.

> "Don't mistake God's patience for His absence. His timing is perfect and His presence is constant. He is always there with you."

> Unknown

Clara's serious faith walk started at conception. Captured in an ultrasound was a rare birth defect. Only one in 44,000 children are afflicted. It was an extra sack containing miscellaneous bone and mass. The extra "baggage" was attached to her tailbone, weighing a couple pounds and the size of a large softball. The mass was huge, considering that Clara was only a little more than twice that weight. She was born Caesarian section. Shortly afterward, the foreign body was surgically removed. No trace of cancer was detected. Praise God!

Roughly sixteen months later, something alarming was discovered. Doctors did an alpha fetoprotein (AFP) scan of her blood. An AFP level of more than ten indicates active tumors are present. Clara's AFP was ten thousand. Further tests revealed scarier news. "Clara has cancer growing aggressively from her tailbone and it has spread to several of her organs." It was traumatizing news.

A course of chemotherapy was charted and this precious little babe was on her way through misery. She lost weight, her hair, and her strength. Hopes were high that the treatment would reduce the size and number of tumors to a point where they could be surgically removed.

If the news wasn't devastating enough for her family, the photos of her during treatment tore everyone's heart out. At seeing her bald, emaciated, head-drooped, and pained face, one could not hold back tears. These photos were sent along with a call to prayer warriors. We pleaded healing and mercy on precious little Clara, and wisdom for her doctors. Little Clara's medical predicament made it to hundreds of emails. Some went as far as South Africa, places in Europe, and Australia to powerful prayer warriors I had met on the Camino. The greatest force was from family and friends at home. We shared the story with them; they shared it with their churches and faith groups who, in turn, sent it their prayer networks. Without exaggeration, a battalion of thousands of mighty prayer warriors were on their knees for sweet Clara.

Over the course of weeks of chemo, the tumors did reduce in number and size. A day before the surgery was to take place, tumor scans showed surgeons where to find the last remnants of the cancer.

The night before the surgery, heaven must have thundered with prayers for God to guide the surgeon's hands in the removal of the last tumors. Testimony after testimony came of people praying their hearts out, fasting, and pleading with Mighty God to spare the life of this little lamb. As the surgery day progressed, prayers continued while a drama was building. Then the news arrived.

The surgeons had made their incision across Clara's abdomen, believing they were at the precise location of the cancer cells. They were utterly bewildered. There were no active tumors. Clara was stitched up and led to recovery.

There are no words to capture the joy in the battalions of pray-ers in hearing this news. It was the combined euphoria of winning the Super Bowl, the World Series, and The World Cup. God be praised! God be praised! Our good God, be praised!

Some might claim coincidence. Some might find fault in the doctor's diagnosis long before the surgery. Some might even be angry that Clara underwent unnecessary surgery. This is speculation that could continue for a lifetime. Here is what is known: Clara had cancer, thousands of people prayed, and then Clara did not have cancer.

For the faithful, it was a display of misericordia. God with Clara. God with family in tense desperation. God with those devoted pray-ers. Those of faith believe it was a miracle; God's sweet voice saying, "Be healed."

God was with Clara. And He was with all her desperate pray-ers. In the misery of knowing and not knowing, life or death, God was with us.

Misericordia is power. We need only call upon Him.

*　　*　　*

Pilgrims rejoice, cry, and stare dumbstruck at first sight of the Cathedral of St. James. The same was true for me. By the time I reached the Camino Pilgrim Office, God surprised me with a profound insight on how my Camino was to end. Read the next chapter, and share my blessing.

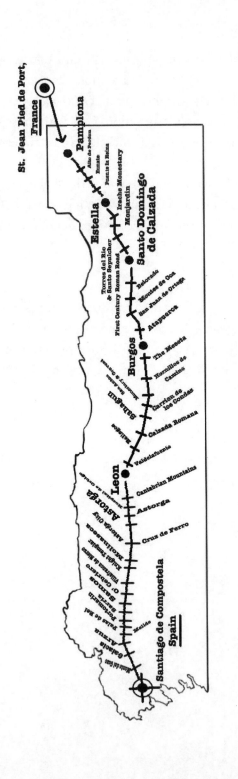

Chapter 19

AD MAJOREM DEI GLORIAM

"A sacrifice to be real must cost, must hurt, and must empty ourselves. Give yourself fully to God. He will use you to accomplish great things on condition that you believe more in His love than in your weakness."

St. Mother Theresa of Calcutta

The Camino

Unbridled anticipation courses through every fiber within the pilgrims during their final days before arriving in Santiago. From Melide to Santiago, the last fifty-seven kilometers (thirty-five miles) pass through a graced natural landscape. Arzùa is the last large town before Santiago, then the province Galicia, Moto Gozo, and finally, the Camino's climax, Santiago.

Arzùa

First impression of Arzùa is that it is just another busy city with kilometer after kilometer of commercial storefronts. But further in and nestled amongst several well-kept albergues is the Fountain Plaza de Arzùa. This fountain is situated within Arzùa's historical center alongside the Church of St. James. A canopy of severely pruned sycamore trees provides welcome shade and escape from the harsh sunlight. The pruning encourages horizontal growth outward while eliminating tree growth upward. It's a perfect oasis for pilgrims to refresh themselves with cool beverages, *pulpo* (octopus), and a platter of the town's favorite cheeses.

The town has widespread fame for its cheeses and its popular annual event: The Festival of Cheese.

Galacia

This famed province stretches from Leòn on the east, the Atlantic Ocean on the north and west, and Portugal to the south. Galacia has strong historical ties to the ancient Celts, the Druids,[64] who lived there. It also marked the Roman Empire's western frontier as far back as 137 BC. In the central section of the province, quaint farms and pastures make these last stretches on the Camino nothing short of enchanting.

The Galacian forest, with its ancient oaks and eucalyptus trees, tower like bark-covered sentinels twenty to thirty meters (sixty-five to one hundred feet) high. The trail is heavily shadowed in places but blue sky can be glimpsed high above through the patchwork blanket of leafy greenery overhead. Sudden winds gust overhead and stir the leaves, creating a mesmerizing, rattling sound of thousands of baby rattles.

Tucked in nature's niches below are small streams and gentle waterfalls. Intriguing little pools collect right alongside the trail and infuse peace in the body, mind, and spirit of the pilgrim in preparation for entry into Santiago.

Monte del Gozo

The last twenty kilometers (roughly 12.5 miles) drums a call to quicken the walking pace—faster—stronger. However, Monte del Gozo, the "Mountain of Joy," is worth a pause before finally walking into Santiago.

The pilgrim crests the hill to see the modern imposingly designed Monte do Gozo, the Monument of Joy. It was built to honor a visit by

Pope John Paul II in 1989 for World Youth Day Mass. Twenty years later, singer-songwriter Bruce Springsteen performed a concert on this hill. What a contrast to traditional Camino experiences!

Within a short distance is the inspiring Monte do Gozo Monument of Pilgrims. A statue of two pilgrims in ancient traditional garb hold their walking sticks with a water gourd hanging at the top. They stand roughly 3.5 meters (twelve feet) tall and are cast in bronze, now aged to a blue and charcoal-grey color. Each strain to view the cathedral towers located nearby in the flatland below.

At the Monument of Pilgrims, the ancient city of Santiago is visible for the first time. Pilgrims' reaction is uncontainable joy, thereby giving the name "Mountain of Joy." Some pilgrims choose to follow a long-standing tradition: they cast off their shoes to walk the final five kilometers (three miles) barefoot. This act of sacrifice expresses gratitude to God as they approach the end of their long pilgrimage.

Santiago

The Cathedral of Santiago[65] honors the name of this apostle of Christ, as well as his remains. The earliest beginnings of the city are marked with the discovery of St. James's grave nearby during the early ninth century. The coffin was kept in a small chapel until the construction of the cathedral began in 1075. As a frame of reference to world history, this was just twenty short years before the first Crusade would begin. The exterior stone facade of this holy place displays carvings of significant characters from the Bible.

The architectural design and structure is in the shape of a Christian cross.[66] The main entrance to the cathedral is located at the foot of this cross. From here, a long aisle, lined with pews, stretches to where the cross's two arms intersect. An aisle crosses from right to left with pews on each side. At this intersection, the main sanctuary and altar are located. Immediately behind the sanctuary and altar is where the burial crypt and relics reside.

The interior of this holy place is magnificent! One can only marvel at its immense hand-hewn stone construction, limestone pillars the size of cypress trees, and the towering arched ceilings stretching twenty-two meters (seventy-two feet) in height. Ancient artifacts and statues of saints line the walls. Down the center aisle are rows of finely crafted confessionals, with just enough space inside for a priest and his kneeling penitent. Pilgrims flock to these in order to rid themselves of the last vestiges of soul burdens before mass begins. Two hundred pipes from one of Europe's largest pipe organs arouse the pilgrims' hearts with joy. Pristine and professionally trained vocals soar above the melody. Pilgrims agree that this is far beyond good church music; this is what one imagines heaven's majestic music and choirs to be. The whole ambience within the cathedral is soul-invigorating!

Just inside the main entrance, pilgrims, weary and emotional after their month-long painful pilgrimage, have their first touch of something holy at their Camino's destination. It is the central marble column called the Portico de Gloria, the doorway to Christ's glory. Inspired by Scripture's tree of Jesse, it depicts Jesus in His glory at the top, His apostles beside, and the apostle James beneath. Some crawl into the church on their knees, others bend over in prayerful humility, all in fervent respect for what the Portico de Gloria[67] represents. After tearful prayers of contrition and gratitude, the pilgrim places a hand on the marble column. Millions of holy pilgrims since the eleventh century have placed a hand on one recognizable spot near the base. Because it has been reverenced by so many, a handprint is now embedded deep within the marble. Amazing!

In the cornerstone of this column is a carving of the head of Maestro Mateo, the mastermind who designed and oversaw the construction of the Cathedral of Santiago in the mid to late 1100s. Mateo is also known as Santo dos Croques, the "head-banging saint,"[68] due to the tradition that pilgrims tap their heads on the carved head hoping that some of Mateo's genius might be transferred to their own minds.

From the Portico de Gloria, down the cathedral's long central aisle to the front, is the main sanctuary's centerpiece: the elaborate marble altar.

To the side of the altar, old world craftsmanship is on display in a wood-carved podium where Scripture is proclaimed and preached.

Behind the sanctuary, perched on a flight of stairs above the central altar is the bust of St. James, cast in human size and shape, peering down. Pilgrims wait patiently in long queues to climb the steps where the bust of the hero saint rests. Each pilgrim pays silent, reverent respect while hugging the statue. Pilgrims then descend beneath the altar to a small chapel where they can view the silver-plated casket containing the remains of the apostle. Most kneel and pay silent respect.

Millions have crammed into this cathedral since its beginning, seeking time for prayer and worship. The pilgrim Mass held at noon each day is the climax of the pilgrimage. Hard wooden benches and kneelers hold no complaint for pilgrims who completed the grueling walk for hundreds of kilometers.

If there is such a thing as a show-stopper during a church liturgy, it would undoubtedly be the swinging of the *botafumiero*.[69] This vessel is a giant version of the small incensors commonly used for special occasions in all Catholic churches. Also known as "the spreader of fumes," this vessel has been used at the end of masses at the Cathedral de Santiago since the eleventh century. Made of silver, it stands roughly a meter and a half tall by a half meter wide (just shy of 5.5 feet) and weighs as much as eighty kilograms (176 pounds).

The *botafumiero* has a long rope, thick as a man's wrist, tied in a huge knot to a ring at its top. From here the rope is strung to a pulley fixed to the cathedral arches far overhead. The rope returns to ground level where the single strand is reconfigured into eight strands and anchored to a massive pillar near the steps to the sanctuary.

At the cathedral's front and center and situated just a mere three meters (roughly ten feet) in front of the main altar, hangs the *botafumiero*. Its path streaks directly in front of the altar at the conclusion of Mass. Eight *botafumiero* servers, called *tiaboleiros*, move to the column, untether the knot that anchored the vessel, slowly lower it to within

a meter's distance (about a yard) above floor level, and keep it suspended there.

The *botafumiero* gets its final preparation for launch. Hot coals are
shoveled into the vessel, followed by scoop upon scoop of incense. Immediately, clouds of sweet-smelling smoke roll upward through the numerous open slots in its design. One *tiaboleiro* stationed at the center of the
sanctuary gives the billowing "spreader of fumes" a gentle push and steps
aside. A swinging pendulum motion begins. In perfect unison, all eight
rope strands are heaved downward at the perfect moment of a swing.
The motion starts in short swings, but not for long. The vessel gains longer and longer strides until, in just minutes, the *botafumiero* is a roaring fireball, billowing fumes of incense reaching a speed of sixty-eight kilometers
(forty-two miles) per hour! The *tiaboleiros's* perfectly timed tugs accelerate
its swing to a precise spot at just under a meter (three feet) below the
ceiling. The pendulum effect causes it to soar in the opposite direction,
guided once again to stop just short of crashing into the ceiling at the
other end of church. On and on it races from one end of the cathedral
to the other until allowed to succumb to gravity and the lack of further
assistance by the men.

The Catholic church has long used incense as a visual representation of how Psalm 141:2 describes that our prayers rise like incense.
However, some might ask why the world's largest *botafumiero* is used
in Santiago. In the Camino's earliest days, pilgrims walked the hundreds of kilometers with rare opportunities to bathe. Gathered in
large numbers at the cathedral, the body odors were significant. The
incense disguised the concentrated smell of those who congregated
there. Today, the swinging of the *botafumiero* is motivated by tradition
and as a tourist attraction.

For the newly arrived pilgrim, having a place to sit and rest for long
periods of time feels awkward. For more than a month, the pilgrim has
walked and walked, always on the move. Some sit trancelike, amazed they
survived. Others stream tears of gratitude. Still others hold effervescent

smiles, their joy uncontainable. A tangible legacy of tradition and grace fills the pilgrim's spirit and penetrates the soul.

My Camino

"I'd rather die whispering your name than live an empty life shouting my own."

Bill Myers

I walked this last stretch toward Santiago like my hair was on fire. The pilgrim Mass would be at noon. I was determined to make it, to celebrate my thanksgiving to God for His care on my Camino. I was also excited to witness the swinging of the *botafumiero* that only occurs after the Mass. I couldn't wait to get there. *Keep pushing, Willie. Push faster, harder!* No coffee break, no lunch, just a power walk that resembled a near-sprint. The first hard climb was manageable. The second, tougher. Then I faced Monte del Gozo, which looked like a climb up an Olympic ski slope eighty meters (260 feet) high. With my head down and trekking poles clawing me upward, I panted my way to the top.

After a very brief view from the Monument of Pilgrims, an alarm went off inside me. I was still five kilometers (three miles) from Santiago. *Don't miss it, Willie. Go. Go. Go!* It was grueling. I was already physically spent. Injuries on both feet howled their pain. I brushed the fact aside and trudged through the commercial outskirts of Santiago, straining to steal a glimpse of the cathedral. Nothing was in sight. I needed inspiration. *How much longer?*

Street after long city street stretched before me. I was so exhausted, I could have tripped over my own gasping tongue. My arms, too tired to lift my trekking poles, let them chatter annoyingly on the sidewalk behind me. A flashback of the movie *Rocky* came to mind. I was moving like the film's final moments when Rocky was slugging away in the ring. My backpack threw my momentum almost uncontrollably to my left, then to my right as pain stabbed between my shoulder blades. But I wasn't fighting the final round of a boxing match; I was fighting my way to my prize— the Cathedral de Santiago.

At long last, the Cathedral towers peaked over the city rooftops. *Almost there, Willie. Don't pay attention to the pain. Keep going!* New energy bubbled up within me. I stumbled ahead a few more city blocks. There it was! The ancient cathedral loomed just a short distance ahead. As tempting as it was to sit and drink it in, I couldn't! It was only ten minutes before mass would end and the *botafumiero* would swing. The alarm in my head sounded again.

Go! Go! You're almost there!

Minutes after weaving through parts of the old city, I froze in solemn reverence. Here before me was the ancient Cathedral de Santiago de Compostela! By God's grace, I had arrived! All that I had dreamed, prayed for, trained for, and romanticized now towered over me. After some tearful reflection, a chuckle lifted my spirit. How I wanted to stop and drink it all in! But reality sobered me. The cathedral bell tower struck 1:00. *No time for this, Willie. Get into that church!*

I shed my backpack and wriggled my way through the crowd standing along the church's back wall. Two minutes later, I learned the disappointing news: no *botafumiero* for me today! It was swung at an earlier mass for some special occasion. I was heartbroken. Crushed!

But I was able to take great consolation in the fact that I would pray that day at the Cathedral de Santiago. What a rare and profound gift! I had just walked the entire Camino, a distance of just over one million steps, and I was safe! I had so much for which to be grateful.

I slipped into one of the ancient pews and relished God's goodness to me. I soaked in the cathedral's ancient history. I drank in the Spirit that was alive in this holy place. I imagined the legacy of millions of pilgrims over the centuries who, like me, walked here and gave God worship—in exactly the same spot I was sitting! The thought alone aroused my spirit.

I took the time to reflect on all of God's blessings over the course of my pilgrimage: His strength that empowered me to climb the 1,500 meters (five thousand feet) over the Pyrenees Mountains; the loss and return of the water bottle; crashing the funeral service; prayers at Cruz de Ferro and the blizzardy descent; the gift of humor and insight born of *Satan Jeopardy!* The memories gave me shivers. It was as if heaven reached down and kissed my soul. After a few hours, peace and rest filled me.

Now it was time to make my pilgrimage official. It was time to get my Compostela, the official certificate of completion of el Camino de Santiago.

The atmosphere in the Camino Pilgrims' Office had the energy of a cork on a champagne bottle ready to pop. One pilgrim after another strutted out, proudly carrying their Compostelas with the calligraphy bearing their names. For those still weaving along this slow-motion stampede to the front desk, there was joy, pride, and gratitude accompanied with short bouts of stunned silence and overwhelming humility. Like proud Olympic champions carrying their medal, pilgrims carried their Compostelas, born of pain and gift.

They made it.

I made it.

Emotions ramped up in me and a heavy lump formed in my throat. Tears were uncontrollable.

It was time for me to be faithful to what God had placed on my heart when I began reflecting upon "my Elvis." Yes, there was more than misery in my pained feet over those days. My soul had ached day after day these past two weeks as I had recalled the darkest day in my life and in our family's life. The details had been branded in my memory.

*   *   *

It was New Year's Day 2009. Our youngest son was home from college. We were watching football games when my phone identified a call coming in from a local hospital. "Do you know Tony Williams?" the caller asked.

"Yes," I answered.

"He's been hurt. If you'd like to see him, come to . . ." and she gave the name of the hospital. My wife, our adult son, and I burst into the emergency room lobby. To our confusion, two of Tony's friends were in the lobby, crying hysterically. Their eyes were swollen and reddened, their breath short. Hospital staff intercepted us at the entrance where we were immediately escorted into Emergency. A hospital chaplain escorted us to a small private room. The news was delivered abruptly. "Your son has died of a sudden and massive heart attack. Ambulance and emergency physicians could not revive him."

A seizing silence followed. We knew what the words meant, but couldn't understand. My wife shouted, "What?! He's dead?"

The chaplain's words drifted before us like one drops a feather, "Yes. He's gone."

The wailing that followed is forever recorded in my soul. It felt like my heart was being clawed from my chest. Agony swallowed me. Agony swallowed us all.

None of this made sense. It was as if time stood still. In slow motion, we were led to view our son's body. My legs were lead, almost too heavy to lift. My every sense was pulsing, searching frantically for understanding. Fear squeezed my chest, making it hard to breathe.

It was surreal to see him lying motionless, lifeless on an emergency room gurney. I could not comprehend it. *This can't be true. He is only twenty-eight years old. Maybe they have it wrong? Maybe he'll move a finger, an eyelid, anything? Maybe they missed something and we'll see him start breathing again. Maybe a miracle will happen, right now, right here? Maybe?*

There was no maybe.

Tony was dead.

At that moment, our family was abruptly and firmly set on a life course they call a new normal. The wake, the funeral, and all the painful goodbyes to the sound of his voice, his hugs, the future of what could have been with him. The grief journey dragged on excruciatingly for years until I accepted God's healing. It came slowly as each new sliver of peace was added over time. Through God's grace, I finally came to a healthy acceptance of his death. When I embarked on my Camino pilgrimage, I believed my grief journey was complete. Turns out, however, God had more planned. I had some unfinished healing from Tony's death to face. And crazily enough, it would occur at the Camino Pilgrims' Office in Santiago.

* * *

As the pilgrim official called me to her desk, I took a deep breath and fought back tears. Echoing back to me were the two words God had originally used to call me to walk the Camino. "Have faith!" They emboldened me then; they strengthened me again here.

It is customary for the official to engage the pilgrim in a bit of inquiry regarding their pilgrimage. She asked me, "Where did you start? Did you walk the whole way? Was it for religious, physical, or other reasons?" Then she studied my Camino Pilgrim's Credentials—my document that had been stamped in each town's albergue where I had stayed. This proved me an authentic pilgrim of el Camino de Santiago. My name was then actually handwritten in the Camino historical record along with the names of millions over the centuries. Next came the moment for the official to artistically pen, as a calligrapher, my name in Latin on my treasured "Compostela."

I interrupted, "Please inscribe these words across the top of my Compostela:

Ad Majorem Dei Gloria"
(All For the Greater Glory of God)

I then asked if she would also please pen this footnote on the document.

"Dedicated to Tony Williams"

I gazed in reverence, a deep fulfillment at seeing my son's name beautifully inked across the Compostela. A quick flashback brought me the memory of Tony's smiling face; I could almost hear his endearing chuckle. He was a talented pianist and singer. To my mind came the joy of his little living room home concerts, which had been silenced for so long. Even though I knew it was impossible, Tony's playing and singing floated back to me. *Ahh, my Elvis.* But more touching than these, the fondest memory of all showered over me. I recalled the feel of his stubbly chin that I held and patted in special father-and-son moments. A comforting thought came.

Tony would be proud of me right now.

The present moment awakened me to where I was and to this Camino moment. A new resolve filled me. All the joys, blessings, and gifts of wisdom gained along The Way—these were now my love offering, a dedication to my cherished son. More importantly, I surrendered the entire gift of the Camino as my humble gift to God.

Ad Majorem Dei Gloriam.

All . . . for the greater glory of God.

Our Camino

"Surrender your own poverty and acknowledge your nothingness to the Lord. Whether you understand it or not, God loves you, is present in you, lives in you, dwells in you, calls you, saves you, and offers you understanding and compassion which are nothing you have ever found in a book or heard in a sermon."

Thomas Merton

Nothing can be more important than God. All that we are, all that we own, all of our life is from God and for God's greater purpose. We were made for His greater glory. Yet ever since Adam and Eve we all try to take sole credit for all the good in our lives and for all our accomplishments.

But life has its ups and downs. When things aren't going according to our plan, we are starved for answers. But whether life is good or not, our

Camino would do well to give serious thought to two critically important faith questions:

Who is God to me?

Who am I to God?

The answers might be found in our answers to other deep-seated questions. Do we cling to life's position? Prestige? Money? Control? Respect? What about holding on to incidents when our feelings were hurt? Are we able to move beyond offenses that were blatantly unfair? Or do we cling to the old wounds and hurts? We can find ourselves wanting to play God by trying to choose how they are resolved.

We might also cling to something that gives us glory. For some it's a God-given talent, a life accomplishment, a job title, college degrees, and, dare I mention, finishing the Camino. Is there anything in our life that gives us glory above God's deserved honor? When we take pride in earthly glory, we court a certain lesson in humility. "Pride goes before destruction, and a haughty spirit before a fall" (Proverbs 16:18).

Our lives can also be chained to a love of things. The jobs we have, the cars we drive, the homes we live in, our high esteem—these can start as intoxicating pleasures only to eventually develop into things we can't live without—life's addictions. These become our life's focus to attain them and then to maintain them.

Or we might place our identity in the roles we play believing they hold our happiness and life's purpose. When the purpose, the relationship, the job, or the career leaves, our lives can become empty and lost. Those who lose a career role they've held for decades, especially near retirement age, often get swallowed in a stormy sea of confusion. Suffering the death of a spouse, a child, a parent, close sibling, or friend can reveal how much our whole life revolved around being a husband, wife, mother, father, brother, or sister. We ask, "What is my purpose in life now?" Only God can fill that void and give us purpose.

His perfect purpose.

Nothing that has happened to us, no material possession, esteemed role, and no person should take a higher importance than the God who made and loves us. Jesus said, "You shall love the Lord your God with all your heart and with all your soul and with all your strength and with all your mind, and your neighbor as yourself" (Luke 10:27).

This is an exclusive love and a selfish love meant for Him alone. It's also no ordinary kind of love for others. It is a sacrificial love with no strings attached. There's no place for a "what's in it for me" when we love another.

How do we know if we're too attached to something?

Try giving it away. Ask, "Is this a God-given gift or something on which I've placed godlike importance?"

Only a fierce, moral inventory will uncover the truth within us to our two essential faith questions: Who is God to me and who am I to God? As the Scriptures point out, "The truth will set us free."

Surrender is the price to pay for freedom. Who does not want to be free?

"Let go, and let God."

These were the painful truths that awoke in me. I found the gift of freedom in my surrender at the Pilgrims' Office in Santiago.

The lesson drilled deeper in me with the memory of an old, classic, 1940s black-and-white movie. Our Camino can be enlightened by it as well.

*   *   *

My favorite movie in the whole world is *It's a Wonderful Life* by Frank Capra. It's been popularly replayed on television at Christmas time for years and years. So many sermons and gems of life wisdom have been drawn from it. Here's mine.

Because I've watched it every Christmas Eve for nearly fifty years, I know this movie classic in detail. The main character, George Bailey, from childhood works, saves his money, and sacrifices for a chance to one day make his dreams come true. Time after time, George surrenders his gains and plans in sacrifice for others' greater needs. With his father's untimely death, George puts his life plans on hold in order to manage the family business, the Bedford Falls Building and Loan.

George Bailey finally saves enough money for his honeymoon and long overdue travel. The Great Depression hits on the same day and the townspeople are in a panic. Long lines have formed at the Building and Loan. George learns that the business is without funds on hand while his customers are desperate for cash to survive. George strains for insight while pacing the office. He finds it in the memory of his hero, his father, Peter Bailey.

Here's one detail you might have missed.

In that particular scene, George pauses his frantic search for an answer on how to save his customers from financial doom. He stands immediately before the portrait of his dad. Inscribed below are his father's words of wisdom. "The only thing a man keeps is that which he gives away." Moments later, George willingly surrenders his years of cash savings to help his Building and Loan customers escape disaster. He gives everything—everything he has.

$$* \quad * \quad *$$

The memory of that scene, a father's legacy, passed on to his son for a greater purpose, ignited the passion within me. In that moment, at the Camino Pilgrims' Office, I wished to give it all. All that I gained on the Camino—the rich pleasures, the challenges, joys, and life insights. I chose to give my all as a love offering for my son. All of it, dedicated to Tony Williams from his father.

This testimony might beg the questions, "Why? For what purpose would a father do this?"

Jesus gives you and me the answer: "unless a grain of wheat falls into the earth and dies, it remains alone; but if it dies, it bears much fruit" (John 12:24).

I saw my Camino experiences as precious seeds—opportunities. The first seed I chose to plant was my heartache over losing our son.

That seed I finally buried and allowed it to die. It took a Camino's effort for that seed to bear this fruit: I was given the privilege of being Tony's dad for twenty-eight years. What a sweet fruit is the gift of healing a broken heart!

I thank God that my Camino was the beautiful fertile soil for this epiphany.

But there was a higher calling God taught me. I must die to self for the greater glory of God. Every accomplishment, talent, or product of intellect—they're all God's generous gifts to me. I did not earn them or deserve them; I simply steward them. They're all pure gifts from a God who loves me and freely gives to me so that I can share with others and point appreciation to my Giver of gifts in heaven.

These gifts I surrender and allow the desire for self-glorification to die in order to give God all the glory. This is what the Lord asks of me. He asks this of all of us. We were created to know, love, and serve Him. We were made for His pleasure—specifically, to love God and be loved by Him.

Unless every gift we receive falls upon the humble soil and dies, our lives will not bear fruit. Jesus did this. His apostles did this. The saints did this. This dying to self out of love is the higher calling asked of us.

We don't live each day in order to one day die. We die each day in order to one day live in the greater glory of God—*Ad Majorem Dei Gloriam*.

This marked the end of my Camino pilgrimage. What an exhilarating and fulfilling journey it had been! I had walked 790 kilometers (five hundred miles) in thirty-three days—not bad for a sixty-three-year old. I recalled all the mountains I walked, triumphs over blisters and knee pains, breathtaking scenery in the Pyrenees and O'Cebreiro, and fascinating history and legends of the Knights Templars and so many others. I reflected upon the powerful discoveries of the Holy Spirit's movement in my life story and the memories of others' faith-walk stories. I owed all these new gifts to when it all began—that intimate prayer moment a year earlier, the moment God called me to walk the Camino and to "Have faith."

It was the gift of faith alone that delivered me to Santiago. I knew from my deepest core that the riches in this experience were not for me to relish alone or gain power, privilege, or prestige. No! The experience was to help others gain insights on how a "have faith" mission can help them grow in faith.

In humility and gratitude, I offered my entire pilgrimage experience for the greater glory of God—*Ad Majorem Dei Gloriam.*

God alone be praised.

"Surrendering to God means giving something over to God and replacing it with something from Him."

Kevin Martineau

*   *   *

For many months after the pilgrimage, people sought me out. I conducted church mission talks and gave sermons that included Camino experiences. Through these, I met many new friends and formed wonderful new relationships. Many wanted to learn about the trail and probed the spiritual insights I gained while on pilgrimage. A good number sought spiritual direction from me.

I couldn't deny that sharing Camino stories enlivened me. Memories of the trail were energizing because of the tremendous gift it was to be in solitude with our Lord while walking in His gorgeous creation. But most of all, I loved that hour-by-hour and day-by-day deep communion with Him on the Camino.

It was a beautiful, once-in-a-lifetime experience. So I thought.

God had other plans. Almost a year later, I had another intimate moment in prayer similar to the one that first called me to the Camino. During this one, He called me to walk the Camino again. His clear message was, "I have so much more to tell you." I vividly recalled what He had to say on my first Camino. I certainly wanted to hear more.

After prayerful discernment, my wife and I agreed that I would walk the entire Camino de Santiago again. For a second time, God gifted me with rich spiritual insights and intimacy with Him while on pilgrimage to Santiago. And wow! He certainly did have so much more to tell me about the depth of His forgiveness and love.

Again, I was convinced my Camino walking days were done. But our God is a God of surprises. Two years later, during yet another intimate moment in prayer, came God's call for me to walk more of the Camino. With it came a mighty and mysterious call: "Catch the thunder." After more intense and prayerful discernment, I embraced the call and walked the last 325 kilometers (two hundred miles) of the Camino, ending at the Cathedral de Santiago.

In my many encounters with pilgrims along three Caminos, I was able to share in their unique and beautiful faith-walk stories. Some claimed their faith walks privately, humbly, or just in their own quiet way. Still others shared their faith walks in bold, conspicuous, and even outspoken ways. The latter was true for James and his younger brother John, sons of Zebedee called by Jesus. Faith walks such as theirs had thunder in their footsteps. Why else would Jesus call them "Sons of Thunder" (Mark 3:17)?

Join me at the end of my third Camino, which happened to be Ascension Sunday and the day the Cathedral de Santiago shook with *thunder*.

Chapter 20

THUNDER

"I go where the sound of thunder is."

Alfred M. Gray

My Camino

Santiago

Not even in my wildest dreams could I have imagined how my Camino would end when I arrived at the Cathedral de Santiago. I was about to serve on the altar as a deacon at that Pilgrim Mass. *Thank you, Lord, for allowing me to serve You at the church bearing the name of my hero, St. James, the "man of thunder"!*

It was Sunday. But it was not like any other Sunday; it was Ascension Sunday! The church commemorates Christ's ascension described in Acts 1. In this Scripture account, Jesus appears to His disciples in bodily form after His resurrection from the dead. This would be their last time to see the risen Jesus on earth. Luke captures Jesus ascending through the clouds into heaven. Every year the church honors this event as a solemn day of remembrance[70] forty days after Easter. Grand and joyous liturgies flourish on Ascension Sunday in churches worldwide. Since Easter falls on different Sundays each year, the celebration of the ascension also changes each year.

Was it a "Godcidence" that I arrived in Santiago to serve as deacon at the cathedral on this special Sunday?

You can guess my answer.

I presented the official document with my bishop's signature, validating that I was a deacon in good standing and giving me permission to serve at the Cathedral de Santiago. I presented my document to a lady, a religious order nun dressed in the traditional habit of black veil and long black dress. As liturgist, she organized all the clergy, musicians, altar boys, and Scripture readers. She directed me to where the vestments were kept—the formal apparel that must be worn by those who served on the altar. It had been weeks since I served; I felt humbled and so, so grateful as I slipped the deacon's garb over top of my hiking shirt and pants. Emotion welled up inside. Soon I learned that I would accompany six priests from four different continents and another deacon from Portugal. *Praise God! He spoke Portuguese and English.*

Special instructions for this mass were detailed. My fellow deacon understood the directions and relayed them to me in English. To my great surprise and privilege, I was chosen to lead the procession. *Yikes! The crowds here! Lord, you led me eight hundred kilometers* (five hundred miles) *without getting lost. Don't let me get lost in these aisles!*

With the troop of priests lined behind me, I walked directly behind a glass-encased bust of St. James, whose image was artistically engraved and adorned in silver. It rested on long, horizontal wood poles and was carried on the shoulders of four brawny men.

In front of them was a small, unusual band of bassoons and French horns. They blared a melody I had never heard before or would have imagined could play together so commandingly. A male cantor led the entire procession impressively with his singing. Piercing the group's musical air was the cathedral's prized organ. This magnificent instrument rolled its notes off twenty-two-meter- (seventy-two-foot-) high arches.

At first sight, it appeared that the soaring _botafumiero_ was streaking directly at its target: me! I instinctively ducked, then shamefacedly realized its path was in fact rocketing a mere three meters (just under ten feet) right over my head! From my close vantage point, I could see the flames like orange tongues lick through the openings while sweet-smelling incense billowed. It was a soaring fireball in a race from one end of the cathedral to the other.

Completely mesmerized by this rare gift from God, I whispered, "Magnificent!"

I was humbled.

Speechless.

The cantor, a professional baritone, led our singing in a deep and resonating voice. Vested in one of the cathedral's floor-length white robes, he carried a long silver staff just taller than his two-meter (six-foot-plus) height. He led the procession, singing with royal dignity. He stepped with great purpose in perfect cadence to the music. At precise moments, he abruptly stopped, and the bassoons, horns, and organ silenced immediately with him. All in the cathedral instantly joined in silent prayer. After a short pause, he dramatically struck his staff distinctly, two times, on the ancient marble floor. Its sound echoed dramatically in the cathedral's silence. The procession once again thundered with song, music, and the organ's pipes echoing off the towering arches. This pattern of worship continued several times during the procession around the entire cathedral.

Will heaven be like this? I put my hand to my chest, feeling the notes rattling inside. Adding to this excitement, our procession passed two thousand worshipers, mouths agape, all leaning in for photos. Although I was on overload, I worked hard to memorize everything I saw, heard, and smelt. The experience filled my body, mind, and spirit.

Then an inspiration, laced with emotion, thundered in me. Dare I call it holy thunder? It rolled above me, behind me, around me, beneath me. It encircled me. God spoke a message, a revelation, not aloud, but in a whisper that rumbled in my soul. It was unmistakably a replay of His whisper to me from a year earlier to walk this year's Camino. *Was God's whisper back then to have more meaning for me now?*

The word "thunder" rolled over and over inside me until a new revelation struck like lightening.

Yes, yes, yes! God called me a year ago to walk this Camino. He had whispered three words: "Catch the thunder." I had no clue the thunder was for me to catch on Ascension Sunday and in the Cathedral of Santiago.

Godcidence?

Without a doubt!

Over time, I have reflected on my experience with God whispers and the times I believe God called me to three different Camino pilgrimages.

My first Camino calling was "Have faith." My second Camino calling was simply, "I have so much more to tell you." This third Camino calling was, "Catch the thunder." I consider them as one call!

"Have faith. I have so much more to tell you. Catch the thunder." Each of these callings has persistently encouraged me and guided me on my Camino journey. They are pearls of grace that have grown even more meaningful since then. I don't take them lightly, as they continue to guide my faith, my life, and my love for Him.

As my third Camino to Santiago reached its end on Ascension Sunday, I recalled Jesus's final words in Matthew 28:20 (KJV), "I am with you always, even unto the end of the world." This was Jesus's promise for all future generations. And this was Jesus's promise for me!

Some have calculated that the total number of footsteps it takes to complete the entire Camino is just over one million steps. I have walked it two and half times, for a total of nearly two thousand kilometers (1,200 miles). Add to this detail the fact that St. James the Apostle ministered in the land known today as Santiago, Spain—the same land all people east of there had believed, up until Columbus's discovery, was the end of the world. A new revelation thundered within my heart.

Jesus kept His promise and walked all two and a half million steps with me to the "end of the world." He was with me then, and He continues to be with me every day of my life, wherever I walk, wherever I am.

And His whispers still thunder inside me, because . . .
He still wants me to have faith!
He still has so much more to tell me!
He still wants me to catch the thunder!

Our Camino

"Deliver thunder, God. If you choose not to talk."

Dejan Stojanovic

I have been immensely blessed to catch the thunder of God's whispers in my life. Those whispers distinctly came three separate times when He called me to walk and re-walk the Camino. To be clear, I don't often get such thunderous messages, but when they come it's always on His timing and only by His will.

I cannot pray a particular prayer in a certain way or for any number of times to force God's hand for another of His whispers. I am certain that they cannot be received by a spiritual cause-and-effect routine. He will not be manipulated. But God speaks, and when He does, hopefully I'm listening and open to His message. This is how His thunder rolls upon me.

Some of you might be thinking, "Well, that's nice for you, but I've never had that. I pray to God, but He doesn't speak to me. I've never had a 'God whisper.' Nothing even close to a whisper that rolls like thunder inside of me."

I get it. I can only share what I know, in hope that it encourages you.

Here are some basic principles about God's whispers that may help our Camino. Let's presume that God does speak to us based upon countless faith testimonies from believers over human history. Some claim that He speaks as a surprise only on rare occasions. Others claim God speaks through the Holy Spirit in little ways throughout everyday life. Still others claim that He speaks, maybe even shouts, when they aren't seeking His voice, but when they are lost in sin. But in whatever way and however often God speaks, the belief that He speaks at all proves that He is active in our lives, speaking His desires over our Camino. This is our hope.

Those who claim, "God spoke to me," are usually quick to add they did not hear an audible voice from heaven. His words might come innocently during a conversation with another. They may come while reading something, spiritual or otherwise, and the words seem to jump off the page as His message. Wild as it may sound, some claim that words on a billboard have been God's medium of speaking. God's ways are mysterious and wonderful.

His voice might be perceived in a certain tone or strength. Some claim His voice is dramatic, and His message hits them like a two-by-four alongside the head. I perceived them as whispers, mighty and holy.

Regardless of how they're heard, they always, always, always ring as something God-pleasing within scriptural truth and bathed in love and mercy. This is God's DNA. This truth is inherent in every God message, God whisper, and God call for our life. If anyone claims they heard God speak a message that is outside of scriptural truths, outside of God's truths, or outside of God's call for us to love and forgive, then that message is outside of any God message. It's not from Him.

Here is one final consideration. Why can't we tune into His voice whenever we need to hear Him? Why can't prayer time bring in His voice as easily as tuning in to a radio station? How convenient would that be— Jesus 111 FM! Hallelujah! God's voice, pure and clear!

But God will not be manipulated. It is our job to tune into God and listen whether it's convenient or inconvenient. Sometimes all we hear is static confusion caused by too many distractions within our hearts and minds. It takes extra effort and practice on our part to say no to minor distractions during prayer time.

What can our Camino do to turn down the noisiest static drowning out God's voice? Here are ways to help tune out the loudest static on our Camino.

Five Ways to Tune Out Static

1. Ask the tough question: Do we truthfully desire to hear God's voice?

Our first response might be, "Yes, of course! Who wouldn't desire to hear God speak?"

But if we're truly honest, we may only cautiously desire to hear from Him. *What if He asks for a big change in the way I live? What if He asks me to sacrifice more? Do something I don't want to do? Something I'm not ready for? Holy enough for?* He may call us to surrender our preferences, our pleasure, our life demands. It seems to be too much, and His desire does not match what we truthfully desire.

We also worry about other people.

What if I tell others that God spoke to me, and that He called me to do something special for Him? What would they think of me? After all, they really know me. They can see right through me . . . judge me for how I've behaved in the past, judge me for how I behave now, see fault in how I speak and in how I live. They will call me a hypocrite.

Such thoughts create fear, which turns up the volume on the static when trying to hear God's voice.

We may struggle with deeper raw truths as well: *Maybe I really don't desire more of God than I currently have.* We may feel torn between the truth of what we should desire and the truth of what we honestly desire. So why not just seek what we personally desire and be happy? Why worry about what God has to say or what He desires for us? Why take God so seriously? *Maybe God doesn't really understand what I need or want! I'll just play it safe and find happiness for myself.*

This is all static from things of this world.

Good luck with that dead-end thinking.

We desire more than static; we are willing to risk more because we know deep inside that His voice makes us rich in love and wisdom. What God speaks comes from His desire for us to have joy greater than anything we could ever dream. He promised it.

"For I know the plans I have for you, declares the Lord, plans for wel-
fare and not for evil, to give you a future and a hope. Then you will call
upon me and come and pray to me, and I will hear you." (Jer. 29:11–12)

If we're still not quite sure of our desire to hear God's voice, we can
pray this prayer: "God, give me the desire to desire whatever You want
to speak to me."[71] The origin of this wisdom comes from the Spiritual
Exercises of St. Ignatius of Loyola, embraced by millions since the six-
teenth century. Praying for a greater desire creates new momentum in
our prayer life while we seek God's voice and discern His will. This prayer
posture pleases God.

2. Clean out the wax.

Metaphorically, earwax is sin. We cannot hear with a wax build-up. Some
wax may have festered and hardened from years by a passionate protection of our pride. Unconfessed sin filters what and how much we want
to hear from God. God speaks to us, but our ears may be plugged with
sin. Owning our faults and asking God's forgiveness cleans out the wax—
the sin—in our lives. Confession opens our ear canals to hear His voice
clearly.

3. Take a hearing test.

Not hearing anything during prayer time? Honest self-reflection might
reveal that we're the ones doing more, if not all, of the talking during
prayer. We need to ask ourselves "How much listening do I do during
my prayer time? How much silence do I permit?" Thomas Keating,
known for his wisdom on centering prayer (a form of contemplative
prayer), wrote, "God's first language is silence; everything else is a poor
translation."[72]

Our prayer time might be consumed with reciting prayers, reading inspirational messages, even reading the Scripture. All are very
important spiritual practices for honoring God. But also worth attention is embracing silence and allowing time for reflection during

prayer—to just listen. Silence is holy ground where God speaks, and we listen.

Can God speak to us when we're drowning in our own noisy life? Definitely. But why would we keep the world's noise at a ten on the volume scale when it's the God of the universe trying to speak to us? The words "silent" and "listen" are comprised of the same letters. We hold the choice to embrace these two elements in our prayer life.

4. Unplug the noise.

Ask yourself, "Is there some background noise still going on in my relationship with Him?" Playing in our mind might be a noisy reminder of something grievous, maybe bitterly unfair, or a costly hurt in our past. These are no small things: a child's untimely death, a loved one's painful suffering, excruciating life losses. Such life traumas drive us to the point where we want to scream, "It's not fair!" Worse yet, we rehearse and relive the hurt and invite the bitter wrong to grow louder and louder in our thinking. Some of us wrestle with the Goliath of "Where were you, God? Why didn't you prevent that bad thing from happening? Why?"

We try to pray; we try to hear God's voice behind the pain and suffering. But the hurt of the injustice is static that drowns any chance to hear God's voice. Some become angry or give up on God altogether.

We wonder, "Is that okay? Am I allowed to be angry with God?"

We look at our lives, the lives of those dearest to us, even the outrageously hurtful and evil events in the world, and we become *angry*!

How do we unplug all this noisy static?

We share these feelings with God. We pour out our bitter hurts, our confusion, our painful loss, and yes, our anger toward Him. He can handle it. It's almost funny to think we can hide our feelings from Him. Hello—He's God! He knows our feelings already, and He yearns for an honest relationship that shares everything. Truth is the cornerstone of a relationship with Him.

We can also find solace in the fact that what breaks our hearts breaks God's heart. He understands injustice; He saw His one and only Son unjustly and brutally killed. When our Camino faces unthinkable injustice, our Father in heaven understands. He hears and feels our pain because He felt the sting of injustice endured by His only Son.

Consider this metaphor: Life experiences, the good, bad, and ugly, are received in our hearts like a radio. It receives its power via a power cord. If the cord is plugged into the world's power receptacle, the world's perspective is amplified with all its anger, resentment, and fuming injustice. The world spews its venom into us as long as our heart is plugged into this power source.

However, if the power source is plugged into the cross, Christ's suffering powers us through our suffering. (I have imagined an electrical receptacle at the base of the cross.) His great love powers us through our weak love. His forgiveness powers us through our inability to forgive. We connect our suffering to the suffering of Christ on the cross. His suffering for love of us powers us through our suffering for love of Him.

Difficult? Amen! However, this is the source of perfect love.

This is precisely what Jesus calls us to do.

You have heard that it was said, "You shall love your neighbor and hate your enemy." But I say to you, Love your enemies and pray for those who persecute you, so that you may be sons of your Father who is in heaven. For he makes his sun rise on the evil and on the good, and sends rain on the just and on the unjust. For if you love those who love you, what reward do you have? Do not even the tax collectors do the same? And if you greet only your brothers, what more are you doing than others? Do not even the Gentiles do the same? You therefore must be perfect, as your heavenly Father is perfect. (Matt. 5:43–48)

If we are hearing heavy static in the background, unplug from the world and plug into the cross of Christ. The noise will subside, and peace will come with His clear voice again.

5. Expect and wait.

As believers, we pray in faith for God's will and wait in expectation. We might pray day after day, sometimes year after year, with a spiritually healthy expectation that God will respond. We've done our part. Why isn't God doing His part? Why don't we hear His voice?

The truth is, sometimes we will hear nothing. And so we must "wait under the beam" we carry. It may be a time of spiritual desolation or God may be withholding His purpose for His perfect timing. Either way, our Camino calls us to accept what He gives at the present as His gift. We are His children and there is nothing He treasures more than us sitting in His presence and waiting. Yes, just waiting for His voice.

David, writer of psalms, advises us, "Wait for the LORD; be strong, and let your heart take courage; wait for the LORD!" (Ps. 27:14).

Our heroes in faith, the saints, found comfort while waiting on the Lord as they encountered all trials and circumstances. We do well to practice their saintly virtues of humility and obedience while we wait in expectation for the Lord's voice.

Our faith grows while in expectation (some would say "in suspense") for His answer.

God still speaks. And when He speaks, wow! It is like catching thunder in the soul.

Zebedee's sons, James and his brother, John, "Sons of Thunder," caught thunder.

My Camino caught the thunder on Ascension Sunday in the Cathedral of Santiago.

And our Camino can catch the thunder; we need only open ourselves to hear it.

*　　*　　*

Our trail ends, but our Camino continues. Where do we go from here?
The final chapter looks at sharing our faith walk through a new lens
called *Ultreia*.

Chapter 21

ULTREIA

"Ultreia just tells the energetic intention to go with courage toward some 'beyond,' to exceed something. By crying '*Ultreia!*' pilgrims actually say **'Let's keep going! Let's go some more, let's go beyond!'**"[73]

Our Camino

"Someone asked, Will the heathen who have never heard the gospel be saved? It is more a question with me whether we who have the gospel and failed to give it can be saved."

C. H. Spurgeon

Everyone has a story. Within each story are episodes when the good, the bad, and the ugly become intense—our personal drama moments. These dramas span a spectrum of emotions that range from the mundane all the way to the excruciating challenges that arrest our attention such as failure or life and death fears.

We all have a story!

God is in that story.

The dictionary definition of "parable" is "a short story that teaches a moral or spiritual lesson."[74] In light of this, our stories can be modern-day parables to teach others of His faithfulness.

Jesus used stories to teach. His parables hit right at the heart of all people's struggles—their drama moments.

Consider the life-changing power of the parables in Luke's gospel: the good Samaritan (chapter 10), the mustard seed (chapter 13), the lost sheep (chapter 15), and the prodigal son (chapter 15). These are more than just stories; they powerfully engage us to examine how our lives align or misalign to the spiritual lesson.

New York Times bestselling author Jon Acuff wrote, "Sometimes God redeems your story by surrounding you with people who need to hear your past so it doesn't become their future."[75]

This is evangelization: A calling to share our story and anticipate that those who don't know Jesus, or are seeking Him, might find Him simply by hearing that Jesus is alive in us. Our personal parables, with their drama, contain spiritual lessons to transform us and to teach others. Our stories have power. Telling our stories is the vehicle to carry that power beyond, to take it further, to take it ahead. *Ultreia!*

This is what taking the good news of God's saving grace beyond, further looks like.

This is Jesus's command: Go to all peoples everywhere and make them my disciples (see Matt. 28:19).

This is what St. James preached to the pagan Druids in far western Spain.

This is how we can win the world for Christ.

This is the mission for us as believers.

This is Our Camino.

This is truth!

Many might think, "The apostles were trained by Jesus. Even talented preachers can do this; they've been trained. I have nooo training in evangelization. I know I should evangelize. I just don't know how. To be honest, I'm afraid I'll mess it up and make myself look like an inept believer, a fool."

These are fair concerns that uncover bigger, looming questions: How do I evangelize without sounding preachy? Without overwhelming the listener? Without turning that person off? How can I evangelize in a way that speaks to the heart of the listener? What should I tell him/her?

What can be our answer?

Tell them your story! Dramas and all. God moments and all, lost and found moments as well. Why? Because our stories have power!

It sounds simple enough. But how do we get to the heart of our stories? How should we organize the details without drowning the listener?

Let's consider this approach. If evangelization is our mission as believers, then two converging approaches can get us there: engaging evangelization and reverse evangelization.

Engaging Evangelization

"Your private struggle is about to become a public testimony of God's grace, favor, and supernatural power to turn things around."

Unknown

The format of this book is actually an ideal pattern for evangelization. The chapters in this book have included three segments: The Camino, My Camino, and Our Camino. The pattern provided an effective way for me to share my pilgrimage experience. The faith walk testimonies included at the end of each chapter illustrate the message undergirding the chapter. They also serve as examples for sharing your own faith walk. Let's look more closely at how this pattern can help.

First, "The Camino" segment in each chapter captures detailed descriptions of the geography at different locations along the Camino. These paint a picture of the landscape and the challenge the geography held for me.

We can use the book's "The Camino" format to share our own faith walk stories. "The Camino" establishes the geography or the setting for our story. Where were you in your life when a particular faith walk event began? What was your mindset?

"The Camino" also contains details of interesting historical events that occurred over the centuries at those locations. Any good faith story includes some personal history. This builds the plot. Describing past details leads the listener to the intense challenge contained in the story. This is critical, as it comprises the story of our journey between being lost and being found again in God's immense love and mercy.

Painting "The Camino" with our personal geography and history is what creates relevant and relatable elements in our story. The listener can see what we both have in common, and this connection sets the stage for engaging evangelization to begin.

Second, "My Camino" in each chapter includes my personal thoughts and reflections. I also highlighted the revelations Jesus used to guide me to follow Him closer. These often contain the exact dialogue between the Lord and me as a model for how to pray reflectively. For engaging evangelization to occur, others need to understand that believers pray their way through life's dramas. Examples of prayer offer a guiding light for the listener and help them find their own prayerful words while they push ahead through their own faith walk, through the tough drama moments, and the lost and found moments as well.

Third, the "Our Camino" segment in each chapter shares the self-reflective insights and spiritual lessons that God taught me. These naturally developed while walking the Camino and deepened as I continued my journey. The Spirit's teaching can be applied to anyone's life journey. When these discoveries are part of our faith walk story, they become believable and relatable. "Our Camino" provides new answers, new direction, and new reason to hope for ourselves and others.

Engaging evangelization is not new. Champion evangelist Paul, writer of thirteen books in the Bible, provides a convincing example. The model of how to tell our faith walk story is illustrated below through his own story, as recorded in the Acts of the Apostles.

The Camino

In his story, Paul paints a picture of his personal geography—where he was at in his life at the time. He describes his background, identity, and way of life. He includes the treacherous deeds he did and where he did them.

The apostle offers us a good example on how to initiate an engaging evangelization testimony by sharing his faith walk story:

> I am a Jew, born in Tarsus in Cilicia, but brought up in this city, educated at the feet of Gamaliel according to the strict manner of the law of our fathers, being zealous for God as all of you are this day. I persecuted this Way to the death, binding and delivering to prison both men and women, as the high priest and the whole council of elders can bear me witness. From them I received letters to the brothers, and I journeyed toward Damascus to take those also who were there and bring them in bonds to Jerusalem to be punished. (Acts 22:3–5)

My Camino

Paul then draws us further into his faith walk story with an incredible account of how God personally and profoundly confronted him and spoke to him. What more drama does one need than to be knocked off a horse, hear God's voice, become blind, and days later have his sight miraculously restored?

> As I was on my way and drew near to Damascus, about noon a great light from heaven suddenly shone around me. And I fell to the ground and heard a voice saying to me," Saul, Saul, why are you persecuting me? " And I answered," Who are you, Lord?" And he said to me, "I am Jesus of Nazareth, whom you are persecuting." Now those who were with me saw the light but did not understand the voice of the one who was speaking to me. And I said, "What shall I do, Lord?" And the Lord said to me, "Rise, and go into Damascus, and there you will be told all that

is appointed for you to do." And since I could not see because of the brightness of that light, I was led by the hand by those who were with me, and came into Damascus.

And one Ananias, a devout man according to the law, well spoken of by all the Jews who lived there, came to me, and standing by me said to me, "Brother Saul, receive your sight." And at that very hour I received my sight and saw him. And he said, "The God of our fathers appointed you to know his will, to see the Righteous One and to hear a voice from his mouth; for you will be a witness for him to everyone of what you have seen and heard. And now why do you wait? Rise and be baptized and wash away your sins, calling on his name."

When I had returned to Jerusalem and was praying in the temple, I fell into a trance and saw him saying to me, "Make haste and get out of Jerusalem quickly, because they will not accept your testimony about me." And I said, "Lord, they themselves know that in one synagogue after another I imprisoned and beat those who believed in you. And when the blood of Stephen your witness was being shed, I myself was standing by and approving and watching over the garments of those who killed him." (Acts 22:6–20)

Our Camino

Paul then shares the profound insight and lesson he learned from his drama moment with God. The crux of Paul's story was being convicted and humbled by God's message. Through this final verse, God's mighty lesson would be taught to us, through Paul.

"And he said to me, 'Go, for I will send you far away to the Gentiles'" (Acts 22:21).

Through Paul's faith walk story, we can identify this engaging evangelization format of "The Camino, My Camino, Our Camino." His insight and lesson inspires "our Camino" to "go far away to the Gentiles" and share what the Lord had done and still does in our lives today! God instills His lessons in us in order that He might teach others through us.

However, this invitation to engaging evangelization is only half as effective unless it's done in reverse as well.

Reverse Evangelization

This term was coined by Peter Rollins, author of *How (Not) to Speak to God*.[76] How does evangelization work in reverse? By inviting someone else to share their story!

We all have a story. And God is in that story. Invite someone to tell their story of some significant life event, dramas and all, lost and found moments as well. The storyteller and listener roles reverse. The listener should be prepared to face one of two very different perspectives regarding attitudes about God and faith. One might be regarded as a person whose faith is sleeping—alive, but inactive. The other might be regarded as a person who has retreated from God and faith altogether. Each requires a different approach. For someone with a sleeping faith, these questions will facilitate the reverse evangelization process.

The Camino: Personal Geography and History

- What was one tough time in your life? Where and what did your thinking revolve around? Where were you with God?

- What was your family background like? What was your life like up to that time? Help me understand you better by sharing a short piece of your personal history.

- Were there any other big life challenges you faced? How did they turn out?

- What is the big story, perhaps some drama, that went on in your heart during that time? Would you be willing to share some of the details? When do you believe you lost your faith? What thoughts and feelings might have been a reason you lost it? What still confuses you about that whole time in your life?

My Camino: What did you say to God? What did He communicate to you?

- What do you believe God might have said to you while you were going through that time? What about after going through that time?
- Were you listening for Him then? Were you prepared to hear what He had for you? Why? Why not?
- What did your prayers sound like during that time? What words did you use? How much room do you believe your prayer offered God in which to work?
- What were your desires during that difficult time?
- What more would you desire that God do for you? Tell you? Have you asked Him about those desires?
- What do you believe was His response?

Our Camino: What insight did you gain? What lesson can you share to help others?

- Have you learned something after having gone through that time in your faith walk?
- If not, why do you think this was so?
- If yes, what did you learn?
- How might that lesson help someone else who is going through something similar?
- What might God be asking you to do with this lesson from Him?

The question list might appear long and daunting, but it's offered just as support and encouragement to help us get to the heart of a story.

An entirely different approach is needed for those who have retreated from God and faith. This guide will help the evangelization process.

- Dear evangelists, it's not your job to convince a person to believe in God! Your role is to share your faith story as an invitation. This is your part. Trust the Holy Spirit to do His part.

- Evangelization is rooted in relationship. This will take time. Don't rush the process; embrace it.

- After you've shared your faith walk story, ask something like, "Where are you with the whole God thing?" And then shut up and listen. Be guided by this line in the prayer of St. Francis, "Seek first to understand, then to be understood."

- Ask, but don't push. Gently question when God and faith fell out of their life. When do you think you just lost the faith? What thoughts and feelings led you to lose your faith? Was it gradual? Abrupt? Was it over some big issue like anger with God? An injustice? Laziness? Equating a relationship with God to church experiences? Seek to understand the true reason why they left God and faith behind. This insight will guide your evangelization efforts.

- Validate their feelings, but don't encourage negative ones. Say something like, "I hear what you're saying. Can you tell me more?"

- Return to step one and repeat each of these steps. Knowing the source of their retreat from God and faith, share another story from your life that connects well with their story. Keep your story simple, relevant, and relatable.

Know this: It's all about the relationship. Showing respect opens the door to communication. A preachy, judgmental, and pushy tone will close the door.

We see reverse evangelization played out in John 9. From the start, everyone knew what was going on—there was a man born blind. Jesus's apostles, the Jewish leaders, and Pharisees were bent on "why" questions regarding this man's life. Jesus showed no interest in the "why" behind the man's life or his blindness; He cared only for the man himself.

As the story progressed, the "what," "how," and "who" questions proved to be game-changers. These helped the blind man tell his story, discover how his life was changed, and discover who helped change it. His faith discovery evolved *while* he was telling his own story. This is the intent of reverse evangelization. Telling our story aloud helps us arrive at our own new faith discovery. The blind man's telling of his story led him to claim, "I believe, Lord" (John 9:38).

Consider National Association of Evangelicals president Leith Anderson's definition of evangelism: "Those who know telling those who don't."

As mentioned earlier, all we are called to do is share our story and anticipate that those who don't know Jesus, or are seeking Him, might find Him simply by hearing that Jesus is alive in us. The supreme hope is that the listener might connect the dots between our story and their story and that the dots lead closer to Him. This is how we spread the good news of salvation through Him!

It's a simple format: Engaging evangelization, followed by reverse evangelization.

By all means, avoid "why" questions. These lean toward judgmental thoughts that can lead to shame and guilt. Inviting someone to wallow in negative emotions sabotages the evangelization process. By contrast, the kinds of questions Jesus asked led others to recognize His love and forgiveness right within their story. Our choice of questions should only assist others to that same self-discovery.

Invite others to share their stories. Respectfully encourage them to share the details—the what, the how, and the who that were involved. Listen and watch how the Holy Spirit will use the details within a person's story to bring a greater self-awareness of God's love and forgiveness.

That's the potential and power within reverse evangelization opportunities.

Let's take a look at this again through Michaelina's faith walk story. Michaelina carried an unimaginable, heavy burden for more than twenty years. Yet her faith walk story offers us a prime example of both engaging and reverse evangelization.

The Camino

Michealina was the firstborn of Italian immigrants, both devout Catholics and fervent followers of the faith. They raised their daughter and younger twins to learn the faith and pray in the practice of the church. This was how it was done in the "old country," so this was how it would be done in their new country. Immigrants identified where they lived in Chicago by their home parish. Her family lived by "St. Gab's"—St. Gabriel Parish.

Michealina excelled in school and finished high school. During that post Great Depression era, four years of high school was a bonus. Instead of finishing school, most girls married young and raised babies—some, many, many babies. Not Michealina.

Michealina went to beautician school and took accounting classes. She was good at both, even though these were not her passion. She loved to dance; the jitterbug was her favorite. On weekends, she'd join a group of friends and head to the dance hall. There, a big band played music of the '40s, and girls would don dance cards on their wrists. Young men would spot a lovely lady and ask to sign their name on her dance card to get in line for their turn for a dance. Michealina's dance card filled fast. She was a beauty, a brunette who wore cherry-red lipstick and flashed a Hollywood smile. But more than that, she could dance!

It was here at the dance hall that Michaelina met the love of her life. He was a sailor, home on leave from Great Lakes Naval Station. He too had a handsome movie-actor look, especially in his sailor uniform. Just two years her senior, his broad grin and southern Illinois boyish charm caught her attention. But it was his swagger on the dance floor that stole her heart.

Two years later, her beau became her husband. However, beneath his groom's tuxedo was a young farm boy where violent physical and verbal abuse was the norm. Michealina's naïve expectation of married life had no warning of the approaching confrontations. Many would say, "It was what happened in those days," and moonshine was the escape for hopeless poverty and domestic violence at home.

A honeymoon baby boy arrived just days after their nine-month wedding anniversary. Both Michaelina and her husband worked full-time jobs to make ends meet. She worked days; he worked nights. Parenting was done in shifts as well. Neither claim to have done it well in those days. Added stress came with the arrival of two daughters in the next few years. Their family had grown from two to five within five years of marriage. With no choice, Michealina quit her job.

Perhaps it was bearing the stress of night-shift work, providing for so many mouths to feed, or the rearing head of his own childhood, but Michaelina's husband struggled. Michealina found herself facing the growing challenge of living with an alcoholic. The pattern of drunkenness included physical and verbal abuse that became the ugly element in their married life.

The years ahead would see the children and their mom tremble in fear of what alcoholic rages meant.

Too many times, Michealina and her children ran for their lives to escape the rage of their madman husband and father. They walked the neighborhood of their Chicago suburb until they believed the emotional storm had subsided. Fearing what might happen if they arrived home before the effects of the booze wore off, they hid in the basement of their home. They sat on lawn chairs hour after hour without so much as a chair squeak, in terror that the sound would give their hiding place away. Abuse was certain, if caught.

Slaps, fist, and belt beatings accompanied binge-drinking episodes. Their son cried through them, but trembled while witnessing them on his mother. At times, Michealina and the kids took refuge in a relative's home. Weeks later, after many promises made, the four would return. They felt cautiously safe, for a while. Then, something would ignite another streak of binging and all safety would disappear like gun smoke. All seemed hopeless.

My Camino

Her children—now ages twelve, ten, and seven—tried to convince their mom to divorce. Michealina would give it no thought. Her response always was, "We must pray." For her kids, this made no sense. It took twenty more years for them to learn their mother's secret prayer—a profoundly powerful commitment shelved in her heart.

She would add, "Besides, if I divorce him that would be a sin. I'm not going to sin by breaking my sacrament of marriage. I will keep praying." And she did. Prayer was the core of her response to her burdens at home. She is remembered by her children for time spent on her knees in church praying her heart out. Her faith was her life preserver.

She pleaded, "Lord, please save my husband. I love him. He's a good man and good provider. It's the alcohol. Break the grip it has on him. Save him."

In hindsight, it was not wise or responsible to stay in harm's way. However, times were different back then, and divorce was a rare and desperate choice. The life she led was deep in faith and stalwart in hope for the God who would save her and her children. This was her burden, one she riveted her hope to faithfully for some twenty years, her "wait of the beam."

While Michaelina's son was away at college, the abuse climaxed. She and the girls, now accompanied by two more sons, moved out. A solemn threat was made to her husband. "Stop the drinking, or the kids and I will leave you!" She meant it this time.

Only God knows why, but this time her husband was scared sober by this last threat. He attended Alcoholics Anonymous, saw himself for the man he truly was, faced the shame of what he'd done, and owned up to the alcoholic he had become. Discovering this truth gave him spine and strength to change. A miracle occurred. He transformed into a new man, a new husband, and a new father. His old self became new. He became soft of heart, generous, and to the utter disbelief of those who really knew his past, he was the gentlest grandpa to his grandbabies.

They enjoyed eighteen years of this new family life together, learning to grow in love and grace while old memories faded. Those years were all Michealina would have before facing the surprise of widowhood. The new husband and father they had gained was short-lived.

Years later, Michealina's firstborn heard a serious calling to follow Christ. He studied and immersed himself in Scripture and prayer. In time, he sensed a calling to be ordained a permanent deacon in the Catholic church. Some thought this was his embrace of God's healing journey from his childhood. He was convinced it was solely from his prayer life, his calling to give his life in service to God and His church.

Or so he thought, until his ordination day.

On ordination day, Michealina revealed the secret prayer she had held so many years. That day she asked her son, "Did you ever wonder why your father finally stopped drinking? Why he stopped all the abuse?"

He responded, "I suppose the ultimatum scared him."

What a question to ask on ordination day! He tried to brush aside any negative reaction to her question. *This was to be a joyful day and to create happy memories.*

Our Camino

Michealina persisted, "There is something you never knew. All those years I prayed through all those tough times, I asked God for something." Her face lit up, and she continued as someone about to hand a surprise birthday gift to a loved one. She shared, "All the time I was praying for your father, I prayed this secret prayer. 'Lord, if you will help deliver my husband from alcohol, I offer my firstborn son to serve you. Take him as my love offering for saving my husband.'"

Michealina's revelation stole the breath of her firstborn. His "yes" to serve God all the rest of his life was all along guided in faith and hope by the fervent prayers of his mother.

That firstborn son is the pilgrim on our Camino and the author of this book. Michealina was my mother.

*   *   *

My mother's story shows how she lived her life and weathered the dramas. Through every lost moment she prayed and listened. She found the faithfulness of God in every challenge. Through her story, God's mighty lessons were shared with me and nurtured my faith. Her story is a great example of how evangelization works.

What was I to do with what I was taught?

Tell my story! Dramas and all, lost and found moments as well.

That's exactly what I've done in this book. Just as my mother's story has lessons for me, I am sharing my lessons, born on the Camino, with you.

Now it's your turn to tell your story. Dramas included. God's lessons included, lost and found moments as well. Share the details so others can see Jesus alive in you. This is engaging evangelization done through your story. Which brings us back to the basic tenet of this book: We all have a story. God is in that story.

We continue His saving work when we, who have found faith, share our story with those who have lost theirs. This is our first step as engaging evangelists of the good news. Our faith-walk story might be captivating and hint of miraculous interventions. However well-intentioned, we must not stop there. A new and deeper transformation occurs when one of His lost ones reflects upon their life dramas, searches for God's presence in it, and discovers the spiritual insight He is offering. This salvation work begins when the "found" invite the "lost" to tell their stories, dramas and all.

Engaging evangelization followed by reverse evangelization brings the salvation story full circle. In this, the faith of the "lost" and the "found" shine their light on a dark world for all to see.

It's time we seize the thunder—that bold courage Jesus recognized in Zebedee's sons, James and John, whom he called "Sons of Thunder" (Mark 3:17).

Our faith walk has thunderous power that draws others to Christ's peace, forgiveness, and love. When we tell our stories, a power is unleashed to change the world for Him.

What's stopping our call to evangelize, our *Ultreia* to go beyond, to go forward with our story? What are we afraid of?

Nelson Mandela's inauguration speech in 1994 may help us break through that fear and unlock the power within us:

> Our deepest fear is not that we are inadequate.
> Our deepest fear is that we are *powerful* beyond measure.
> It is our Light, not our darkness, that most frightens us.
>
> We were born to make manifest the Glory of God that is within us.
> It's not just in some of us; it's in everyone.
> And as we let our Light shine,
> We unconsciously give other people permission to do the same.
> As we are liberated from our own fear,
> Our presence automatically liberates others.[77]
>
> Fellow pilgrims, tell the world your story, for it is thunder.
> Let's be . . . *powerful!*

DIG DEEPER, RISE HIGHER PERSONAL REFLECTION AND DISCUSSION QUESTIONS

Introduction

Prepare to receive it:

Quiet your body and mind for five minutes. Focus on God being present with you. Reflect upon moments when you believe God called you to follow Him in a new way. Thank Him for that. Pray your regrets, fears, joys, and sorrows related to living out God's call in your life. Look forward in hope for the courage and grace to accept His next call for your life. Close your prayer in gratitude.

Think it out/Talk it out:

Reflect upon a time when you believe God called you to do something special for Him. What was it?

1. How did you feel at the time?
2. How did you respond to His call?
3. In hindsight, what do you believe He wanted you to experience? Learn?
4. How open are you to a new calling from Him? What do you imagine that could be?
5. Who are two people you will talk to this week about a future ministry in which you're interested? Schedule some time with them.

Pray it out:

Use the ACTS Prayer:

Adore: Claim a reason why you adore God.

Contrition: In general terms, for what do you need God's forgiveness?

Thanksgiving: For what do you want to thank God?

Supplication: What do you need God to do for you?

Chapter One—Measure of a Man

Prepare to receive it:

Quiet your body and mind for five minutes. Focus on God being present with you. Reflect upon moments when you believe you were called to make a sacrifice for your faith. Thank Him for that. Pray your regrets, fears, joys, and sorrows related to the costs of your discipleship. Look forward in hope for the courage and grace to accept the next sacrifice for your faith. Close your prayer in gratitude.

Think it out/Talk it out:

Reflect upon a time when following God's call cost you.

1. How did you feel at the time?
2. How did you handle the sacrifices?
3. What did the sacrifice actually cost you?
4. What grace or spiritual insight did you gain by way of the sacrifice you made?
5. What two sacrifices can you make this week for your faith?

Pray it out:

ACTS Prayer
   Adore: Claim a reason why you adore God.
   Contrition: In general terms, for what do you need God's forgiveness?
   Thanksgiving: For what do you want to thank God?
   Supplication: What do you need God to do for you?

Chapter Two—Of Thunder and Stars

Prepare to receive it:

Quiet your body and mind for five minutes. Focus on God being present with you. Reflect upon moments when you believe God called you to be strong for someone. Pray your life's regrets, fears, joys, and sorrows for how you bore their burdens. Pray in hope for the added courage and grace to be strong for the next heavy-burdened person you'll be called to help. Close your prayer with gratitude that God keeps calling you to carry your cross and bear another's burden.

Think it out/Talk it out:

Reflect upon a time when you helped someone carry their life burden. What was that burden?

1. What thoughts and feelings came while bearing their burden?

2. What role did courage and humility play in your burden-bearing?

3. Reflect upon a personal experience when someone helped you carry your burden. What was the burden? How did that person help?

4. How did receiving that help humble you? What life lesson did it teach?

5. Who are two people enduring heartache you will check in with this week?

Pray it out:

ACTS Prayer

Adore: Claim a reason why you adore God.

Contrition: In general terms, for what do you need God's forgiveness?

Thanksgiving: For what do you want to thank God?

Supplication: What do you need God to do for you?

Chapter Three—The Lure of Heaven's Melody

Prepare to receive it:

Quiet your body and mind for five minutes. Focus on God being present with you. Reflect upon moments when you witnessed something of God's awesome power. Prayerfully savor the memories of those signs of His majesty you witnessed. Were these found in nature? Life events? A person's kindness? Pray your regrets for not fully appreciating God's majesty that surrounds you. Close your prayer in joy and gratitude for times you witnessed God's mighty power in your life.

Think it out/Talk it out:

Reflect upon where and when you witnessed a sign of God's awesomeness. Describe it.

1. What were your emotions at the time of this occurrence?
2. How did your witness of God's awesomeness influence your thinking about Him?
3. What lesson do you believe God wanted you to learn from what you witnessed?
4. Finish this statement: "God's majesty means . . ."
5. What two examples of God's awesomeness will you share with someone this week?

Pray it out:

ACTS Prayer

Adore: Claim a reason why you adore God.

Contrition: In general terms, for what do you need God's forgiveness?

Thanksgiving: For what do you want to thank God?

Supplication: What do you need God to do for you?

Chapter Four—Grace

Prepare to receive it:

Quiet your body and mind for five minutes. Focus on God being present with you. Reflect upon moments when you've experienced what you called "a gift from God." As believers, we claim these gifts as His grace—an undeserved favor. Pray your regrets for taking for granted how gracious God is. Close your prayer in gratitude for the many graces you've received throughout your life.

Think it out/Talk it out:

Reflect upon a special moment of grace that came when you needed it most.

1. What difficult circumstances were pressing in on you?
2. What emotions were alive in you?
3. How did you experience the gift of His grace? What emotions were alive in you then?
4. Which gospel story best illustrates a grace-filled event to you? Explain.
5. What two things will you do this week to open yourself up to receive more of His gifts of grace?

Pray it out:

ACTS Prayer

    Adore: Claim a reason why you adore God.

    Contrition: In general terms, for what do you need God's forgiveness?

    Thanksgiving: For what do you want to thank God?

    Supplication: What do you need God to do for you?

Chapter Five—Humility

Prepare to receive it:

Quiet your body and mind for five minutes. Focus on God being present with you. Pray your regrets for prideful moments in your life. Reflect upon humbling moments that have happened in your life. Close your prayer in gratitude for the spiritual gifts that came by way of your humbling experiences.

Think it out/Talk it out:

Reflect upon one event in your life that was particularly humbling.

1. What circumstances led you to that humbling event? Had your prior choices played a part? How so?
2. How did you feel at the time? Was pride involved in your life lesson about humility?
3. How have humbling experiences made you a stronger person and a stronger believer?
4. Why do you believe Jesus spoke so often about living in humility? Explain.
5. What are two things you will do this week to exercise greater humility?

Pray it out:

ACTS Prayer
    Adore: Claim a reason why you adore God.
    Contrition: In general terms, for what do you need God's forgiveness?
    Thanksgiving: For what do you want to thank God?
    Supplication: What do you need God to do for you?

Chapter Six—Offer It Up

Prepare to receive it:

Quiet your body and mind for five minutes. Focus on God being present with you. Reflect upon times you truly suffered. Pray your regrets for any poor ways you might have handled your suffering. Pray in gratitude for any spiritual gifts that came through the suffering. Close your prayer by asking God's healing for someone you know is suffering.

Think it out/Talk it out:

Reflect upon an event when you suffered greatly. Describe what your suffering entailed. What circumstances led up to your suffering? What made your suffering so painful?

1. How did you pray through your suffering? How did God respond?

2. Did the notion of offering up your suffering to God enter your prayers? Why? Why not?

3. Could you feel the prayers others offered up for you? If so, how?

4. Jesus offered up his suffering on the cross for us. How might uniting your current or future suffering for others join you to Christ's salvation work?

5. During this week, for which two people will you offer up your current suffering?

Pray it out:

ACTS Prayer

   Adore: Claim a reason why you adore God.

   Contrition: In general terms, for what do you need God's forgiveness?

   Thanksgiving: For what do you want to thank God?

   Supplication: What do you need God to do for you?

Chapter Seven—A Mountain of Forgiveness

Prepare to receive it:

Quiet your body and mind for five minutes. Focus on God being present with you. In light of the sinful nature of mankind, reflect upon the immense mercy of God. Pray your regrets for past sins. Pray in gratitude for the mountain of forgiveness God has shown you. Close your prayer praising God for His love expressed through His mercy.

Think it out/Talk it out:

Reflect upon an event when you truly felt God's forgiveness for some heavy-burdened sin.

1. What did it take before you sought forgiveness for the wrong you committed? What influenced your reluctance to admit the wrong and ask forgiveness?

2. What makes accepting your forgiveness so easy? What makes granting forgiveness to others so difficult for you to do?

3. How difficult is it for you to forgive yourself? Explain why you think this is so.

4. Which Scripture passage best speaks to your heart about seeking and granting forgiveness?

5. From whom will you seek forgiveness this week for something you've done? To whom will you grant forgiveness (in your heart) this week for something they've done? Ask God to help you unburden yourself.

Pray it out:

ACTS Prayer
  Adore: Claim a reason why you adore God.
  Contrition: In general terms, for what do you need God's forgiveness?
  Thanksgiving: For what do you want to thank God?
  Supplication: What do you need God to do for you?

Chapter Eight—A Leap of Faith

Prepare to receive it:

Quiet your body and mind for five minutes. Focus on God being present with you. Reflect upon times when you depended upon your faith to sustain you through a tough time in life. Pray your regrets for times when doubt and fear nudged your faith away. Pray in gratitude for the gift of your faith. Close your prayer reflecting upon events and people who have inspired you to seek a stronger faith.

Think it out/Talk it out:

Reflect upon an event when your faith was strongly tested.

1. What was the challenge? Describe it in detail.
2. How did fear and doubt challenge your situation? How did your faith help you?
3. How difficult is it for you to act on faith alone? Explain why you think this is so.
4. What current situation are you in that requires a leap of faith? What's holding you back? Explain.
5. What two baby steps (not leaps) of faith will you make this week?

Pray it out:

ACTS Prayer
    Adore: Claim a reason why you adore God.
    Contrition: In general terms, for what do you need God's forgiveness?
    Thanksgiving: For what do you want to thank God?
    Supplication: What do you need God to do for you?

Chapter Nine—My Encircler

Prepare to receive it:

Quiet your body and mind for five minutes. Focus on God being present with you. Reflect upon a time when you felt so close to God that His loving presence seemed to surround, even encircle, you intimately. Recall the emotions you felt. Pray your regrets for times when doubt, fear, or anger pushed away God's attempt to encircle you with His wisdom and love. Close your prayer sharing your desires to experience God as your Encircler.

Think it out/Talk it out:

Reflect upon an event when you felt God's presence so strongly it was as if He was encircling you. What events were present in your life at the time? Describe the experience in detail.

1. Did you pray for God's presence to enter or was His presence a surprise gift?

2. What word captures the emotion you felt? What did the experience do to influence your faith? Explain.

3. Which gospel story best illustrates God as an Encircler?

4. In what current situation do you desire to experience God as your Encircler?

5. God desires to encircle us with His love and grace. What two things will you do this week to make yourself more open to the Encircler's presence around you?

Pray it out:

ACTS Prayer

    Adore: Claim a reason why you adore God.

    Contrition: In general terms, for what do you need God's forgiveness?

    Thanksgiving: For what do you want to thank God?

    Supplication: What do you need God to do for you?

Chapter Ten—Voice Lessons

Prepare to receive it:

Quiet your body and mind for five minutes. Focus on God being present with you. Reflect upon a time when you heard a message that you believe came from God. Some describe this experience as "I heard God speak to me." How open are you to hearing God speak to your heart? Close your prayer seeking the grace to hear Him more clearly and often.

Think it out/Talk it out:

Reflect upon a situation in your life when you needed God's direction. What was the background to your life's situation? Describe in detail what you believe God spoke to you.

1. What led you to believe the message was from God?

2. If you haven't had the experience of God speaking a personal message to you, what do you wish God would say to you? Do you truthfully desire to hear Him?

3. How did or would it feel to have God speak to your heart? What words would capture the emotions of hearing God speak to your heart?

4. God desires to speak to the hearts of all His children—believers and nonbelievers. What might prevent you from hearing what God wants to speak to you? Fear? Sin? Pride? Lack of self-forgiveness? Sloth? Anger? Control?

5. What two things will you do this week to make yourself more open to hear from Him?

Pray it out:

ACTS Prayer

    Adore: Claim a reason why you adore God.

    Contrition: In general terms, for what do you need God's forgiveness?

    Thanksgiving: For what do you want to thank God?

    Supplication: What do you need God to do for you?

Chapter Eleven—Godcidence

Prepare to receive it:

Quiet your body and mind for five minutes. Focus on God being present with you. Reflect upon a time when you were in a difficult spot in your life. You prayed, and some miraculous answer to the prayer occurred soon afterward. Some would claim the event to be mere coincidence. For the pray-ers, they believe God intervened. Lorraine Nunley coined the experience a "Godcidence: a circumstance that looks like a coincidence, but is obviously a 'God thing.'" Close your prayer reflecting on Godcidence stories that you've heard.

Think it out/Talk it out:

Reflect upon a situation in your life when a Godcidence occurred. Describe the event in detail.

1. What led you to believe the event and its outcome was a Godcidence?

2. How often do you believe Godcidences occur? Explain.

3. What do you believe is the difference between luck and a Godcidence?

4. Based upon advice from the Our Camino section in this chapter, where is your favorite "Divine wifi hot spot" for a Godcidence?

5. What two things will you do this week to make yourself more attuned to Godcidences around you?

Pray it out:

ACTS Prayer
    Adore: Claim a reason why you adore God.
    Contrition: In general terms, for what do you need God's forgiveness?
    Thanksgiving: For what do you want to thank God?
    Supplication: What do you need God to do for you?

Chapter Twelve—From Stuffed to Starved

Prepare to receive it:

Quiet your body and mind for five minutes. Focus on God being present with you. Reflect upon a period in your life that was filled with many good things. Health, wealth, and happiness may have been some of the things that stuffed your life and made you happy. Reflect further on a time after this period of abundance when that happiness bubble popped. One situation changed everything. Life went from being stuffed with so many good things to being starved for things to return. Close your prayer reflecting on times you experienced both of those life situations.

Think it out/Talk it out:

Reflect upon the details contained in your "stuffed life" and your "not-so-stuffed life." What forced the shift?

1. Where was God during the transition between both experiences?
2. What did your prayers sound like during the transition? Explain.
3. How did God answer your prayers? Did you find yourself starved for anything from God? Explain.
4. What life lesson did you learn?
5. Ask yourself: On what comforts or luxuries or dependencies or things are you stuffing yourself? What are two things you will do about how you currently stuff yourself with things?

Pray it out:

ACTS Prayer

    Adore: Claim a reason why you adore God.

    Contrition: In general terms, for what do you need God's forgiveness?

    Thanksgiving: For what do you want to thank God?

    Supplication: What do you need God to do for you?

Chapter Thirteen—Holy Spirit Backdraft

Prepare to receive it:

Quiet your body and mind for five minutes. Focus on God being present with you. What thoughts come to mind in regard to the Holy Spirit? Reflect upon this Scripture regarding the fruits of the Holy Spirit: "love, joy, peace, patience, kindness, generosity, faithfulness, gentleness, self-control" (Galatians 5:22–23). Close in prayerful gratitude for the fruit of the Spirit that's most alive in you right now.

Think it out/Talk it out:

What emotions surface when you consider who the Holy Spirit is?

1. Describe an experience when you believe the Holy Spirit was present with you.
2. What led you to believe it was the Holy Spirit's presence?
3. Which Spirit "fruit" from Galatians 5 was provided?
4. Who is the most Holy Spirit-filled person you've met? Describe the holiness you feel being with him/her. Which qualities are most apparent in that person?
5. What are two situations in which you will look for the Holy Spirit's intervention this week?

Pray it out:

ACTS Prayer

    Adore: Claim a reason why you adore God.

    Contrition: In general terms, for what do you need God's forgiveness?

    Thanksgiving: For what do you want to thank God?

    Supplication: What do you need God to do for you?

Chapter Fourteen—Wait of the Beam

Prepare to receive it:

Quiet your body and mind for five minutes. Focus on God being present with you. Reflect upon the virtue of hope. What is a characteristic of a hope-filled person? What leads you to believe this? Do you consider yourself to be a hopeful person? How so? Close your prayer sharing with God the strongest hopes you have.

Think it out/Talk it out:

Reflect upon a time when you carried the heavy weight of some very difficult life challenge. Scripture claims these are our crosses (beams) to bear (Matt. 16:24). How would you describe a cross (beam) you carried or are still carrying? Explain in detail.

1. How long did you wait before your prayer was answered? Or are you still enduring under the "wait" of that beam?

2. Describe your challenge in waiting for God's answer to your prayer. What lesson did you learn or are learning from waiting for God's answer to your prayers?

3. Which of the "Eight Ways to Nurture Hope" in the Our Camino section of this chapter comforts you most? Explain.

4. Which of the "Eight Ways" challenges you most? Explain.

5. What two things will you do this week to become a more hope-filled person?

Pray it out:

ACTS Prayer

   Adore: Claim a reason why you adore God.
   Contrition: In general terms, for what do you need God's forgiveness?
   Thanksgiving: For what do you want to thank God?
   Supplication: What do you need God to do for you?

Chapter Fifteen—Junkyard-Dog-Like Kindness

Prepare to receive it:

Quiet your body and mind for five minutes. Focus on God being present with you. Reflect upon the virtue of kindness. Recall examples when Jesus demonstrated kindness. Which gospel story best illustrates kindness to you? Close your prayer imagining being present during that gospel story.

Think it out/Talk it out:

Reflect upon a time when someone was overwhelmingly kind to you. What were the details surrounding the experience?

1. What qualities did this person demonstrate to you? What words capture a purely kind person?

2. What would acting kind outside of your comfort zone require?

3. Finish this statement: Sacrifice is to love as _____ is to kindness.

4. Give an example of someone who demonstrated a fearless display of kindness to you.

5. What two things will you do this week to grow yourself into a more fearless provider of kindness?

Pray it out:

ACTS Prayer

Adore: Claim a reason why you adore God.

Contrition: In general terms, for what do you need God's forgiveness?

Thanksgiving: For what do you want to thank God?

Supplication: What do you need God to do for you?

Chapter Sixteen—What Are You Here For?

Prepare to receive it:

Quiet your body and mind for five minutes. Focus on God being present with you. Reflect upon what you believe God's purpose for you was at different times in your life. How has your life's purpose changed? Describe your feelings when your life's purpose is clear and focused. If your purpose in life today were a weather report, how would you describe it? Close your prayer meditating on your life's purpose and asking God for greater clarity with it.

Think it out/Talk it out:

Reflect upon a time when your purpose in life at a given time was crystal-clear to you. Describe your feelings surrounding the experience. Contrast that to a time when your life purpose at a different time was not clear. What were your feelings then?

1. What good can there be in having a period of time when you don't know your life's purpose?

2. How do your passions drive your life's purpose? Are passions alone reliable guides to follow in order to reach your life's purpose? Why? Why not?

3. What does going all in for God mean to you?

4. What would be the cost of going all in for God? What holds you back from going all in?

5. What two things will you do this week to go further in for God?

Pray it out:

ACTS Prayer

Adore: Claim a reason why you adore God.

Contrition: In general terms, for what do you need God's forgiveness?

Thanksgiving: For what do you want to thank God?

Supplication: What do you need God to do for you?

Chapter Seventeen—Satan Jeopardy!

Prepare to receive it:

Quiet your body and mind for five minutes. Focus on God being present with you. Consider the tension between the influence of Satan's evil and the power of God's desire for good. Reflect upon an event when you have witnessed evil overtake someone else or yourself. Reflect upon what Satan's game plan was. Close your prayer asking God to help you overcome Satan's next temptation to sin.

Think it out/Talk it out:

Reflect upon the role Satan plays in the world. What do you believe are his objectives?

1. Why is the temptation to sin so tempting?
2. Some believe that Satan's temptations slide us into a state of sin while others claim that temptation causes an irresistible fall into sin. What does your fight against temptation suggest? Explain.
3. With which of the "Eleven Bare Truths about Temptation" in the "Our Camino" section of this chapter do you most agree?
4. Which of the "Eleven Bare Truths" is worth committing to memory? How does that advice help you right now?
5. What two things will you do this week to avoid playing "*Satan Jeopardy*"?

Pray it out:

ACTS Prayer
  Adore: Claim a reason why you adore God.
  Contrition: In general terms, for what do you need God's forgiveness?
  Thanksgiving: For what do you want to thank God?
  Supplication: What do you need God to do for you?

Chapter Eighteen—Misericordia

Prepare to receive it:

Quiet your body and mind for five minutes. Focus on God being present with you. Consider the virtue of compassion. How would you define the word? What story have you heard, witnessed, or personally experienced that demonstrated pure compassion? Which gospel story best illustrates compassion to you? Close your prayer imagining being present during that gospel story.

Think it out/Talk it out:

Reflect upon events in your life through the lens of compassion. Are expressions of compassion growing in you? How do you feel about your answer?

1. What does showing compassion to another cost? What causes a reluctance to enter into another's misery? What's the possible price involved?

2. Reflect upon a time when someone showed sacrificial compassion to you or someone close to you. Describe the feeling of compassion you experienced.

3. Consider gospel events when Jesus entered into certain people's misery. Which Scripture event touches your heart most and why?

4. How might sharing in someone's misery be a witness of Christ-like love? Can you offer an example?

5. To which two people will you show sacrificial compassion this week?

Pray it out:

ACTS Prayer

    Adore: Claim a reason why you adore God.

    Contrition: In general terms, for what do you need God's forgiveness?

    Thanksgiving: For what do you want to thank God?

    Supplication: What do you need God to do for you?

Chapter Nineteen—*Ad Majorem Dei Gloriam*

Prepare to receive it:

Quiet your body and mind for five minutes. Focus on God being present with you. Reflect upon life events that brought you esteem. Consider the feelings that come by way of praise from others. How well do you deflect praise of your accomplishments to give the glory to God? Close your prayer asking God to help you hold praise from others lightly and humbly.

Think it out/Talk it out:

Reflect upon three life roles, job titles, and life accomplishments of which you are most proud. Recall the accolades you received for a job well done.

1. How do you see these three as gifts from God?
2. What advice would you offer to a younger version of yourself on how to handle these roles and job titles humbly?
3. What advice would you offer your younger self on how to handle success and the accolades from others in a humbler fashion?
4. How does the story of the rich young man (Mark 17:31) challenge you to give all the glory to God for the successes you've enjoyed in life?
5. What two actions will you take this week to live freer and more humbly for God's greater glory?

Pray it out:

ACTS Prayer

    Adore: Claim a reason why you adore God.

    Contrition: In general terms, for what do you need God's forgiveness?

    Thanksgiving: For what do you want to thank God?

    Supplication: What do you need God to do for you?

Chapter Twenty—Thunder

Prepare to receive it:

Quiet your body and mind for five minutes. Focus on God being present. Reflect upon times you heard the sound of thunder. Consider how its sound is attention-getting. What emotions arise from hearing thunder? Use your imagination and try to connect the sound of thunder to God speaking. Are there qualities the two have in common? Close your prayer reflecting upon what it takes for God to get your attention.

Think it out/Talk it out:

Reflect: Reflect upon an experience when some insight came to you from God. How did God get your attention?

1. Does the metaphor of hearing thunder and hearing God speak connect? How so? If not thunder, what other metaphor relates a different attention-getter for how you hear God speak his warnings and advice to you?

2. Does a stronger attention-getter from God gain stronger obedience on your part? Why or why not?

3. Which of the "Five Practices to Tune Out the Loudest Static" in the Our Camino section affirms you most?

4. Which of the "Five Practices" challenges you most?

5. What two actions will you take this week to tune out your loudest static over God's voice?

Pray it out:

ACTS Prayer
   Adore: Claim a reason why you adore God.
   Contrition: In general terms, for what do you need God's forgiveness?
   Thanksgiving: For what do you want to thank God?
   Supplication: What do you need God to do for you?

Chapter Twenty-One—*Ultreia*

Prepare to receive it:

Quiet your body and mind for five minutes. Consider the call all Christians share to evangelize. Reflect upon Jesus's command to go to all people everywhere and make them His disciples (Matt. 28:19). Why is evangelization so critically needed in the world today? In the world around you? Close your prayer asking God to help you overcome any fear you have to evangelize others.

Think it out/Talk it out:

Who was instrumental in evangelizing you to the Christian faith? What was his or her approach?

1. Engaging evangelization occurs when we share our faith walk story in a relevant and relatable way. What thoughts and emotions deter you from sharing your faith story?

2. What thoughts and emotions motivate you to share your faith story? Why?

3. Reflect upon your faith walk story. What drama moments were involved?

4. How did God reveal His call for you to follow Him? Share details of certain events that explain this part of your faith walk story.

5. With which two people will you share your faith story this week? How will you invite them to share their story with you as well?

Pray it out:

ACTS Prayer

Adore: Claim a reason why you adore God.

Contrition: In general terms, for what do you need God's forgiveness?

Thanksgiving: For what do you want to thank God?

Supplication: What do you need God to do for you?

ACKNOWLEDGMENTS

Sir Isaac Newton wrote, "If I have seen further, it is by standing on the shoulders of giants." *Lost and Found along The Way* was completed as I stood on the shoulders of countless family, friends, and immensely talented people. These are my giants, who loved me and supported this writing.

First and foremost, my bride, Barb, for sacrificing time together for me to walk three Caminos and the seven years it took to write this book.

My children Nick, Frank, Rocco, and Angela who forever give me their love and support.

Brady, Clara, Mila, Lily Mae, Giada, and Leo—my precious grandchildren who were my inspiration throughout my Camino adventures.

Maureen Fox, a lady of mature faith, who skillfully offered editorial advice over the years in writing this book. Her spiritual wisdom and literary expertise informed my manuscript to become more insightful, lean, and heartfelt.

Jennie Steinbeigle, my aunt, was my most enthusiastic encourager. She prayed daily, and in earnest, for me to hear God's wisdom to guide this writing.

Jeff Tegge, who works in the book distribution industry, read early drafts of the manuscript and spurred me on to keep writing. Jeff's professional advice guided me to reach the publishing stage.

Mark and Dave Miller, owners of Prince Industries where I work as a Corporate Chaplain, were generous supporters of my Camino pilgrimages. To all employees there, my fond appreciation for your warm friendship.

The faith community of St. John Neumann Parish prayed for me while on my Camino pilgrimages and eagerly welcomed my stories along The Way.

Fr. Michael Sparough SJ, my spiritual director, gifted me with his wisdom about seeing the Lord in my consolations and desolations. His love for Jesus inspires me to love Him more.

Bishop Eric Pike and his wife, Joyce, my dear soulmates, enriched my life while walking the Camino. Their steadfast faith and tender love for our Lord humbles and inspires me.

Bill Roth and David Kellen added the gifts of their artistic talents to the creation of website and the video productions for the book's digital marketing.

Steve Donis, the gifted illustrator, brought the Camino and its experiences to life through his maps and beautiful sketches.

Tony Hyler, John Showalter, Barb Williams, Peg Stevens, Charlie Strack, Bob Hughes, John Blieszner, Betty Vitale Naso, and Jim Naso poured hours into analyzing all my blog entries in order to discern which stories would make the best choices for the book's chapters.

The folks at Deep River Books, my new and dear friends, believe the message in *Lost and Found along The Way: Stories for Your Faith Walk from the Camino de Santiago* will build the kingdom of God here and especially, now.

CONTACT THE AUTHOR

If you'd like to learn more about my Camino, visit the daily blog I wrote on The Way

- williesfaithcamino.blogspot.com

If you'd like to learn more about the book's mission, check out videos about Willie's Camino insights, and connect with him, visit

- www.lostandfoundalongtheway.com

ENDNOTES

Introduction

1. http://www.theroadtosantiago.com/the-camino-de-santiago.html.

2. https://www.stjames-cathedral.org/Prayer/jameslegend.aspx.

3. https://www.newadvent.org/cathen/08279b.htm.

4. https://www.stjames-cathedral.org/Prayer/jameslegend.aspx.

5. https://www.stjames-cathedral.org/Prayer/jameslegend.aspx.

6. https://www.stjames-cathedral.org/Prayer/jameslegend.aspx.

7. https://www.red2000.com/spain/santiago/history.html.

8. This information was shared on the Finnesterre tour.

9. https://en.wikipedia.org/wiki/Camino_de_Santiago.

10. https://www.red2000.com/spain/santiago/history.html.

11. https://en.wikipedia.org/wiki/Camino_de_Santiago.

12. https://www.newadvent.org/cathen/08279b.htm.

Chapter 2—Of Thunder and Stars

13. http://www.bbc.co.uk/thepassion/articles/joseph_of_arimathea.shtml.

Chapter 6—Offer It Up

14. https://caminoways.com/introduction-to-the-le-puy-way.

15. John Brierley, *A Pilgrim's Guide to the Camino de Santiago*, 11th Edition (Forres, Scotland: Findhorn Press Ltd, 2014), 44.

16. http://www.xacobeo.fr/ZE2.06.CF_description_en_01.htm.

17. http://www.xacobeo.fr/ZE2.06.CF_description_en_01.htm.

Chapter 7—Mountain of Forgiveness

18. Anna Dintaman and David Landis, *Camino de Santiago*, Village to Village Guide (Traverse City, MI: Village to Village Press, 2017), 67

19. https://www.sanfermin.com/en/party-guide/what-is-sanfermin.

20. Kevin O'Brien, *The Ignatian Adventure: The Examen* (Chicago: Loyola Press, 2011), 75–77.

Chapter 8—A Leap of Faith

21. Dintaman and Landis, *Camino de Santiago*, 79.

22. Brierley, *A Pilgrim's Guide*, 77.

23. https://www.caminoadventures.com/camino-frances/pamplona-to-puente-la-reina.

24. https://www.caminoadventures.com/camino-frances/pamplona-to-puente-la-reina.

Chapter 9—My Encircler

25. https://kathwilliamson.blogspot.com/2009/10/celtic-spirituality-circling-prayers.html.

26. Brierley, *A Pilgrim's Guide*, 90.

27. Dintaman and Landis, *Camino de Santiago*, 91.

28. Dintaman and Landis, *Camino de Santiago*, 98.

29. https://vivecamino.com/en/the-miracle-of-the-rooster-and-the-hen-one-of-the-most-famous-legends-of-the-camino-no-173.

30. https://kathwilliamson.blogspot.com/2009/10/celtic-spirituality-circling-prayers.html.

31. http://irishfireside.com/2015/02/03/history-symbolism-celtic-cross.

32. http://irishfireside.com/2015/02/03/history-symbolism-celtic-cross.

33. https://www.ourcatholicprayers.com/st-patricks-breastplate.html.

34. https://www.loyolapress.com/catholic-resources/ignatian-spirituality/finding-god-in-all-things.

Chapter 10—Voice Lessons

35. Brierley, *A Pilgrim's Guide*, 119.

36. Dintaman and Landis, *Camino de Santiago*, 127.

37. Brierley, *A Pilgrim's Guide*, 131.

38. https://www.dreamstime.com/statue-jesus-christ-cross-died-us-santa-maria-cathedral-burgos-spain-europe-statue-jesus-christ-image132166159.

39. Steven Curtis Chapman, "Listen to Our Hearts," https://genius.com/Steven-curtis-chapman-listen-to-our-hearts-lyrics.

Chapter 11—Godcidence

40. Dintaman and Landis, *Camino de Santiago*, 142.

41. Brierley, *A Pilgrim's Guide*, 145; Dintaman and Landis, *Camino de Santiago*, 148.

42. Brierley, *A Pilgrim's Guide*, 145; Dintaman and Landis, *Camino de Santiago*, 148.

43. Dintaman and Landis, *Camino de Santiago*, 167

44. Rich Mullins, "Awesome God," https://genius.com/Rich-mullins-awesome-god-lyrics.

Chapter 12—From Stuffed to Starved

45. https://followthecamino.com/en/blog/roman-walls-of-lugo.

46. https://www.google.com/search?q=calzada+romana+roman+wall++history&tbm=isch&ved=2ahUKEwiEkd669frqAhUS0KwKHVwgD8wQ2-cCegQIABAA&oq=calzada+romana+roman+wall++history&gs_lcp=CgNpbWcQDFCHSliHSmCkV2gAcAB4AIABXYgBXZIBATGYAQCgAQGqAQtnd3Mtd2l6LWltZZ8ABAQ&sclient=img&ei=X9olX8TlDZKgswXcwLzgDA&bih=819&biw=1280&rlz=1C1AWUA_enUS778US780#imgrc=R51BUnwlh678RM&imgdii=xbVeZT17C26sxM.

47. https://whc.unesco.org/en/list/987.

48. http://www.sacred-destinations.com/spain/leon-cathedral.

Chapter 13—Holy Spirit's Backdraft

49. Brierley, *A Pilgrim's Guide*, 196.

50. Dintaman and Landis, *Camino de Santiago*, 193.

51. Noted from literature at the site of Hospital de Òrbigo

52. http://turismoastorga.es/walls-of-astorga.

53. https://www.casabatllo.es/en/antoni-gaudi/sagrada-familia.

54. https://mercortecresa.com/en/blog/what-is-a-backdraft-and-how-does-it-work.

Chapter 14—Wait of the Beam

55. Dintaman and Landis, *Camino de Santiago*, 208; https://www.fundacionjacobea.org/en/ways-of-santiago/202.

56. Michael Card, "God's Own Fool," https://genius.com/Michael-card-gods-own-fool-lyrics.

Chapter 15—Junkyard-Dog-Like Kindness

57. Bill Walker, *The Best Way: El Camino de Santiago* (Lexington, KY: Skywalker Publishing, 2012), 178–180; https://www.authentic-journeys.com/blog/who-were-the-protectors-of-the-way-of-st-james-in-ancient-times.

Chapter 16—What Are You Here For?

58. http://santiago-compostela.net/camino-frances/24-from-ponferrada-to-villafranca-del-bierzo.

59. http://blog.turismo.gal/destinations-en/santa-maria-a-real-scene-of-a-miracle.

60. http://whispersintheloggia.blogspot.com/2008/09/give-god-per-mission.html.

61. https://focusoncampus.org/content/how-do-i-discern-my-vocation.

Chapter 17—Satan Jeopardy!

62. http://www.moodycatholic.com/confirmation_renewal_of_baptis-mal_promises.html.

Chapter 18—Misericordia

63. https://followthecamino.com/en/blog/melide-on-the-camino-de-santiago.

Chapter 19—*Ad Majorem Dei Gloriam*

64. https://www.britannica.com/topic/Druid.

65. Michael Jacobs, *The Road to Santiago*, 3rd Edition (London: Pallas Athene, 1999), 188–189.

66. Dintaman and Landis, *Camino de Santiago*, 272.

67. Jacobs, *The Road to Santiago*, 188–189.

68. Jacobs, *The Road to Santiago*, 188–189.

69. https://www.atlasobscura.com/places/botafumeiro.

Chapter 20—Thunder

70. https://www.calendarpedia.com/when-is/ascension-day.html#:~:text=The%20Solemnity%20of%20the%20Ascension,ascension%20of%20Jesus%20into%20heaven.

71. https://www.ignatianspirituality.com/desire-for-what-you-want.

72. https://www.spiritualityandpractice.com/explorations/teachers/thomas-keating/quotes.

Chapter 21—*Ultreia*

73. http://santiagoinlove.com/en/ultreia-meaning/#:~:text=Ultreia%20just%20tells%20the%20energetic,%3A%20ultre%C3%AFa%2C%20ultreia%2C%20ultreya%E2%80%A66.

74. https://www.christianbiblereference.org/jparable.htm.

75. https://www.azquotes.com/quote/1497335.

76. https://www.patheos.com/blogs/jesuscreed/2015/01/07/reverse-evangelism-by-jonathan-storment.

77. https://www.africa.upenn.edu/Articles_Gen/Inaugural_Speech_17984.html.

Canola Fields

Shepherd's Fields

Godcidence Water Bottle

Elvis

Rabanal to Molinaseca

Cruz de Ferro

Botafumerio

Cathedral de Santiago

Finisterre